The Directors Guild of America
Oral History Series
David H. Shepard, General Editor

1. Byron Haskin. 1984.
2. Worthington Miner. 1985.
3. Curtis Bernhardt. 1986.
4. King Vidor. 1988
5. David Butler.
6. Stuart Heisler.
7. Henry Koster. 1987.

A *Directors Guild of America Oral History*

KING
VIDOR

Interviewed by Nancy Dowd
and
David Shepard

The Directors Guild of
America and
The Scarecrow Press, Inc.
Metuchen, N.J., and London
1988

Library of Congress Cataloging-in-Publication Data

Vidor, King, 1894-1982.
   King Vidor / interviewed by Nancy Dowd and David
Shepard.
      p.   cm. -- (The Directors Guild of America
oral history series ; no. 4)
   Includes indexes.
   ISBN 0-8108-2161-3
   1. Vidor, King, 1894-1982--Interviews. 2. Motion
picture producers and directors--United States--
Interviews. I. Dowd, Nancy. II. Shepard, David.
III. Title. IV. Series: Directors Guild of America
oral history series ; 4.
PN1998.3.V54A3   1988
791.43'0233'0924--dc19   88-18250

King Wallis Vidor, 1894–1982

King Vidor died peacefully at his ranch in Paso Robles on November 1, 1982. As his family subsequently gathered his belongings from various homes and storerooms, it became clear that he had preserved an amazing collection of personal and professional papers. One small trunk became the basis for Sidney Kirkpatrick's best-selling book <u>A Cast of Killers</u> (1986), and the entire collection was subsequently donated to the University of Southern California where it is available to researchers. Other collections of Vidor papers may be found at the UCLA Research Library and at Brigham Young University in Provo, Utah. The volume of material is daunting, but would make possible a definitive biography of a pioneer film artist who was also a beautiful and extraordinary human being.

INTRODUCTION

When The American Film Institute's oral history project was active in the early 1970s under sponsorship of the Louis B. Mayer Foundation, King Vidor was among the most significant artists chosen for interviews. Vidor's autobiography, A Tree Is A Tree, had appeared in 1953; however, AFI wanted to supplement the book. Not only had Vidor completed years of subsequent professional activity; MGM had completed a restoration program which made it possible to discuss most of his best films in the stimulating environment of a fresh look.

I recommended that Nancy Dowd, who had become interested in Vidor's work when a student at UCLA, be commissioned as oral historian, and I witnessed the excitement when they viewed films like Happiness, Wild Oranges, and Show People -- she for the first time, he for the first time in almost half a century. The freshness and immediacy of the interview is due in large part to those screening opportunities provided by AFI with the cooperation of MGM and other producers.

Before the project was completed, Nancy Dowd and AFI parted company, AFI's oral documentation program changed direction, and the 46 completed tapes gathered dust for years before Ms. Dowd delivered them to the Directors Guild of America for finishing into the present volume.

In the edited transcript, Mr. Vidor's remarks were somewhat rearranged to reflect the chronology of his career, rather than the random order of the original film screenings which stimulated the interview sessions. The inevitable trailings and inconsistencies of transcribed speech have been silently corrected, and many isolated reflections on various subjects have been moved to locations to which they seemed more logically suited. As the Nancy Dowd interview ended with King Vidor's last commercially produced motion picture, I recorded a final session early in 1980 summarizing Mr. Vidor's career and discussing his personal films produced since 1959.

The transcribing of interviews was accomplished under Directors Guild auspices while Edward Schilling and Adele Field did all of the organizing, checking and editing. I functioned as general editor throughout the project; however, readers should note that while we have made the manuscript error-free to the best of our collective ability, neither King Vidor nor Nancy Dowd passed final judgment on this written record.

-- David Shepard

DOWD: Could you describe your family situation in Galveston?

VIDOR: My grandfather was born in Budapest and came to America as the press representative and general manager of a prominent Hungarian violinist named Rimini. He stayed in New York for a year or so, until the violinist returned to Hungary. Then he came by boat from New York to Galveston, Texas, and went into the cotton business. I think it was called cotton factoring. He married and established his home in Galveston. My grandmother on my father's side was from Key West, Florida, and she was of Scotch and English parentage. I don't know much about my mother's family, but they were all Texas people. They were prominent in politics. One of them was a mayor of the town, and my grandfather was on the Board of Commissioners.

Galveston was a very cosmopolitan type of place, strange for Texas and strange for the United States. On the block where I lived there was a French speaking family, and across the street lived a German speaking family. Galveston was an island, and it was a tremendous cotton port, so it attracted people of all nationalities. The houses were very close together, and I grew up in this atmosphere of many languages and cultures. To a boy, the town had tremendous atmosphere.

Because of all this activity, and since it was an island, it was sort of a resort town and almost considered beyond the law. The gambling and prostitution went on long after it was outlawed in other Texas towns. I have very graphic memories of activities around the town such as the drayage of cotton, a street called The Strand, the mule teams and the cotton wagons, the noise -- and it was all tremendous.

I was interested in photography almost immediately. When I was old enough I got a camera and learned to develop negatives myself. My father was in the lumber business, and he sort of thought that I would follow in his steps. I tried it for a while, and worked as a treasurer or accountant in his sawmills, but it wasn't for me. I was interested in photography and movement even before I started photographing things with a camera. Various kinds of movement held my attention, and of course when motion pictures came to Galveston, it was only natural that I would jump on this means of recording the things that I felt.

In 1900, at the age of six, I went through a flood and hurricane in which the island was completely inundated with ten feet of water. It was one of the major disasters of the time. Throughout my life I understood that out of a population of twenty-nine thousand, ten thousand were either drowned or killed. All of the wooden structures of the town were flattened. The streets were piled high with dead people, and I took the first tugboat out. On the boat I went up into the bow and saw that the bay was filled with dead bodies, horses, animals, people, everything. The town was isolated immediately, and shortly after that the hurricane began. The house I was in came apart, all except for two rooms. In one room there were about thirty or forty negroes who had been pulled out of the storm, and in the other room were all our friends and family.

DOWD: Do you think of yourself as having a pictorial imagination?

VIDOR: Yes, very much. I still know that certain images remain over everything else. It was absolutely vivid each minute, each hour of the storm, and even when I came into adulthood, I could remember it all very well. I was just constantly aware of the drama and graphic interest. Then the town was raised up to sixteen feet. The grade of the level of every house or building was lifted up in the air. This meant canals, going to school in rowboats, and sand being pumped in.

The whole extraordinary process of the thing fascinated me and probably established a desire to record it all. One of the first things I did with motion pictures was to become associated with a fellow who had built a camera, and with him I later recorded a storm in 1909.

DOWD: Was this Roy Clough?

VIDOR: Yes. He later became the mayor of the town. We stood up on the sea wall and recorded the buildings beyond the wall breaking up into pieces. I had the job of taking tickets at the local theatre, and I got experience running the projection machine, and I was hooked with the interest of motion pictures. It just seemed to fit into all of the things I liked. I was interested in the theatre, in photography, writing, acting, and this graphic work with photography -- then here was photography in movement, and it was a perfectly natural sequence of my interests. As a young boy I was building stages in the basement, as so many kids do. The combination of acting and my fascination with the theatre and the movies answered all of this. I wrote stories and tried to sell them.

DOWD: It must have been pretty unusual at that time for someone to take an interest in motion pictures in Galveston.

VIDOR: There wasn't anyone else. Later on in Houston one man, who had been to New York and had been a chauffeur, had a motion picture camera. There was no one else in either Galveston or Houston with one. You just couldn't go around town and buy a motion picture camera in those days, even if you wanted to. You had to send to New York or Chicago to have the film developed.

DOWD: How did your family feel about your interest in motion pictures?

VIDOR: I think my family was really enthused about it. My father was, at least. When he finally sold out all of his interests in Galveston, he moved out to Hollywood and helped me build the first studio I had. They thought as long as I knew what I wanted to do, they better go along with it. It was a

4

tough struggle, though. I built a stage in Houston with another fellow, but we never did anything with it.

DOWD: Was that Eddie Sedgwick or John Boggs?

VIDOR: Boggs was the chauffeur with the camera. Sedgwick came along with his family, and we made two one-reelers in Houston, which I later took to New York and showed around. I tried to sell them, and turned them over to a company, but the company went broke and we never got them back. Then I made one film, In Tow, in Galveston. It was a two-reel film made in conjunction with the races. I wrote it, directed it, and even played the lead.

DOWD: This was in town?

VIDOR: Yes, in town.

DOWD: But before you went to Houston you were working for Mutual Weekly as their representative, right?

VIDOR: Yes. "Weeklies" were what the newsreels were called then. I worked some for my father, but still didn't have enough money to buy equipment. I just telegraphed off when some event was going to happen and got the job of representing Mutual Weekly. I had no camera, so I went to Boggs and made a deal. When he was working, he didn't have time to film, but I had the time, so we arranged a deal that I was able to borrow his camera. It was a hundred-foot Ernemann camera. We had to get 35mm black-and-white film in hundred-foot rolls and load it into magazines and boxes. So, I got one of these assignments and went out and photographed a movement of troops. That's all described in the book (A Tree is a Tree).

That was my first actual use of a motion picture camera. You had to crank it by hand, and Boggs was going to go along to photograph it for me. Eleven or twelve thousand troops were marching from Galveston to Houston. They were preparing to go into Mexico on some expedition. It was the largest march of troops in American history. When I got the assignment they said they would pay sixty cents per foot for anything they used.

Now this march was to take place early Sunday morning. When I got home Saturday night there was a note on my door from Boggs saying that he had to work the next day. The note also said that the camera was at the corner drugstore, and he listed the directions for using it: Two turns per second, and if the sun was shining use f/11, if it wasn't, use f/8. Those were all the instructions I had to operate the camera. I stayed up half the night with a practice reel, trying to practice two turns per second by hand. My uncle and I got up the next morning and set up to shoot about six o'clock on top of a cotton warehouse. We were ready to shoot and tilt up when the troops came along. When I say "tilt up," we had no tripod that had a tilt head on it. We would somehow drag the leg back slowly and that would be the tilt.

Well, the line of troops came by and I started to crank the camera. Suddenly, it jammed. I didn't want to lose the fifteen or twenty feet of film I had already gone through, because that was the beginning of the march. So, I ran down into the warehouse and stood up some cotton bales and improvised a darkroom so that we could take out the film we had already shot. We had to do this because we didn't have any magazines to use as a take-up once one had jammed. We either had to open it up and destroy it, or take it out and put it in a can to save it. Eventually that did go to Mutual Weekly and we got sixty cents per foot, and it was distributed throughout the world.

DOWD: Did you ever see it in a theatre?

VIDOR: Yes, I think I did. They didn't use much, though, only about thirty or forty feet.

DOWD: What else did you shoot for the Mutual Weekly?

VIDOR: Well, soon after that I set up a "local," a local weekly newsreel around Houston. It was in conjunction with the local paper. Eventually I dropped the Mutual Weekly. I don't know if I shot any more for them. I might have shot one or two other events, but they don't stand out. However, we did make the local newsreel for a while. A man who became prominent as a title writer inaugurated the idea of it.

DOWD: Ralph Spence?

VIDOR: Yes. I think he was one of the editors on the Houston paper. Later on he did one of my films.

DOWD: I think he titled <u>Show People</u>. He was from Galveston, then?

VIDOR: Yes. Then we made this one picture, <u>In Tow</u>, and that was never shown anywhere but in Houston and Galveston. It had some awful mistakes in it. Boggs photographed that, and made some very bad mistakes in the exposure. He stopped down when he should have opened up, and he opened up when he should have stopped down. That meant overexposure in some places, and underexposure in others. He cranked slow when he should have cranked fast, and vice versa. When an automobile was supposed to speed up, he slowed it down, and so forth.

We set up a lab and developed and printed the stuff ourselves. We even tried to tint it. That's how I happen to know about tinting. Even with my first feature film in Hollywood, <u>Turn in the Road</u>, we had a lab right on the lot. We didn't have an open-air stage, but we did have a lab.

DOWD: How many people were working with you in Houston?

VIDOR: I had one man who was very ingenious about building stuff. He would work on the set doing general construction. Usually we used what was available, but when we had to build something, he would do that, and then he, the cameraman, and I would go into the lab and develop the film. We didn't shoot for very long, so in a few days we would be through and then would work on the developing and printing.

DOWD: I suppose you would just make one print and distribute it.

VIDOR: We made one print, which I took to New York. The Sedgwicks acted in it, but they weren't experienced in film acting. They had been in vaudeville before, though. I made two one-reelers with them.

DOWD: Do you remember what the plots of those were like?

VIDOR: No, I don't remember the plots. But you know, there was a certain one-reel comedy technique like the Sennett one-reelers. After that I made a documentary for a sugar company in Houston.

DOWD: Was it a documentary about refining sugar?

VIDOR: Yes. The tragedy with that film was that there was static. We had static exposures on the film, and it looked like lightning all over the place. In that day there was no definite frame line position and we sent away to Chicago to have titles made. It so happened that the titles came back with a different frame line than the camera. There was nothing we could do about it, so we got them out and cut the titles into the film. Every title jumped out of frame, and by the time the projectionist framed it, the title would be over with. I gave the projectionist my last dollar and told him to keep his hand on the framer so that he could immediately put the title back into frame when we screened the film for the sugar company.

DOWD: Were you married at this point?

VIDOR: Yes, I think I was. I met Florence because she was a beauty and another fellow wanted to meet her. I arranged somehow to find out for myself who she was, and then introduced her to the other fellow. We found out she had a big ambition to get into films, and I was immediately sympathetic. The other fellow faded out quickly, and I think we were married not long after that. We lived in Houston for six or eight months before we decided to come to California, where the action was.

I remember my mother particularly objecting. A lot of people were telling us that we were going out into that "terrible Hollywood" and that the films were so crude. My reply was that if the films were so crude, that was just a good opportunity for someone to come in who was not so crude. I said that it was just more of a chance for me to get started because someone new with a little different attitude might be appreciated. The films then were unreal. They were in bad taste, almost as much as they are today. It seemed a good place for us to go. Florence was very much a lady, which would help us even more.

DOWD: Now on your trip from Texas to California you were shooting for the Ford Motor Company, weren't you?

VIDOR: Yes, that was a scheme I had. How were we going to pay our expenses to get out there? My family was comfortable, but not wealthy. I had a strong independence whenever I wanted to do something, and by that time, my father's business had gone downhill quite badly. I didn't ask for help.

We bought a Ford automobile with a twenty-five dollar down payment and I figured out that if I could shoot enough footage for the Ford Motor Company to use in their films, we could make sixty cents per foot and be able to finance the trip. By this time I had a camera of my own. I didn't have enough money to buy a tripod, so I bought a surveyor's tripod instead.

I wrote to the Ford Company and they replied that they would buy any usable footage from us at sixty cents per foot, in the same way Mutual Weekly bought footage. We went out and bought five hundred feet of film, and along the way we took pictures of this Ford Model T and different locations. They used some, but very little. We eventually ran out of money long before the trip was over. It turned out that they didn't pay until sixty days after getting the film. It was six weeks before we got any money.

DOWD: That trip must have been rough.

VIDOR: The only money we spent was to buy gas. In the wild, remote places it was thirty-seven-and-a-half cents per gallon.

DOWD: Did you ever see any of the material you shot for the Ford Educational Weekly on this trip?

VIDOR: Yes, I'm sure I did. One time we were stuck in Fort Worth for four days. I set up a thing to look like we were photographing a car theft. I parked our car out in the street with the keys in it, and set up the camera in a store window and waited for someone to steal it. No one ever tried to steal it, so I got someone to act the part of the thief, and found a policeman to chase him on his motorcycle. It didn't fool the Ford Motor Company, and they didn't buy the film.

DOWD: People must have been pretty amazed to see a cameraman way out in the boondocks.

VIDOR: Oh yes. It was 1915, and anybody with a camera set-up was just everything. I remember one time I saw a newsreel crew shooting and I watched them photograph a cornerstone dedication. I noted when the fellow was shooting he read the words out loud. Well, there was no sound recording then, but having him read it gave him an idea of how long he should shoot the scene.

That's where I picked up how to shoot titles. If we shot a title or any sort of reading matter, a letter or something, you'd pick it up and read it out loud while you were filming, and then soon after you finished, you'd estimate how fast or slow an audience would go. Usually when you finished speaking you'd crank the camera a few more times, and that was the way you got the proper length of the shot.

The reason I mention this is because each technique in the development of filmmaking was discovered in some remote way or perhaps discovered accidentally. There was no other source, nobody to talk to, no school to go to, nothing. Everything had to be discovered.

DOWD: So you were discovering as you went along?

VIDOR: Yes, you had to. That is why I took a job as an extra when I came to Los Angeles. I had never before been on a motion picture stage.

DOWD: So that is what you did when you first came to Los Angeles?

VIDOR: Yes.

DOWD: Where were you living?

VIDOR: At the end of that trip we stopped in San Francisco. We were absolutely broke with twenty cents between us. I sold my automobile and that gave us enough money to come to Los Angeles by boat. Florence had some relatives in San Gabriel, and when we arrived we stayed with them for a few days, but that was too far away. We came to Santa Monica because I had known Corinne Griffith in Mineral Wells, Texas, and we stayed with her.

She had wanted to be a movie star, and I had written a letter to a rather remote second or third cousin who was married to a comedian named Brennan, I think, and he was working with the Vitagraph Company. The letter was successful in getting Corinne a contract for two days a week at five dollars a day. She took Florence over to the Vitagraph studio in Santa Monica and introduced her to the head director, and they put Florence on at five dollars a day for two days a week, and moved Corinne up to three days a week.

We rented a little apartment on the beach. Having written scripts in Texas, I was trying to write and sell scripts in between time. I had a camera, but I wasn't prepared to get into the studio as a cameraman. Before long, the Vitagraph Company moved to Hollywood. We moved with them. They moved not far from the D.W. Griffith Studio on the corner of Prospect and Talmadge. Right up the street towards the hills we had a little two-room apartment in a boarding house. Florence was by then beginning to star in some films for them. That's where I worked as an extra, but I did sell a script to them. I don't remember which one it was.

DOWD: Was that <u>When It Rains, It Pours</u>?

VIDOR: Yes. I guess I sold that to them for thirty dollars.

DOWD: Do you remember what it was about?

VIDOR: No, I don't. But when it rained in Los Angeles the companies couldn't work. They all had outdoor stages with canvas overheads. Everyone would be out of work, so it was my idea to write something they could shoot in the rain.

DOWD: Do you remember any of the films you worked in as an extra, or what you played?

VIDOR: I didn't play anything. What I was trying to do was watch what kind of lighting they had, particularly the electric lamps. I was trying to learn where the lights were, and how many, and whether to use daylight. I remember that I was an extra in a courtroom audience. I was in the front row of the audience watching the director, Roland Sturgeon. I worked on others, but this one impressed me because it gave me a chance to sit there and watch everything that was going on, and I didn't have to do anything else. I tried the same thing on Intolerance, and I don't think I ever had to put on a costume. I do remember several days when they shot the Babylonian scene. It was right across the street from the studio.

DOWD: Had you ever heard of D.W. Griffith before you came to Hollywood?

VIDOR: Yes. I was following the directors in Houston. I was aware of Griffith, and I think De Mille when I arrived in San Francisco at the end of the trip. The Birth of a Nation was showing then, and reserve seats were two-and-a-half dollars, and that was a tremendous price. When we sold the automobile we had enough to go see The Birth of a Nation, with just enough money left over to get down here.

DOWD: So you actually saw Griffith directing on the Intolerance set?

VIDOR: Yes.

DOWD: Were you impressed by this?

VIDOR: Yes. Remember, this was like the top of all things for a young man from Texas trying to learn about movies. Griffith had a camera in a balloon, and he had chariots way up in the air, on top of buildings. They had all sorts of tremendous acts and big crowds. I still don't know how they got those horses on top of the walls. I think I had to crawl under the fence to get in. There was a canvas fence all around the set, but it wasn't very difficult to get in. There were enough technicians walking around so they didn't know I was a visitor. I remember very well the balloon with the cameras in it, simulating a helicopter shot. You couldn't think of a greater experience or opportunity than to be on that set. I would have done just about anything to get in and watch what was going on.

DOWD: The tables were turned later on.

VIDOR: Yes. Griffith didn't know I was there on the set, I'll tell you that.

DOWD: What did you think of Hollywood when you first came here? Were you optimistic?

VIDOR: The whole thing to me was just one great Disneyland. It was a place where I wanted to be, and I wanted to be part of it. I was very ambitious. I told Florence that I knew how to direct films, and she said, "How can you say that? You haven't even been in the studio more than a few times." Well, I sort of felt that I wanted to be a director. Just to be in a studio, that's how important it was to me. Don't think that I didn't need the money, either. I was doing it to be able to live and eat. Nevertheless, I had a goal, and it was a very definite goal. Everything to do with movies fascinated me. I didn't have thoughts about anything else.

DOWD: So you worked at Universal as a writer?

VIDOR: I got jobs at Universal just to be on the gang, to be the prop man, or even the assistant prop man. Later, I had a job at forty dollars a week as a writer in the shorts department. They made animal shorts and comedies. I was thinking of being a director, but I thought that it would be good to know all this stuff.

I worked for two days as a cameraman for Judge Willis Brown. He was making some sort of travelogue, and I went down to San Diego to photograph things for him. Later he made <u>Juvenile Court.</u> He was a juvenile court judge, and he had a thing set up where the boys all sat around the table. He did not sit at the bench; he was at the head of the table, and he took the boys' problems. He wrote a series of approximately twenty two-reelers about the problems that the boys had. I got to know him when I worked as a cameraman. He came to Universal and saw me in the writing department and said, "How would you like to direct?" Of course, I then went to work.

DOWD: He must have been quite a colorful character.

VIDOR: Yes, he was. He had long hair and was very athletic, nothing like a judge. He was very eager, quick moving, and determined. He played the part of the judge in the series of films.

DOWD: In the films, would you actually see the boys sitting around the table?

VIDOR: Yes, that was the basis for the films. He would ask, "How did you happen to get into this trouble? Tell me about it." Then we would go right in and show the story. At the end he would come back and say, "I am going to think over your problems and tell you what to do." There would be both white kids and black kids, and they would tell a very human type of story.

To cast the pictures, I picked kids up off the street selling newspapers, or wherever I could find them. Sometimes as I was heading to work for Culver City from Hollywood, I'd see a kid selling newspapers on a street corner. I'd stop, buy all his papers, and then say, "How would you like to be in a movie?" Then we'd go down to the studio, and he'd start work that day.

DOWD: You've done that through your entire career.

VIDOR: Yes, because I would have a vivid picture in my mind about the characters. There's no telling who I picked up in those groups.

DOWD: Were these pretty good films?

VIDOR: Yes, but I don't know if I still have any reviews of them. It gave me a chance to feel out the human qualities of films because the stories were all very human. At that time they were not making many other human stories, especially in the short films. The one- and two-reel films were mostly comedies then. These films gave me a chance to establish myself and get a feeling of how to treat things humanly in short form.

The big job in front of me was to step up to feature director. If you were considered one kind of director, if you made just two-reelers, then it was a big step to become a feature director. So, I had the idea of taking two or three of these two-reelers and putting them together to make six reels, which was feature length, and then making them look like one story, with the tie-in of Judge Brown and the juvenile court.

I put them together by taking off the titles, and had my agent take them out to the Goldwyn Company, or wherever they were looking for a feature director. Then the agent was supposed to say, "Here is a feature he is directing," which I suppose he did. However, I didn't get away with it. I couldn't convince them.

Today they would have been accepted very readily just by the quality of their directing, but the goal was to be able to maintain interest throughout, and to be able to handle the money involved in a full-length film. Features were a different sort of animal, requiring a different sort of training and ability. This is a rather interesting point -- that it wasn't just the direction of one scene, or of one sequence that qualified you, but it was being able to assemble the whole thing, lasting approximately an hour and a half. Today this differentiation is not thought of. It was very much thought of then. You just had a terrible time making the jump.

DOWD: Where was Judge Willis Brown's studio located?

VIDOR: It was located across from where the Selznick studio later was, in Culver City on Washington Boulevard.

DOWD: Was it his own studio?

VIDOR: He didn't have enough money to build it. The people who financed the films furnished the money. The studio was called Boys' City. That was his idea, to have a boys' town, and they worked on the films and lived there. These films were released by the biggest company then, General Film. They owned all of the patents. I actually had some good reviews off of these two-reelers. There was some attention called to them, but not enough to give me the status of a well-known director.

DOWD: So now you were trying to get into making features?

VIDOR: Yes, that was the big jump. I finished the boys series, and then I realized that in order to get a job as a full-length feature director, I had to write my own story, and make it good enough for someone to buy it. I would only sell it if I could direct it. That was the plan. Well, I went to a play called The Light of Asia up in the Hollywood Hills at the Kratona Institute. It was the story of the Buddha's search for the truth. During the performance I thought, Why not have a young American search for the truth? I went home and wrote the whole story that night.

It was a silent story, and it didn't take long to write. I wrote five or six pages first, and then turned that into a script. As usual, I had trouble conveying my ideas on paper as to what I wanted to do on film. I've always had the difficulty of trying to explain what I wanted to do without making the picture. A girl who worked for William deMille read it, and recommended that someone else do a rewrite. I went to the doctors who put up the money for the boys films and I sold them the idea of making this feature. We formed the Brentwood Film Company. They belonged to the Brentwood Country Club and we played some golf there, so we called it the Brentwood Film Company.

DOWD: There is a brief description in your book about the plot of Turn in the Road, and it says that the wife loses her life in childbirth, then the man despairs, and he goes off in search of the answer.

VIDOR: Yes.

DOWD: Exactly what did he do in the film?

VIDOR: I had him run out of the house on a rainy night because the wife's father was a minister and had tried to pacify him. The man's answers didn't satisfy him, so he went out around the world. I was going to have him go to India, China, or the Bowery of New York, but we didn't have enough money to shoot these episodes, so we had to leave them out. But he was going to different places and different cultures that might be able to give him the answers. I picked him up again as a tramp who rides the freight trains, still searching. Then he came back. It was on a rainy night, and he crawled into a barn. It happened to be the barn of the house where the girl he married had lived, and in the end it was his own six-year-old boy who told him the answers he was looking for.

DOWD: Do you remember what the answers were?

VIDOR: I was a Christian Scientist, and they were basically metaphysical. It was a simple thing of truth, or God, good predominates; and the shadows . . . I remember I illustrated a scene with the little boy who got up and opened a window in the barn loft and said, "The darkness is only the absence of light." Just to be conscious is a miracle in itself, just as life and the awareness of consciousness of living is itself harmonious and good. All the fear and suffering could be dissolved just like the darkness by opening the windows of our minds.

DOWD: Was your family Christian Scientist?

VIDOR: My mother was. I guess I was influenced by my mother. My father was, more or less, but my mother definitely was Christian Scientist. I got interested in it when I was fifteen or sixteen years old, after going to many doctors and discovering that they didn't seem to know what they were talking about. I was disillusioned with doctors and medicine because I had a nervous problem and they couldn't agree on what the problem was. I wanted to grab hold of something more general, more basic, something that affected the whole man rather than just pieces of the anatomy.

DOWD: So this was happening to this man in the film?

VIDOR: Yes. He then came home and the little boy came up to him in the barn loft and sort of gave him a few simple things of what he was looking for. In other words, just by his own fireside hearth were the things he was looking for.

After having made it and shown it, we only had enough money for one print. We opened in Los Angeles and I got an offer from every star and every company. For the fun of it I got a written offer by every film company to direct films. It was great after having such difficulty getting a job as a feature film director.

DOWD: Every company in Los Angeles?

VIDOR: Yes, New York and Los Angeles.

DOWD: Did you shoot this in Los Angeles?

VIDOR: Yes.

DOWD: What were some of the details of the shooting?

VIDOR: The Brentwood studio was on Fountain Avenue. I suppose we thought we could save money by building our own studio. When I say "building a studio" all I mean is renting a house for probably fifty dollars a month, and then building a stage in the back yard. But this studio did have a small lab, and it had a carpenter's shop. The offices were in small bungalows on Fountain Avenue, I think, between Western and Vermont. They tore it all down to make the Cedars of Lebanon Hospital. It must have been a studio before we used it, probably built and then disused until we rented it.

In talking about the financing, I thought it was very amusing that the men who put up the money for the Judge Brown stories backed <u>Turn in the Road.</u> There were nine active doctors who each put up a thousand dollars. Then one of the doctors took the script home. His wife read it, and he came back the next day, and during a board meeting he said, "My wife tells me there's a lot of Christian Science in this picture." There wasn't any Christian Science, but there was a miracle and some metaphysical talk in it.

There was nothing labeled Christian Science, but at the time there was a general feeling of antagonism between doctors and Christian Scientists. When they had the meeting, I said that there wasn't any Christian Science in it, although it did parallel it a bit. They told me, "We don't want to make a picture about Christian Scientists!" We argued, but I won, and we made the film.

It was immediately successful, and it played in Los Angeles for eleven weeks. As I said, we only had enough money for one print, and one of the officers wanted to take it back to New York and get a big distribution company. They had to pull it out of the theatre in the eleventh week, with standing-room-only crowds going around the block.

When I wrote the next picture, the doctors read it and took it home to their wives, and the president of the company came back the next day and said, "We read the script last night, and there is no Christian Science in it. We want you to put some in!" I said, "No, I'm not going to do that, because the picture doesn't call for it." They insisted I put some in, and I insisted that I wouldn't do it. We finally compromised with the agreement that I would put some in the next picture, which was called The Other Half.

As to the details of the shooting of Turn in the Road, we took a peaceful valley and then filled it with steel mills and pollution. We used the San Fernando Valley, which at that time was a beautiful green valley. Griffith had used it a lot in The Birth of a Nation. I had shots of that before and after the pollution.

Another interesting thing was I used a little boy, Ben Alexander. He was a small boy then, but he done a part in Hearts of the World for Griffith. I had him come into the grandfather's room and stand there with his hands on each sliding door, and it never occurred to me that with the spotlight we had behind him, it made a cross on the floor. He was the symbol of spiritual thought, but I was quite surprised to read in one of the reviews about my symbolic treatment of the cross of light on the floor with the boy standing in the doorway.

This was the beginning of people interpreting things in a picture that the director may have just done naturally. The imagery you want does derive from the meaning, but it also comes from just being involved with the story and communicating it at the same time. I remember several occasions during the silent era when the titles used in the story began to be used in everyday life during the making of the film. In other words, there would be enough material in the film to supply inspiring quotes during the day while making the film, cutting it, and so on.

Well, we went on from Turn in the Road, and it was indeed a turn in the road for me. From then on I didn't have any problems in getting a job as a feature director. The technique of direction was probably similar to the two-reelers that I'd made, except that I didn't have to get so melodramatic in the feature films. I remember saying, "When someone in your family comes home and says they had a flat tire out on the highway and had to walk a mile and a half, it's a big dramatic situation. But if a boat sinks in some remote island and three hundred people are drowned, it's not nearly as dramatic." This was the thinking I was doing at the time. I realized that I didn't have to blow up things so much if I could just make them more believable.

At that time we had no provisions to buy stories. I got two or three hundred dollars for supplying the stories that we filmed. We didn't go looking to buy a book or a story, so I ended up writing all three or four stories that first year. I had offers from all the companies, but I felt a loyalty to these nine doctors and I stayed for a year and made four films with them.

The second film was called Better Times. When I had been an assistant director, I had discovered ZaSu Pitts on a bus, and I wrote this story around her. Then I got David Butler out of a theatre in downtown Los Angeles and made this comedy called Better Times.

DOWD: You made three films with ZaSu Pitts: Better Times, The Other Half, and Poor Relations. What kind of character does she play?

VIDOR: Well, she was very eccentric and Griffith had her over to rehearse for some picture. He used to have his cast, his stock company, watch people who came in to rehearse. She had such strange individual movements with her arms, hitting people with them as they swung about, that they stole her movements and gestures and used them in their films. In those days you didn't have to pay someone to come in for rehearsals, and they would make people rehearse all day long. I think it was Dorothy Gish who they used with the Pitts mannerisms.

Anyway, the next picture was The Other Half, which was getting back into a little bit of my metaphysical beliefs. The last one of the four we made the first year was called Poor Relations. I don't remember too much about that story, except that I wrote about basic human interests, and all four of those pictures that year were like that.

II

DOWD: The next film you made was called The Jack Knife Man. Wasn't that taken from a book?

VIDOR: Yes, a book with the same name. It was written by Ellis Parker Butler who had written a short story called "Pigs is Pigs." I think my father had read that book and told me about it, or someone I knew called my attention to it. I read it and I said, "This is the kind of film I want to make."

At the end of the first year with the Brentwood Film Company I had gone to New York and had written offers from every film company, but I selected First National Exhibitors, which financed theatre chains. I felt that I would have more freedom -- even at that time I was thinking about freedom -- and I made a contract with them for four or six pictures with an option that they could take up after two. I came back to Los Angeles, having no studio to work in -- I didn't even own a home -- and I had seventy-five thousand dollars to make a film. I suppose I had already discovered Jack Knife Man, and we bought that book, adapted it, and made the film. The next film was called Family Honor, in which I used Florence Vidor.

I made one of the films for only sixty-two thousand, and I sent the rest of the money back to First National Exhibitors. They didn't like the fact that I hadn't spent all of the money, or gone over budget. I didn't understand then. They wanted bigger pictures, and they wanted me to spend all of the seventy-five thousand dollars. I didn't know at that time that their main interest was getting the pictures as glamorous and as big as they could be. They wanted me to get stars and big drama so they could fill their theatres.

21

In Jack Knife Man it's just a couple of old fellows and a little boy, everybody unknown. There was no glamor whatsoever. It was just kind of a down-to-earth story without much of the usual motion picture pattern. They told me they would not pick up my option because I had sent the money back, rather than spending it. Well, I wouldn't have known how to spend any more money on Jack Knife Man. I forget whether we could have spent any more on Family Honor. I don't think so.

I remember that we didn't shoot any scenes for Jack Knife Man in Los Angeles. We went on location and started the picture in Stockton, near the Sacramento River. We had gone up there before and found that they had shanties and houseboats on the river that we could rent and use in the background. This was right outside of the town. Stockton isn't too far from the Mother Lode-Bret Harte-Mark Twain country. We photographed scenes in the snow in a very small town called Angels Camp. We got in there one afternoon and photographed the scenes without snow, and that night it snowed. The next morning we photographed the snow scenes.

DOWD: Is this the scene where the man and the boy spend the night in the barn?

VIDOR: Yes. Most people were saying what bad luck we had with the weather. Mark Twain always said, "Most everyone talks about the weather, but nobody does anything about it." It occurred to me that it was time for me to do something about it. So, I went to work mentally on the idea that we needed no snow for this first afternoon of shooting, but that it would be nice if we had snow the next day. That's what I was thinking as we first arrived in Angels Camp. And that's what happened. If you don't put a block in the way, very often things will happen that way.

DOWD: How did you direct the little boy in the film? It must have been difficult.

VIDOR: We cast the little boy and when we got up to Stockton on the first day of shooting, it was terrible. He refused to do anything. He was just such a spoiled brat that everything had to be tricked or dragged out of him just to get the scene. After one day of this, I thought, My God, I'll have to recast the part of the boy. We had the company on location, so we really didn't have the time to start interviewing all over again. We thought about local boys, but that was taking too much of a chance, so we just went ahead.

The kid acted with this sort of disinterest and refusal, but it seems to be an asset after looking at the film. When he kicks his feet up and down, yelling "no, no!" it looks very natural. That's the beauty of seeing these films many years later. You forget what a terrible struggle it was just to get the scene on film.

We used every trick in the world to get him to work. We offered him food, candy, anything to get him to do the acting. When you'd win him over, he'd do it. Well, it gave me a terribly strong lesson to try to make tests to find out whether a kid would do anything. Anyway, we pushed ahead. I think until the last scene of the picture he was still objecting, refusing, kicking, and going into tantrums. His mother could do nothing at all. But as you see, those things fade away.

DOWD: What about the delirium scene where the woman looks at the old man and his face is out of focus? How did you do that?

VIDOR: It could be that it never had been done before. I think we put a piece of plate glass in front of the camera and we breathed on it, you know, like you do with eyeglasses. When the camera was going, we fogged it up, and then it would clear through gradually. I don't remember ever seeing that done before.

DOWD: You said when we saw it the other day that you wanted to talk about collapsing time.

VIDOR: Oh yes. The old man cuts a toy out of wood and you can't have him sit there and just keep the camera going while he whittles. No matter how fast he can do it, it will always be too slow. How do you speed up the time? Today we know that we could just jump from the thing being started to halfway or three-quarters of the way through it. You'd just jump through the process, jump cut and get right to the end in a hurry. We didn't know that you could do this way back then. We thought the audience wanted a literal time, so we did it by cutting away. We discovered by cutting to the other close-ups of the boy looking, or the old man working, that you could actually progress through the actual time it took to cut the toy out of the wood.

That's why you see many scenes in those pictures of someone arriving in a carriage, getting out, walking through the gate to the front door, knocking, and when the door is opened, going into the house. Well, eventually we forgot the carriage and the automobile, and we even forgot about going up the path. You just go inside and they are there. That was a series of developments that took audience acceptance. That's why titles all appear superfluous now. At that time they seemed necessary to explain the action.

DOWD: At the time it didn't appear superfluous?

VIDOR: No, not at all. It seemed that you had to lead the audience and explain for them. These people would read titles out loud, and they just weren't conditioned to figure it out immediately. It was just like the cliché in the theatre, where the curtain used to go up and the butler was always at the telephone explaining whose home it was, what time it was, when the lady was about, and all that. This was a development that came along and it is being developed each year. The audience becomes more wise and more apt to accept the techniques and you can keep leaving out things.

DOWD: Jack Knife Man is one of the first films where we see your concern for the underdog. Did you have a deliberate concern for that person?

VIDOR: No, I didn't, and I wasn't aware that I was starting a series of films about the underdog. The only thing I was aware of was that I had a natural affection for all sorts of people and I never felt any isolation from any type of people or group, including the blacks. Even though I was born and raised in Texas, I just felt close to them. My concern was not conscious. It was just a way I felt then, and still feel today. I know that I didn't accept the glamorous, well-smoothed-over attitude about the rich or anything like that. It's not in my character at all to be impressed by a Rolls-Royce.

DOWD: After Jack Knife Man, you made Family Honor, and then you made The Sky Pilot.

VIDOR: Florence Vidor was becoming a big star. She was a tremendously beautiful woman. As a result of her being so outstandingly beautiful, dignified, and having a style that was quite individual, she later went on to star in quite a few C.B. De Mille pictures. Anyway, after Family Honor we signed a contract with Associated Producers. I think (Thomas) Ince was one of them, and so was Allan Dwan. They were a group of about four or five producers who combined along the lines of United Artists and had a distributing company. They made a contract for me to make four Florence Vidor pictures.

By then I had started to build my own studio. My father left Texas and moved to Hollywood. Together we built a studio on Santa Monica Boulevard. We bought a square block of land for fifteen thousand dollars and built a studio which we called Vidor Village. The idea was that since I was making mostly American types of film, I would build the stage to look like a courthouse or city hall, and the other offices would look like homes so that they could be used for shooting.

DOWD: What did the stage look like?

VIDOR: It was a regular closed-in stage. It had to be lighted by then. The Brentwood stage was open with what we called diffusers. We used to nickname them "confusers." They had a light muslin type of cloth on wire scrims that pulled over for daytime shots, and black ones which were used for night shots. There was a series of telephone poles with wires between them, with ropes and rings so that you could slide the cloth back and forth.

By the time I had built my own studio we were resigned to the use of complete artificial lighting. With the daylight lighting, if it rained, you were out of luck. Everything was sitting out and you had to carry it all in every night. Artificial lighting was used mainly to protect yourself against the weather and daylight. The use of daylight was not good. It was really bad photography. But by then we were away from open-air stages, with the diffusers being blown up and down in the wind, letting streaks of sunlight in, all of that.

DOWD: When you were in Truckee making The Sky Pilot you had to deal with other problems, didn't you?

VIDOR: Yes. During production of The Sky Pilot we ran out of money and were waiting for the snow at Truckee. I had to get people to cooperate by promising them that they would get their money when the picture was delivered. I did keep them all, the cast and crew. Probably there was just enough money left for railroad tickets home.

Then it snowed when it wasn't supposed to. Looking at it the other day, it's probably the sequence where the church burns down in the snow. Again, I was trying to do something about the weather. We were praying for it to snow, and it snowed a day too soon, and far too much. I hadn't finished the non-snow sequences when the big blizzard came and snow was all over the place. We had to go ahead and shoot the snow scenes, but we couldn't complete them because it meant burning down the church, and I still had a sequence to do with the church without the snow.

When we finished the snow scene, they had to scrape all the snow away for one day's worth of scenes without the snow. Since we couldn't put the real snow back for the burning scene, we moved in a carload full of salt and spread it all around. The natives said that these people were absolutely mad -- two days before, these people had been shoveling snow away, and now they were putting salt all over the countryside.

We finally finished the picture, cut it, and then I took it to New York. However, I kept the negative locked up someplace in a vault and told them I was indebted to quite a few people to finish paying their salary, and I wouldn't deliver the negative until we got the money. First National gave me a check, and I came back and paid off all of the people, and that was it. I just got a salary for directing the film, but I was also responsible for the production. I mention this because of the feeling of cooperation that existed then. Perhaps later, with the unions and the guilds, you couldn't do this.

DOWD: The other day, Colleen Moore remembered a scene she did for you where she was twisting a handkerchief and batting her eyes. She said she was "Gishing" it. Were you conscious of this phenomenon, or the Griffith influence at that time?

VIDOR: No, I wasn't. In silent films when you had to express some emotion, you'd pantomime gestures. I still do. Just as a writer would write down words to remember, I kept a mental memory bank of gestures that meant certain things. Yesterday I saw a man on the street making certain gestures that meant something, and I tried to figure out what they meant.

In a Griffith picture Lillian Gish would put her finger against herself and that would mean, "You mean me?" When somebody in a Sennett comedy pointed upstairs, that meant, "My husband's upstairs," or "My wife's upstairs." So, if Lillian Gish or Griffith would do some gesture that would come through as having the same meaning as a sentence or paragraph, everybody else would pick it up. As director, I would also pick these up. You never knew exactly what gesture you were going to use to express something. I'm puzzled today, wondering how Gloria Swanson and Garbo and all of those people earned such tremendous salaries when they couldn't speak. Well, they had certain ways of doing things, certain expressions and gestures. In today's world of underacting, it all looks quite humorous.

DOWD: Colleen Moore had been with Griffith before, hadn't she?

VIDOR: Yes. She'd sit in a trance with music going for a Lillian Gish type of performance. If you were an actress, some of it was bound to rub off on you.

DOWD: Let's talk about Love Never Dies. The other day you were telling about how you convinced Ince to make the picture.

VIDOR: After Sky Pilot we were pretty well out of money at our studio. When I say "our studio," I mean my father and myself. We didn't have enough money to go ahead and make another film. I've always been a terrible promoter and money raiser. It just isn't one of my assets. So here we had a studio with nothing much in it, and we only had an art director, a construction man, or maybe sometimes both at one time. They were waiting for us to get another film.

I probably had an option on the book Cottage of Delight. It had a train wreck in it. Some fellow volunteered that he would just go ahead and build this train wreck on the stage. It wasn't a question of my hiring a crew for him, he built the whole thing himself. This included the bridge, the model of the train, everything. We photographed it with very little money. We had just enough money to film that one scene.

Then I took the episode to Thomas Ince. I think by then Florence was an Ince star. At least she played in some big pictures for him. He was one of the Associated Producers, so I took the film over there and left a few scenes for him to look at. He saw them and said, "Very interesting. Let's read the book, and let's make the film." I then moved out of my studio and made the picture at Ince's studio.

DOWD: You closed your own studio?

VIDOR: Yes. I went around and made pictures on the outside to make enough money to keep my own studio going, pay the mortgage and so forth. I made a picture with Clara Kimball Young called The Woman of Bronze, another picture called Peg o' My Heart with Laurette Taylor, and I was out working just to keep this studio going. Somewhere along the line we got the contract to make the four Florence Vidor pictures.

DOWD: And you produced these four films?

VIDOR: I produced and directed all except one, which was Booth Tarkington's Alice Adams. That was directed by Rowland V. Lee.

DOWD: You said the other day that the courthouse scene in Love Never Dies was shot in Sunland.

VIDOR: Yes, the grove of oak trees in Sunland was a typical setting of a small town with a good old hotel, a church, a small park, and some other trees. It was not too far away, and yet it had no semblance of progress. It was the perfect type of location for the films I made.

DOWD: Were you using the metronome in your direction of the final scenes?

VIDOR: We had music on the set. I discovered if you wanted actors to work fast, you would let the music play fast, and if you wanted them to slow down, you slowed the music down. My biggest influence in music came from Griffith because I saw the Griffith films in downtown Los Angeles with the big symphony orchestra. Griffith worked on different themes for different characters in a picture. I was impressed with Hearts of the World, how Lillian Gish's theme was from an opera. He used Brahms' Lullaby in another picture. It helped my growing impression of music in silent films. I wasn't into the use of the metronome until I made a picture called Three Wise Fools.

DOWD: You have been called a director who was fantastic at doing parting scenes, and there is a beautiful parting sequence in Love Never Dies where the man goes back to his wife, and she's married someone else and they leave. You said this was shot in Beverly Glen. Are you aware of that in your own works?

VIDOR: "Parting is such sweet sorrow." I wasn't aware of that until recently when somebody mentioned it. I know of some partings in my own life that just stand out vividly. In The Big Parade one of the highlights was the parting, but I was not conscious of it. I think maybe it was an opportunity that appealed to me. For the one in Love Never Dies I remember building the fence and putting up a huge scrim twenty feet wide to soften the background. It was not used that much, but it would soften the background so that the figures would stand out. I remember my poetic feelings about that and I presume the music was also quite effective.

DOWD: One last question about Love Never Dies: Would you like to talk about the scene where they were going down the river? That looks pretty frightening.

VIDOR: That was the shot on the Feather River. The town's name is Belden, and that's in the high Sierras, northeast of Sacramento. This was a very fast rushing river filled with rapids, and we were living in a railroad camp right on the banks of the river. The natives had said that if anybody fell into the river, that would be the end of him.

We had to do this sequence of a river crossing, so we bought a raft and rented a skiff and a small boat. We had to build a big boat for the scene, and we only had one grip. I remember that very well. He put this big barge together with nails. The little boat was put together with screws. Well, we were always working right above those darn rapids, and when it came to using doubles, we didn't have one on the small boat.

For some reason we never got a stunt double for Lloyd Hughes, the leading character. He said he would do the scene anyway, so we got this huge barge across the river by pulling and pushing it, and some big men we had were supposed to grab it when it bumped the other shore. It came over and somehow they missed grabbing it. The barge turned and went into the heavy rapids. As we stood there petrified, it just sort of broke in half and the whole river poured into the boat while Hughes was standing in the back half of it. He and the whole thing went under water.

For a minute I remembered everybody saying, "Nobody comes out alive!" We started yelling and running down the river. It was a terrible task, and as we ran up and down I imagined the headline notifying his mother and family. I saw all the tragedies of the thing while we were racing up and down looking for him. Finally somebody looked down in the shrubbery and there he was, hanging onto a branch with some cuts and a bloody arm. We dug through the brush and pulled him out. He was none the worse for the experience, but the boat was in splinters, with nothing left but little pieces of wood. Lloyd had managed to grab one of those branches as he went rushing by.

DOWD: Sounds like a scene from Sail of the Tide.

VIDOR: Absolutely. Those things happen, and occasionally they turn into tragedy. But he got out of that one in good shape. We were just so short-handed when we went on location, and they had no requirements as to the number of people you had to have. We would run this small boat through a couple of rapids, and we often had to carry that damn thing back up a trail along the river a quarter of a mile.

DOWD: Before we go on to Conquering the Woman, I want to ask you if you could talk a little bit about Thomas Ince.

VIDOR: Ince was very dynamic. He wasn't very large, but he had a tremendous amount of energy. He reminded me somewhat of the same sort of character as Dino de Laurentiis. He was very fond of sailing, and he had a big yacht. His office was fixed up so that there was a private apartment adjoining it. That was the studio where Selznick was later on, and where we made Duel in the Sun. That's also where we made Love Never Dies.

Florence starred in one of his big films. He directed occasionally, but he was putting all of his energies into being a producer. I remember when I went to see him the first time. He was so dynamic and direct, and I was so nervous, that when I shifted in my chair and crossed my legs, I accidentally kicked his desk. This embarrassed the hell out of me, and I said, "Oh, excuse me," as if I had kicked him.

He later got into some sort of trouble. He was named and talked about in the Hearst press. There were stories going around which I never believed -- stories about Louella Parsons getting a lifetime job with Hearst because she kept something a secret. It was all supposed to have been hushed up. It was one of Hollywood's scandals, so I'd rather not talk about it.

Anyway, we were able to get this contract with Associated Producers to make four starring pictures with Florence. In those days, and even much later at Metro, they would go out and sell the pictures as a series. They'd sell four pictures directed by me with one star name. It wasn't until The Big Parade that I was able to break this thing. In fact, Metro had already sold The Big Parade as part of a John Gilbert series.

So, here we were selling four pictures as a series with Florence. Conquering the Woman had Roscoe Karns and David Butler, who was in my second full-length feature. It was a story about an unruly girl whose father got this cowboy to take the daughter on a cruise to bring her down to earth. They got off the yacht and onto a desert island. They found tremendous footprints on this island, much further apart than a man could make. I don't know what the cowboy did. I don't remember all the details of the story, but I remember that the idea was to conquer her dominance and break down her hard shell to a human being. Florence was a good type for this because she came over rather cold. It was a real adventure.

DOWD: Dusk to Dawn came after this, didn't it?

VIDOR: Yes. I remember that Dusk to Dawn was an experiment. The original story was called The Shuttle Soul, and the idea was that the soul of the character played by Florence would be an American girl during the day, but at night would become an Indian girl in India. The same soul went back and forth every time she went to sleep. We discovered someone had shot a lot of good scenes in India around some maharajah's palace with a big wedding procession using about forty or fifty thousand decorated elephants. We actually wrote the story around the spectacle of all these elephants climbing up a hill, and the wedding itself. Then we would come back to America. I've forgotten what the American setting was. It went back and forth, with Florence playing both Marjorie Latham and Aziza, the beggar girl. Sidney Franklin was also in the cast.

DOWD: That's not Sidney Franklin, the director, is it?

VIDOR: No, it was a different one.

DOWD: Now we come to <u>Alice Adams</u>. You didn't direct that, did you?

VIDOR: No, Rowland V. Lee directed it. These four pictures with Florence were made very quickly, all in the same year. They didn't make much profit, either. This simply meant that at the end of those four pictures we didn't have any other means of making films.

I had been such a Booth Tarkington fan, I thought that everything he wrote should be made into a film. I had taken an option on <u>Penrod</u>, which really was a boy's story. Finally Tarkington had a chance to sell it, I think it was to Marshall Neilan. I let him buy it back at the same price I'd paid for it. I was then able to get an option on <u>Alice Adams</u>, one of his more recent stories.

We somehow got the money to make the film, but at the same time I had a chance to make <u>Peg o' My Heart</u>. That was a story with Laurette Taylor that was a very popular play at the time. She was also a big star. This was a new adventure for me, to take an established star and a well-known play and see what I could do with it. I wanted to see if I could make it faithful to the theatre, or whether I should transform it into a motion picture. In the theatre, remember, it was all talk. In movies it was deadly if you had too many titles. Films would just not be released if they had too many titles. I decided to take the job and perhaps use the money to keep my studio going.

We got Rowland V. Lee to direct <u>Alice Adams</u>. The way it worked out, I had a few conferences with Rowland before the film started, and perhaps put more time in on the script than supervising the direction. I had a theory that if the director agreed on the way it should be handled, if we were in accord, that I should let the director make the film.

In the <u>Peg o' My Heart</u> situation, the Metro Company had its studio in Hollywood, so that was where I was working. I tried to be as faithful to the script as possible, but the usual situation, where somebody would write a script and throw out anything that was any good from the original, cropped up again. Writers wanted to show they had written something, so they wouldn't stick to the original material. I studied the play and I got a different writer, although I usually took the script over and re-wrote my stories myself.

I had never met Laurette Taylor, nor had I ever seen her onstage. As I remember, she was forty-two years old at the time, and the girl in the story was supposed to be eighteen. She had such a lively personality, individuality, and character, and was such a wonderful actress that she was able to overcome this age difference.

The interesting thing was that she got D.W. Griffith's cameraman, Billy Bitzer, and they made a photographic test of her. They sent the test out to me, and I gasped. I thought it was just impossible. You could not make a picture with a woman who looked as old as she did in the test trying to play an eighteen-year-old. It was frightening. She had on this terrible wig, the lighting was not good, and I just thought we couldn't do it. Soon after that, they decided to come out and make the test in the studio. When I saw her again, my hopes fell. She had done quite a bit of drinking in her time, and I didn't know how she could do it.

I had the lucky remembrance that in Love Never Dies the stills had looked excellent. I thought, Why couldn't we use the lens on the eight-by-ten still camera? George Barnes, the cameraman on Peg o' My Heart, said we could. We had to set up the still camera lenses in front of the motion picture cameras, but there was such a long telephoto lens on the still camera that for a big close-up, Laurette Taylor was all the way across the stage. However, Barnes worked out a type of rifle lighting. He used a key light that he put sights on, just like a gun. Wherever she went, the electrician followed her with those sights.

DOWD: Was it just on her?

VIDOR: Yes. It was at such a height that it threw a false shadow around her chin. This eliminated the wrinkles around her throat. It made her face into a round, pear-shaped face. In this trick lens it was distorted just enough to make her face more round than long. The distortion wasn't supposed to be apparent, it just happened. The result was that after several days of tests, we finally accomplished a test where she looked very young and very lovely. We took the wig off, and she had beautiful hair of her own. In running the film today I noticed that her long blonde hair was just beautiful, and made all the difference in the world.

Laurette and her husband, Hartley Manners, seemed to like me, which worked out just fine. We were in a very hot location near Sherwood Lake one day. We had all been getting along just fine. The owners of the property wouldn't let us build a fake front, so we had to build a real house for the location. The prop man brought out geese and wild goats and other animals the night before and put them into this house. I guess it was also supposed to be used as a dressing room for Laurette. It was a little Irish hut overlooking the lake.

We got out to the location together that morning. Hartley was wearing his white shoes and Laurette brought her maid and her dog along. We had to climb a very steep, dusty trail to the top of the hill where the house was. She damn near quit the film while climbing the hill and slipping and sliding in the dust. The usual Hollywood cast never thought anything about the hardships on location.

On the set Barnes had bright tin reflectors and the sun was very, very hot. One of the actors said some silly line instead of what he was supposed to say, and Laurette got very angry. She said, "I just can't stand the reflectors, and I just can't turn on hot and cold emotions when you say so." She finally passed out. They carried her into the house and laid her down on the floor. When she came to, there were all the goats and geese all over the place. Laurette saw the mess and jumped up and said, "It's impossible. I'll never be able to do it." She rushed out the door and down the hill with her maid and dog trailing behind.

I went to work and tried to smooth out all of the feelings, and the following day we went back out and started all over again. I told the actors to please say the right words and not do any more mumble-jumble. Everything went fine from then on. When she was in a good mood, when she was laughing or smiling, her face was up and right and round, and when she was sunk, her whole face and expression would go down. Every scene was shot by kidding and laughing and making jokes and doing all kinds of things to keep her amused.

She fell in love with me as a result of this. She ran the film over and over for the rest of her life. She would screen it for me whenever I came over to visit, and she'd sit and hold my hand because I had made her look eighteen. She had a print of it in New York and she used to call people up just to show it. I remember what Ethel Barrymore said when Laurette asked her to dinner. She said, "I'll come over to dinner if we don't have to sit through Peg o' My Heart again afterwards." I suppose she asked people to dinner and ran the film every night. Well, you can imagine the gratitude I felt from her. We were great friends.

I was hired out as the director of some other pictures before Happiness. I still had the studio, but by this time we had fired our lawyer who knew all of the tricks and was also the only one who knew where all of our accounts were. He got a sheriff's detachment to lock up the gates of the studio. My father was with me and he was able to take the brunt of managing the studio while I worked on the outside. I remember the sheriff even took our automobiles. We were living on Selma Avenue then, and I think I had somebody pick me up, and I got a job directing Clara Kimball Young.

DOWD: Where did you make Woman of Bronze?

VIDOR: The studio was a Spanish looking building over near the Mack Sennett Studio. That district was called Edendale then. I think it was a short block off Glendale Boulevard on the opposite side of the street from Sennett. It was a small studio, as so many were in those days, just set up for one star and one production company.

DOWD: It wasn't Metro, then?

VIDOR: It might have been distributed through Metro. It says "The Metro Company" on the film. That picture was also from a stage play. William O'Connell was the cameraman, and he had done pictures for me before. In those days we kept the same cameraman. We got to work very closely with each other. You always felt more at home if you had the same cameraman. We followed the practice as much as we could. Anyway, John Bowers, who had been in Sky Pilot, was in that picture. Kathryn McGuire and Edwin Stevens were also in it. It was sort of a triangle. She was posing for a sculpture. The big scene was where one of them got very angry and smashed up the whole clay form of the sculpture.

It was out of my line, sort of out of my category, but I was becoming more and more known as a director, and different stars and different companies were making me offers. We made a settlement with our old attorney and we opened up the studio again after that, but we didn't make any films, and it was very soon after that that I sold the studio to Sol Lesser. He was a producer, and I think we sold the studio for $125,000. The real estate had gone up and made up for the loss we had incurred in running our own studio.

I had seen a play of Three Wise Fools and one day when I was coming out of the Cocoanut Grove, Major Edward Bowes, who was one of the top executives at Goldwyn Pictures, stopped me out on the steps. He asked if I had any ideas of a film I wanted to do. I said, "Yes, I would like to do Three Wise Fools, the play." He said, "Well, that sounds good to me." So the next day I went down to the Goldwyn Company and Bowes introduced me to a man named Abe Lehr who was running the studio. They went ahead and bought the rights to the play.

Eleanor Boardman, one of their rising young contract players, was to star in the picture. They were trying to develop her into a star. I had never met her, but the play was over at the Pasadena Playhouse, and I asked her if she would go with me to see it. We went, and she was delighted with the possibility of playing the part, so I made the picture at Goldwyn.

It wasn't very long before I was separated from Florence, and I fell in love with Eleanor. I had actually fallen in love with her from a big advertisement for the Eastman Kodak Company. They had a picture of a girl on top of a hill in a wheat field, with a striped dress on which was being blown by the wind. She had posed for it. So it was a fast romance from then on. In that picture we had my old friend ZaSu Pitts, and William Haines.

DOWD: You said this was the first film in which you used a metronome. Would you talk about how it was used?

VIDOR: Going back to The Birth of a Nation and Intolerance, I was so much aware of Griffith's handling of mounting excitement. I was trying to get the same sort of an effect, and that's how I ran into speeding up each scene. You can't remember from one day or one week to the next how fast one scene went. Sometimes you couldn't be sure if you were speeding up or slowing down. I was very conscious of the music played on the set and the effect it had of speeding up or slowing down the acting. I was very conscious of tempo. In fact, I felt that the most important thing about motion picture directing was tempo.

In order to have an exact diagram of speeding up the end of a film to reach an exciting climax, I worked out the metronome idea. I simply made each scene progressively faster, according to the beat of the metronome. Now, there was nobody walking and keeping exact time to the metronome, but it gave me a basis. I could tell just by listening how fast the scene should be played. It gave me the tempo and I could have the music played according to the metronome. It affected how I set the camera. If I said, "Camera, action, fast!" that meant the actors would all move faster.   Then if I slowed it up and said, "Camera, action, slow," that meant I was thinking of it in terms of slow performances, slow tempo.

In the climax of Three Wise Fools we had a runaway armored car built for the convicts to make their escape in. I remember reading and studying all of the famous prison escapes, about the different ways -- the railroad trains, how they passed notes, and all of that. We had an adaptation of the play, but I tried to get in an exciting climax.

Cedric Gibbons designed this car and crashed it through the prison gates, which were actually the MGM studio gates. We used an airplane in pursuit, but the airplane was an old World War I Jenny, and it couldn't keep up with the car. We had to keep slowing down the car, then we'd have to speed it up once we got ready to shoot again. They were dropping bombs on the car to stop it and halt it. The camera was never very set in its speed. I suppose with this film Eleanor Boardman emerged into stardom.

DOWD: By now you had directed about twelve features. Could you describe the method you were using at this point to direct? Would you talk to your actors while the cameras were rolling?

VIDOR: I've just talked about how the speed with which I would say "Camera, action," would be a way of directing tempo. My voice didn't carry too much, and I had a theory that if you talked too much you would distract the actors. We used a sort of shorthand by saying, "That's good," or "Enough," or you might say, "More," or "More of that," and try to say it quickly and unobtrusively so that it wouldn't distract, wouldn't pull the actors away.

In fact, with Gilbert I developed almost a type of telepathy. We knew each other well. It was also partly by gesture. Maybe he'd see a gesture of mine outside the corner of his eye, as a person in an orchestra sees a small gesture the conductor makes. He claimed he knew what I was thinking.

Some directors did lots of talking, and lots of acting. I would try to make it very clear to the actors exactly what it was that I wanted from them, but if something were to develop during a scene, which often happened, I would keep the camera going. This is particularly true of comedy. We'd keep the camera going and the actors would know that we had run onto something and I would say, "Don't stop now, that's great!" I gave encouragement. That was very important.

I felt that those actors who had been on the stage were like children and they missed the applause of the audience. The director had to take the place of the audience. The director is like a psychiatrist. The women stars are always falling in love with the director because he gives the whole reaction of whether they are good or bad, and I don't think anyone who has ever been an actress isn't precarious about her performance.

DOWD: Did you rehearse?

VIDOR: The rehearsal was to know exactly where they should go, where they should stand, just to get the blocking straight. I did take it to the point where I thought the next rehearsal would be the best performance. If it wasn't, I would stop and correct it, but I always felt that there was one take that would be the right one, and from there they would all go downhill.

I would try to set up everything to photograph the good take so it wouldn't get stale. I never did indulge in too many takes because I thought the actors would get mechanical. I always tried to capture some spontaneous quality in the acting. They may supply something better than you had planned.

What you do is tell the actors exactly what you want, not from the acting standpoint, but what idea it is that you want communicated. I avoided giving them a performance as an example. That is getting in and acting and expecting them to copy you, which is what Griffith did. I wanted it to come from them so that each person would have a different individuality, rather than just copying my performance. All of the Griffith people looked alike. He had been an actor at one time himself.

DOWD: What kind of music did you have on the set for Three Wise Fools and Peg o' My Heart?

VIDOR: We had a portable organ and a violin. That was the standard music on the set. In the case of Marion Davies, she had a quartet which included a cello, bass fiddle, and two violins. It was marvelous, just beautiful. It was surprising how much you could control by the music you selected.

DOWD: Were you the one who selected the music to be played?

VIDOR: Yes. Sometimes if a star had to do an emotional love scene, they would play a special song. John Gilbert, for example, liked a piece called "Moonlight and Roses." He selected that himself. Sometimes a star would come along and say, "The piece that affects me the most is 'Love's Old Sweet Song,' " or something like that. They would ask me if we could play it during the take.

DOWD: Then would you go over and consult with the orchestra?

VIDOR: In the case of Marion Davies, I had a long talk with them. Sometimes I would hear a piece on a record, or go to a symphony concert and tell them, "Would you come prepared for that music tomorrow?" In The Crowd we used a phonograph and a record of Tchaikovsky's sixth symphony, the Pathétique. Sometimes when you were pressed for money, the first thing to go would be the orchestra. In those cases you would then bring a phonograph to the set.

DOWD: You wouldn't take the orchestra on location, would you?

VIDOR: Oh, yes.

DOWD: On something like Sky Pilot, would you have an orchestra there?

VIDOR: I've forgotten. Well, not if you just had cowboys running by and stagecoaches and all that. But if you had any kind of emoting going on, the stars would say, "Where's the music?" This was as important as the dressing room. The star almost had to be your wife or something before they'd give up the music to help them emote. They had to stand still, they couldn't do their crying by making noises with their mouths. As I remember, we took the orchestra on location most of the time, except if the shooting involved strictly action shots.

DOWD: Do you remember if Eleanor Boardman had any favorite things she used to use?

VIDOR: No, I don't remember.

DOWD: Let's go on to Happiness, which we screened recently.

VIDOR: As a result of Peg o' My Heart, Laurette Taylor and the Metro Company were a big success. The Metro Company wanted me back to do another one of Laurette's husband's plays, Happiness. She had also done this play, but without the success of Peg o' My Heart. By now I was very much in love with Eleanor and I did not want to be away too long. However, I did stay in New York long enough to shoot all of the necessary scenes. The rest of it we shot in the studio. That thing on Fifth Avenue, the sequence where we were running over the tops of the automobiles, that must have been done on the studio lot, because it's pretty hard to tie up Fifth Avenue with traffic unless you have some kind of special technique.

          I didn't feel at the time that I had concentrated enough and dedicated myself enough to get everything there was to get out of this picture, but I was wrong. Looking at it today, maybe it was a good idea that I didn't take it too seriously. I sort of light-heartedly went through it. Well, there was a love affair going on between Laurette Taylor and me, and there was a wonderful rapport and spirit between us. It seemed to show up in the film, because there was a sort of delighted expression on her face all of the time, and she moved with the freedom I like to see actresses and actors move with, a certain unexpected freedom.

DOWD: I noticed in the film that there were lots of comic bits, little actions that she would do which I'm sure she probably didn't do in the play. There were quite a few of these visual gags.

VIDOR: Most of the gags were probably mine, because I think as a kid along those lines. There was a wonderful spirit we had going, and somebody asked me not too long ago why we didn't make more films together. I think she only made one other film that I know of, a film called One Night in Rome, from another one of Hartley Manners's plays. It was directed by Clarence Badger.

          When we were working together she stayed in one of those bungalows at the Beverly Hills Hotel. We played tennis on Sunday and then we would have dinner there. She loved to play all sorts of games, mental games especially. I saw her afterwards in New York one time. She was doing another picture at the time. We still remained good friends. Years later on a New Year's Day she was at her daughter's home, and her daughter called me and said, "Be prepared for a shock." When I went through the door I saw how old she had gotten to be. It was a shock, but I stayed with her and we talked for a long time. It was the last time I saw her.

DOWD: The cameraman on Happiness was Chester Lyons, but were you using that same shotgun spotlight technique?

VIDOR: Yes, but I don't think we had to use that lens. The lens I talked about in the other film was only for close-ups. We didn't have so many big close-ups in Happiness because the age thing was not so apparent. In that film there was no age stated, except that she was going to be married to a young guy. We did use the spot, though.

DOWD: In the opening scene when everyone is dancing on the sidewalk, she is wearing that mask. It reminds me a bit of Street Scene. Was this business of her wearing the mask in the script?

VIDOR: It surprised me when I saw it, because I had forgotten about it. That scene was not in the play, but she may have come in with the mask on, I don't really know. It did remind me of Street Scene, but it was not done on New York streets. It was done on the studio lot in Hollywood, because I recognized the organ grinder. He was a Hollywood figure at the time, and that's how I can place it in Hollywood.

DOWD: She reminded me of Marion Davies in The Patsy. I think you were developing a comic style at this time, because Happiness is very similar to Show People and The Patsy.

VIDOR: Yes, you see Marion Davies did a similar type of comedy. You talk about Marion Davies and Laurette Taylor being similar in their comedic styles, but I can't say they were exactly the same. They touch the same little humorous twists, but it's a slightly satirical and slightly imitative style, and it's perhaps based on blasting conventionality or hypocrisy. This was done by undermining it, by saying something that takes the foundation out of conventional form.

DOWD: You seem to do very well at blasting preten-tiousness.

VIDOR: Yes, it's based on that. I find myself going just so far in accepting what they call "conditioned thinking." I'll tolerate it just to a point, and then when it gets too pompous and when the person says something with authority on some point as if it were law, I won't attack by antagonizing it, but I will attack it by commenting on it. I suppose in this way their sense of comedy was about the same.

In The Patsy, I think Marion Davies imitates Lillian Gish. Laurette was quite an imitator, too. We'd each have a sympathetic understanding. When you have that, you can find comedy in everything you're doing.

I noticed that if you made a more serious pic-ture, there was something applicable to about every situation. In Three Wise Fools there was a line that would apply to any situation in life. It was a strange thing, and I have difficulty describing it. It was a line that fit anything you could do, whether it was getting up in the morning, or eating a meal, or ordering a drink. I applied that to mean that this picture had the scope of life. The picture covered enough of the vital things of life to have a line, a reference to almost anything you could do.

DOWD: I wanted to ask you some more questions about Happiness. Did you write the final title -- "So an endless chain of Jennies goes on in all big cities, courageous in defeat, hopeful in adversity, fighting the battle against poverty, taking their fun where they find it, and knowing happiness is looking forward"?

VIDOR: I must admit when I read it during the film that it sounded very much like me at the time. I can't be sure, but it certainly hit me. The line "... succession of Jennies ..." was a similar line to one in Jack Knife Man that went like:

"These buddies all over the world . . . " Later on, I think we'll see where I have a character, just a bit character, and he is repeated over and over again in the same way.

--- --- --- --- --- ---

DOWD: Let's talk about <u>Wine of Youth</u>. This was another Eleanor Boardman picture.

VIDOR: This again was from a play. I am surprised at how many of these pictures were from plays. I think I read this play in a compiled collection of all the plays from the year before. I didn't see the play, I'm sure of that. I'm quite amazed at the restrictions, and surprised at the thinking -- the naïveté that went on. In making a film of this sort, which was about trial marriage, there were so many inhibitions and restrictions that it really took the guts out of the idea. I felt we had to do too much avoiding of saying what we really wanted to say.

I'm sure this is the first film I made with the combined forces of Metro, Goldwyn, and Mayer. The studio was the Goldwyn studio, and Metro moved out from Hollywood, and they also moved their stages over. Then Mayer brought in Irving Thalberg, and this was the first film that I made in conjunction with Mayer and Thalberg.

Colleen Moore's <u>Flaming Youth</u> was a big hit. It was during the flapper age, and she became the original flapper. The ideas that they expressed, looked at in today's light, are not very daring. Even the fellows in dinner clothes all seem rather dignified, and the way they're seen in the performance was very dignified.

By the end of the next film, <u>His Hour</u>, the Hays Office had formed. This threat of censorship and the false puritanism was hanging over our heads, and Mr. Mayer was quite sensitive about anything that suggested the slightest bit of off-color disrespect. He and Gilbert used to go round and round because Gilbert wanted to make a picture where he slapped his mother. Well, to Mr. Mayer, a mother was a sacred object. You were walking on eggs all of the time.

Here I was, trying to do a film about trial marriage, which is so much the issue today. Parents are trying to make children follow the same line of thought that went on in their generation. That was the basic idea of the film. It just had to be watered down.

I had to be more suggestive. That was another thing that went on, especially in silent pictures, because that was the nature of silent pictures. So many things had to be inferred or suggested. You just couldn't come out and say anything. They'd take it out, cut it, and censor it. They were always afraid that all the women's clubs would rise up in anger, which would bring around censorship legislation.

DOWD: I remember Eleanor Boardman's performance in the film was quite remarkable. She appears to be an extremely intelligent woman when you see her in this film.

VIDOR: Yes, I thought so. I don't know whether she's the right type. I had blinded eyes at the time. I was in love with her, and we weren't married yet. She just seemed beautiful to me. She certainly wasn't the flapper type. She was an intelligent, thoughtful actress. Actually she was a little bit miscast, but she was an MGM star, and they were developing her. That was the way they thought in those days. A star series of films was what they wanted.

This again was from a play, and our efforts were always to get the story moving, get it outside, out of the confinement of the rooms. We were always faced with getting off the couch and into some action.

DOWD: In Happiness and Wine of Youth your camera was beginning to move around.

VIDOR: Yes. I was getting away from the straight line-up. Once or twice I noticed in Happiness that the actors seemed to line up straight across the screen, but I'd been getting away from that type of thing, which was still going on at the Sennett Studios. The question was, were you willing to shoot at someone's back? Were you willing to get different angles, rather than just profiles? Those old shots were called "fifty-fifty" which meant that two people were facing each other. I began to say no to fifty-fifty shots. I wanted to get over someone's shoulder and show the other person's face.

When the dialogue came along, it freed all of us because you could play a scene with someone's back to the camera and still have a very effective scene. I discovered later you could have everybody's back to the camera if you wanted to. At least people could be in a circle. Up until then we just thought that you must see a person's face at all times.

It was the same thing with lighting. We couldn't get lighting that was too effective, because the more light you used on a person's face, the more it helped tell the story. The faces and expressions told the whole story. You just couldn't have anyone's face in the shadows. Many times some producer would say, "Oh, you're going to have to retake that. You couldn't see what was going on."

DOWD: There is a lot of depth in Wine of Youth. You'll see a character in the foreground and there will be something going on in the background. I noticed that although this film was made only two years after Love Never Dies, it was much more sophisticated.

VIDOR: We were going through the development stage of compositions. Another thing you notice is that they weren't photographed with just long shots. We were into the set more. You didn't get back and look at the set in long shots. In the past, if you had gone and built a huge set, everyone wanted to make sure that the whole thing was photographed so they could get credit for it. If you built it very deep, they always wanted to have a walk-up shot so they could have the character go from one end of the set to the other. But we got over that. The audience always thought you were photographing it in a real location, anyway.

In this film we had a beautiful set with a large banister, which allowed us to photograph people sliding down the entire length of it. I must have become conscious of the fact that I had to get more intimate in my use of the set, as well as my treatment of the characters. I probably was motivated by some social consciousness. I was really motivated by the parents trying to govern the children. That's the guts of the story as I saw it.

DOWD: I noticed that you used speeded-up and sloweddown camera techniques, as well as out-of-focus effects in the drunk scene.

VIDOR: You didn't use too much of that in this type of film. Maybe I hadn't done any of those things before, but it was a common practice in some types of films to speed up the action. The films from Europe started to come over at that time, and I certainly began to think about camera techniques very strongly.

DOWD: Were you influenced by any particular European directors that you can think of?

VIDOR: Well, I was quite surprised looking back at the night scenes of The Crowd. That was shot during the daytime without any tinting. I don't know whether the tints were being used at that time. We used heavy filters, later, for the dayfor-night shots, but in this film we didn't seem to use any of that. It wasn't tinted in any way, as some of the other films from the same period were. Perhaps the original copies had been tinted, but the ones around today aren't. I don't think this was a result of any specific directors I had seen, but I do remember that I was strongly influenced by their films.

DOWD: You've never been fond of using that German shadow technique. In your films of this period the lighting is all very clear and precise.

VIDOR: I think you'll see this soon in Hallelujah, which was my first sound film. In that picture, I begin to have some shadowy effects.

DOWD: I think Show People was just beautifully lit. I don't recall any shadows in it, but it was beautifully clear.

VIDOR: I must say that in looking at my silent films in retrospect I was pleased with the clarity of them. The cameraman was more concerned with getting a certain roundness in the lighting. You see, films are two-dimensional, they're not stereoscopic. The idea was to light them to make them appear as stereoscopic as possible. That was what the best cameramen were doing. It pleases me especially with these silents to have them clear. In fact, with Chaplin comedy, the technique was to put all the lights in front. We were trying to make the characters stand out from the background. Everybody thought Technicolor was going to take a lot longer, perhaps twenty-five percent longer, to shoot. After a few years they discovered it didn't take as much time because the colors took care of the roundness and background. You can really shoot color photography faster than black-and-white.

DOWD: Were you really influenced by Chaplin at this time? I know you and Chaplin were good friends.

VIDOR: I saw all of his films, and I saw all of the Sennett films, as well as Harold Lloyd's. There really wasn't a direct influence with Chaplin as a person. It didn't come until later. I suppose the reason we were friends was because we could talk the same language as far as films were concerned. You see, even with the Griffith films, a Sennett film always ran as a second feature at the Philharmonic Auditorium. The Sennett studios came out with a new film each week. They were more slapstick, and Chaplin was not entirely slapstick. As he always said, comedy and tragedy are very close together. His films had a lot more tragedy in them. You couldn't help but be in this mood, you know. You couldn't help but pick it up and be influenced, just as I was influenced by Griffith, too.

DOWD: Do you think there is any characteristic of this period of the twenties, one that you could name with one word? I believe you once mentioned that it was a "naïve" period.

VIDOR: I hate to generalize. There was a great bubbling enthusiasm. In the book The William Desmond Taylor Story, I think something is said about it. People were doing these things and they couldn't help but think that it was a bubble that would burst, and it would all come to an end. There were so many people out from vaudeville and various places that were having great joy and fun in all of this work, turning out all these films, sort of setting the world on fire because they were getting world-wide recognition. Yet, they had to pinch themselves to believe it was all happening, so they kept themselves in a great spirit of keyed-up gratitude. That's how it seemed to me in perspective. A lot of people would say that I wasn't playful about it, and I was very serious. However, the general mood at the time was playful. It was based to some extent on their fear of the dawn, and that they would all be back on the vaudeville stage once again when it was all over.

III

DOWD: In relation to His Hour, which you made at
Metro in 1924, I wanted to ask you a few things. It was Irving
Thalberg who gave you the assignment to direct the picture,
which was an Elinor Glyn screenplay from her own novel of
the same name. That does not seem to be the kind of film you
would be suited to direct, at least it doesn't seem to be your
type of film. I wanted to ask you what your reputation was at
MGM at the time? What did Thalberg think of you? How did
you get along with him, and can you compare him to other
producers you have worked for?

VIDOR: Well, the situation as I remember was this: I had
gone to Culver City to work for the Goldwyn Company. I think
they were in a little financial trouble, and although I made
Three Wise Fools and Wild Oranges, there was a big publicity
campaign as to who would direct the next big picture, Ben
Hur. I was called in one day, and since I had sold myself to
them with the first two pictures, they gave me the big assignment of making Ben Hur in Europe. In fact, I remember
reading it either coming to or going back from Florida as I
was making Wild Oranges. That film got very good reviews, as
I suppose Three Wise Fools did.

        I was well liked and thought of by the Goldwyn
Company, but apparently their financial position was not too
strong, although they were starting production of the film in
Italy. Maybe this was one of the schemes to amalgamate with
Metro anyway. Suddenly, along came this amalgamation and
MGM was formed. Metro immediately picked up a rather medi-
um-sized and somewhat questionable operation, the Goldwyn
Company. Goldwyn himself was not with the company at the
time, they were just going on with his name. I think they
lacked any kind of decisive management, and along came

51

Louis B. Mayer and Thalberg, with the combined forces of the Metro Company to take over executive management. I suppose Wine of Youth was the first picture under that arrangement. That picture was done to offset Colleen Moore's Flaming Youth, which was very popular.

His Hour was made because of the great popularity of Glyn's Three Weeks, which I think was made at Goldwyn, and had a very big sex appeal factor. All of Elinor Glyn's writings at that time had big sex appeal. The whole idea was her approach, a sort of romantic Victorian, but nevertheless very sexy. I think one was called His Moment. So, MGM got His Hour.

Well, I had not yet made The Big Parade, and was not so confident of myself. I was glad to go along with the new administration and become acquainted with the new executives, but I was not in any position to dictate what I would or would not do. I was glad to continue on with the new management and sell myself to them.

Making His Hour was an assignment and a real challenge. We had a lot of humorous feelings about it. When Elinor Glyn arrived she wanted to read me the script. She rented a suite at the Ambassador Hotel. I took my assistant director up, and she (Glyn) read the entire book, from beginning to end, all in one evening. She acted out all of the voices, the different characters, and actually performed it. We had a terrible time just staying awake. If anybody reads to me, I fall asleep, and to read this whole story with all of the inflections was really a job. So, we drank a lot of coffee and stayed awake with great difficulty. She insisted on this.

The whole thing was getting along with her and whatever contributions she decided to make. She had been in Imperial Russia, which was where the story took place. Of course I hadn't been there myself, and she had many suggestions. Some of them were ridiculous, but I went along with them. She was a very popular authority, as well as a big-selling author at that time. It was also a big enough picture that an aspiring director like myself would not turn down the assignment.

DOWD: Was that the first film you directed John Gilbert? Could you also talk about your relationship with him?

VIDOR: I suppose Gilbert and I got along very well on His Hour. He was a dashing type of fellow. I remember thinking up pieces of business to play love scenes that he would like. Gilbert was the great lover and we got along very well. The other picture we worked on was Wife of the Centaur. We seemed to become good friends right away. In fact, I had one of the first houses in the hills in back of Beverly Hills, and he moved in with me. We played tennis together and were part of a group that included Joe Cohn, the studio manager, Donald Ogden Stewart, the writer, myself, and Laurence Stallings. John built a house right next to mine. We were together a lot, even outside of the studio. I suppose the first big change in Gilbert's life and our association was not until The Big Parade.

DOWD: Gilbert had been a director before. Was he still a frustrated director as an actor?

VIDOR: No, I don't think so. In fact, I don't think he had ever talked to me about being a director. He might have said, "I directed a picture once," but this was very normal. Many actors had once directed a picture like some of the stars today -- Kirk Douglas, for example. They flaunt the idea that they want to direct, but Gilbert never spoke of it to me.

        Anyway, Thalberg came in and was put in charge of the studio. The order of power at that time was Mayer, Thalberg, and then Harry Rapf. He would call up the different directors, Thalberg would, and have talks with them, and he was going to be the top executive at the studio eventually. I was perhaps a little older than he was, but we became very good friends. We went on many boat trips and parties together. I was an usher at his wedding to Norma Shearer. I was at his house a lot, and he was at mine, I suppose. He had a feeling for my work. He wanted me to be one of the stable of directors there, of which they had quite a few. These were men such as Robert Z. Leonard, Jack Conway, von Stroheim, and Niblo. At this time they had recalled the Ben Hur project, recast it, and put in a new director.

DOWD: Why did you finally decide not to direct Ben Hur?

VIDOR: Well, I was in love with Eleanor Boardman, and I didn't want to be separated from her. Also, I didn't feel that I was ready to tackle a story like Ben Hur. The realism of it wasn't inherent. There were a few false things that happened. The basic theme of the story didn't get to me. I didn't want to be in a strange land, living away from the girl I had fallen in love with. I thought I was getting along well enough at home. I wasn't exactly afraid of it, but it just didn't seem to touch me.

DOWD: You were also asked to do the second version of Ben Hur, weren't you?

VIDOR: Well, the first one was the one I saw in the theatre at home in my youth. After War and Peace, Zimbalist, the producer, was going to make a call after they had seen the picture and offer me the present-day job of doing Ben Hur. I had been in Italy about a year and a half, and again I wanted to stay in America, and I didn't want to go rushing back over to Italy again, and I didn't want to undertake such a big picture without working on the script. They always say, "We want to start the picture in a month." They never, ever do, but I believed them and I thought I wouldn't want to embark on this project quickly without having worked on all of the scenes myself. When Wyler finally got onto it, he didn't start in a month. He probably started eight months later. I was just naïve enough to buy their story. Later on I began to wonder why I had turned it down. When I was in Spain doing Solomon and Sheba the reason we weren't working in Italy was because all of the Italian stages were occupied by Ben Hur. Many times I've thought what a fool I was to turn down Ben Hur for a less important picture. Many times I've thought of that.

DOWD: Wife of the Centaur appears to be a lost film, unfortunately. Can you remember anything about the story?

VIDOR: I remember starting to read the book. It was by Cyril Hume. He wrote very well. He appealed to me as a writer, and I remember when I first read the book, the first few pages had a love scene taking place while the characters were returning from a funeral. Gilbert and Eleanor Boardman were in the back seat of the car, and there was something that impelled them, some romantic feeling, or a physical feeling between them, that was taking place. I remember this just intrigued me no end. I was excited about the possibilities of this scene.

I had also seen a documentary on skiing. Gilbert couldn't ski at all, but we'd get him in and out of the shot for the picture. I thought that if we could use this skiing stuff in the picture, it would lighten up some of the episodes. I remember that the man would leave his home, and he would go skiing through the woods, up and down mountains, to another woman and another love affair. It was probably a triangle affair, a man between two women, which is the basis of many of my pictures. I think he was married, and he had a mistress on the side. I suppose it was the same situation as you would see in The Crowd when she says, "I think I understand you." The basis is probably the wife accepting Gilbert having some love interest other than herself. I think the other woman was Aileen Pringle. I would think that was the way the casting would go. Eleanor was certainly more the wife type than Aileen Pringle.

To get back to Three Weeks, one time we were all called up to the projection room by Mr. Mayer. He started to run about a thousand feet of film for all the directors at MGM. They were all clips from our pictures, and he was illustrating why they had employed Will Hays and why they were setting up the Hays Office. I remember it started out with a couple of hundred feet from His Hour, with John Gilbert kissing Aileen Pringle. His arm was under her robe, and there was just a tremendous amount of energy while he was working her over. This was lifted out as one of the scenes that illustrated why they had to have the Hays Office. You see, cashing in on sexual themes is not that new.

DOWD: How did you feel about the Hays Office? How did you react as a director? I think it was established around 1922. These pictures were made around 1924.

VIDOR: The reason we had the meeting with Mayer was because the picture had been released before the demonstration. There were so many strong threats and reactions about cuts, feelings that the cuts would hurt the pictures in certain places. I just felt that it was something we had better go along with. If we didn't they would just start cutting the pictures themselves. We didn't want the films cut. We didn't want to have them barred. We also didn't want stricter laws being passed. One of the threats was that they would just bar movies entirely. At that time movies were not established as a necessity. We actually believed that they could stop the production of movies.

DOWD: The film you made after Wife of the Centaur was Proud Flesh. Were there any projects you wanted to do, but couldn't, or was there something before the idea of The Big Parade came that you had in mind?

VIDOR: Just let me say a few words about Proud Flesh. There were two things I remember. It was set in San Francisco, and I wanted to get the atmosphere of the steep streets and hills. Again, I was trying to go to real locations to get the advantage of the settings. How much we got in that picture I've forgotten, but I know we did travel to San Francisco. I was always talking about going to places that the stories were set in so that it would look more convincing.

        After that we went down to Carmel and Pebble Beach to get some coastline shots. I remember the fog came in, and when I wanted to shoot, I couldn't. I asked, "Why couldn't we have the fog in the shot anyway?" We finally convinced the cameraman that we could just shoot a few feet, just to be safe. There were some gulls flying overhead, and I said, "We'll take a shot of the gulls!" That shot was later mentioned in a lot of reviews. There was a symbolism working in the fog, creating a better atmosphere than shooting in sunshine. It was a great plus to the scenes we went there to shoot. I did that many times. If there was fog, use it! The same thing applies to rain.

DOWD: At this point did you have a preferred cameraman?

VIDOR: I had George Barnes. I don't think I carried him on into Metro. They had their own cameramen, though. That was always a problem. You wanted a cameraman to work with you, and you never got them in time. Here was a company making fifty films a year, and they would give you whoever was available. They had a good stable of cameramen, a great bunch, but you got the ones that were not working on any other pictures at the time. Also, you were not in a position to pull the good ones off another picture. Somebody like Garbo or Marion Davies could, but as a rule, you couldn't do that. It would be rather an insult to the director of the other film, and they couldn't really show that favoritism. They might, in the case of Norma Shearer, hold a cameraman in abeyance, but the other directors would be given whoever was free.

We would make a picture, Proud Flesh, for example, and it would come to town and they would only play it for a week. Some films played two weeks, if you were lucky. The first picture, Turn in the Road, ran eleven weeks in a theatre on Broadway. But most of the films would just come to town, play the big theatre downtown for one week, and then would be gone. I thought about how hard we worked on them, how careful we were, and then somebody would go in for seventy-five cents or a dollar, see it, say, "Oh, it's pretty good," and then it would be forgotten. I went to Thalberg and said, "I would like to make a film that runs longer than just one week. I would like for a lot of people to see it, because films only play for a week and hardly anybody sees them." So he said, "Have you got something in mind?" I said, "Wheat, steel, or war." He said, "Well, you better start looking for stories." Right away I started on a war story.

DOWD: Was this a project you had in mind for a while?

VIDOR: I had been thinking about it in terms of photographic environment. These three ideas intrigued me because of the photographic fields and subjects to be explored. We had a scenario department and you just asked for all the submitted stories about the war. All war stories up to that time had been ones that glamorized war. The leads were all played by handsome officers in highly polished boots, tailored uniforms, and wonderful hats. My idea, of course, was not to glamorize war, but to just have a GI, a common soldier who didn't want to make war. He didn't think enough against it to start a campaign against the war, but he still felt badly about it. This was my idea, a more realistic thing.

DOWD: In The Big Parade you can't see John Gilbert's leg strapped up.

VIDOR: I think I had seen Lon Chaney in The Penalty with both of his legs strapped up and we figured that if Chaney could do it, Gilbert could do it. We worked out some sort of harness. His leg must have been very slender to do that. I looked at him in profile, and I still couldn't see the leg. I know it was painful being strapped up for long periods of time. We would try to do just one scene and then let him get out of it right away.

There was also something that happened to me that was very important. I don't want to seem jealous about Thalberg, but it's just one of those things that happens in filmmaking. Thalberg got a lot of credit for doing certain things to add to the bigness of The Big Parade. One of them was a night battle which he had insisted upon, and it is after the last scene with Gilbert in a shellhole when the Germans and Allies all rise up and have a big battle at night. That was his one contribution. The ironic thing is that the pages I had written for the beginning and end were rejected when we first shot it, and I had to do it a different way. Then we showed the picture and they began to say that the beginning should go a certain way, and the end should go a certain way. All I had to do was pull out the original pages I had written. But then I had to hear for years and years how the film was saved and how other people added to it. When you're involved with it, it's very important. . . . I didn't have the cut-off leg. It was more satirical than ironic. The interesting thing was that I had to reject these pages in the beginning. Later on I just pulled them out again. Not many people know about that, only Harry Behn and Stallings. But that's how films are made.

DOWD: I want to talk about the casting of Gilbert. It was quite an unusual casting in that he had been billed as a great lover by MGM. He seems to have been very modern, unlike the Gilbert I've seen in other films. In this one he's terribly confused. Usually he doesn't have that confused air about him. In this film he reminds me of Dustin Hoffman in The Graduate. The father says something to him with perfect straightforwardness and sincerity, and Gilbert looks at him as if to say, "Are you nuts?"

VIDOR: My motivation for the thing was reaction. Some of the stars make their careers on an aggressive, positive approach. They don't like to play scenes where they react to things because they've made their careers by being aggressive and certain. They motivate things and they cause things. When you get a big aspect of war, no actors are going to come in there, motivate the war, and solve everything. That was my idea.

My approach was to have him reacting to things he saw and experiences he had. He's looking at the father and thinking, What sort of fellow are you? Then he looks at the mother and thinks, What sort of woman are you? When he gets into the shellhole he looks at the German and thinks, What sort of person are you? He falls in love with a French girl and forgets about what he's over there for. Then, suddenly it comes time to move up and they look at their first encounter in battle with a sort of "What should I think of this?" attitude.

Gilbert was playing a part he never played before. He never had dirty fingernails before, and he'd never done a part without makeup before. Then he found that he liked it. I had dictated the methods and the ways he should be dressed, and so forth, and after it was a successful box-office film, he would willingly go along with anything I suggested. There was a lot of talk about the casting. Even when it was finished some said that he wasn't a typical doughboy. You gain so much by putting an individual in the part, like Gilbert, and letting the other people be the typical doughboys. I don't suppose the others are typical, either. However, the typical people always seem to fade into the background.

DOWD: Did Gilbert want the role from the very beginning?

VIDOR: Yes, he did.

DOWD: Did you think of him from the very beginning? Was he your first choice?

VIDOR: No, I think we probably thought of a more ordinary fellow, more like James Murray in The Crowd. I don't remember that this went on very long. They were putting the combination of stars together and they figured it was going to cost a couple hundred thousand dollars. They wanted material for their stars, and it started out as another John Gilbert starring vehicle. They had to go around and buy all those exhibitors off who insisted that they should have this film as another picture of Gilbert's series.

VIDOR: Did you discover Karl Dane?

VIDOR: Yes. We were looking for a strange type like that. We would hold casting interviews and we'd be sent a dozen people to be interviewed for each part. When he came along I jumped right at him. He hadn't done a film before, and I understood later that he was a carpenter, but I grabbed him. He was a star.

DOWD: I think the titles about patriotism, the origins of it, and how it sort of was an easy-come, easy-go thing are very ironic. Were these your titles, or were they Joseph Farnham's?

VIDOR: I think they were Farnham's. I don't think I wrote the titles, but what we wanted to say was from Stallings and me. One of the most outstanding scenes that was talked over and remembered was this close-up of his feet beating time to the band. The rhythm of the band is how he happened to go to war and leave the automobile standing right in the middle of the street. Reviewers all talked about how the rhythm of the band was what got him going off to war.

DOWD: Also, the girlfriend comes along and says, "Hasn't he told you?" He probably hadn't even decided then that he was going to go, but you see that he can't lose face with his parents, so he says, "Yeah."

VIDOR: Now he had signed up, he had enlisted, but by then he'd cooled off a bit and didn't want to make a big thing of it. He was cynical about signing up, but he jumped in with a bunch of friends and enlisted before he knew it.

DOWD: There is a great sequence with the walking barrel. Gilbert comes walking over with a barrel over his head. I think that's one of the first times he sees Renée Adorée. Was that really Gilbert under the barrel?

VIDOR: Yes. I can't help thinking about Chaplin. Chaplin was a big item at that time, and his films were tremendous when he used pantomime. What I remember very distinctly was how wonderful it was to have a girl who could not speak English, and a man who could not speak French -- there was the excuse for all of the pantomime that you could want. I thought at this time that I was going to have people in all of my pictures who couldn't speak the same language.

The other thing I thought of at the time was how important every scene becomes when death is being faced around the corner. It gives a power to every scene you do. The love, the romance, it's all carefree for the time. It's an uninhibited type of lovemaking and romance that was current at that time.

DOWD: I really thought that The Big Parade made such a beautiful use of all the differences in the two languages. So many of the scenes between Gilbert and Adorée are based on the fact that they can't communicate in terms of words.

VIDOR: Yes. I remember one particular scene when he gets the photograph from home. You could have put all of the dialogue you wanted there. You could have had sound and words, and it would have not added one bit to what was going on. He was so articulate with the pantomime, with her mood, about how he should go home to the American girl, how she was just a passing fancy and so forth. You could not add anything to it at all.

Time and time again, it just seems that the visual is so much more important than the words. When sound first came, I was very much aware that the most important lines could go by if you based the picture on exposition, and it would be completely unnoticed. A visual thing, no matter how short or how brief, would not go by unnoticed. If you try to put in the right spoken lines, it seems to be coming out of a loudspeaker somewhere, and it can be ignored, not heard. But if you put it up there on the screen and have it right in the composition, it'll be remembered. It will be remembered not only for the length of the picture, but for years afterward as well. I've seen it time and time again.

DOWD: I think that is particularly true of the scene where Adorée takes the rose and rubs it on her neck.

VIDOR: Yes.

DOWD: Would you talk about Donald Ogden Stewart and the chewing gum scene?

VIDOR: We had a line in the script: Love Scene Between the Two. That's the way a script would read. You'd have to go out the night before and have a romance if you wanted to do the scene well the next day, if you wanted to get something new. Well, some mornings I would arrive, maybe I'd gone to a party or something the night before, and I didn't always have something prepared. I was standing around and the cameraman was asking me where I wanted him to put the camera. Stewart said something like, "Come, let's get going." I looked up at him and saw that he was chewing gum. I said to the prop man, "Get me some gum in a hurry."

        The scene with the American soldier introducing gum to the French girl was improvised right there. I said, "Take the gum out and give it to her. She doesn't know whether to unwrap it or swallow it, and he teaches her how to chew gum." I guess that scene ran three hundred feet. It was all done in one set-up. It wasn't cut up with any close shots, and they don't move around, they just sit on the bench. It was basically a pantomime. To let a shot run three hundred feet was an absolute innovation in motion picture making then. You were supposed to let them stand up, move around, or go for a walk or something, but a take that long just was never done. I just let them sit there on the bench, and it was terrific. It was talked of and written about for a long time.

DOWD: Did you have any pressure put on you later to cut that scene?

VIDOR: No, I didn't. The going-away scene was another great scene that was talked about for years. The most talked-of moment is the scene where the fellow wants to throw her something, and then throws her his own shoe. The fact that he reached back and tossed her his shoe, and that she grabbed it and held it to herself was talked about for twenty years.

DOWD: When Renée Adorée picks up the picture of the other girlfriend, she doesn't get mad. She says, Yes, I understand, just with gestures alone. Then she runs off and cries by the trees. Then seeing the troops going away, she has no malice at all. That's such a beautiful sequence.

VIDOR: Yes, it is. There's no time for malice, no time for jealousy, none of that. I was reminded after seeing it again that I was thinking very much in terms of symphonic treatment. I had begun to use the metronome and I began to think in musical movements. I know that these scenes were planned sitting in the Philharmonic Hall in Los Angeles while listening to the orchestra.

In the background you can see horses, trucks, and men, with all sorts of things going on, all in the back of the close-up. This whole movement is almost choreographed. In observing an orchestra with one group of instruments, the violins are doing the pizzicato, the cellos are doing something, and the tympanies are doing something else. In the picture there are motorcycles going back and forth, trucks are doing a different thing, and horses are moving at still a different pace. It's all paralleling to musical actions. They build up to a certain climax with a long line of trucks, and then the camera drops down to a lone girl on the roadway, completely complacent, and tranquil. Even with the lighting, we went back late in the day to get the long shot of the girl. Here a minute before had been thousands of men, trucks, and machines, and a little bit later there was only a young girl left alone in the empty roadway.

DOWD: Would you talk a little about the directing of the march of death?

VIDOR: All of the men are having a hell of a good time in this French village. They are all clowning and laughing it up, and pretty soon a bugle blows and they go up and we get closer as they are going to enter the woods, which are filled with German soldiers. I didn't want to show the German machine gunners first. So, what do you do after the line comes on, "Fix your bayonets"? I was looking at eighty reels of Signal Corps footage and on came a scene with soldiers marching at a tempo that looked like death. It was a funeral procession, but the first scenes just showed soldiers and then pretty soon you were able to see the flag-draped coffin on the carriage. The tempo was death. So, I got the metronome into the projection room, marked down the speed, and then I thought I would do the whole walk through the woods in this tempo.

We actually had men who had musical experience in charge of each platoon of men. We had a big bass drum, but we didn't have loudspeakers, so we hit this drum to keep the proper tempo. If you got hit, if you were to fall part of the way down to the ground, you had to wait until the next beat of the drum. Everybody was instructed that no matter what they did, they must do it in time to the beat. Everybody's footstep was on a beat. It's all so relentless. Even though men are hit by machine guns and drop on all sides, the body of men keeps walking forward.

DOWD: You had specific instructions as to how this would be played in the theatres, didn't you?

VIDOR: Yes, I wanted to cut out all of the music, but it got away from me during the general scoring. In the Egyptian Theatre in Hollywood I was able to have just a muffled bass drum beat. It was very effective, so much more so than any type of music. I tried to get it done in New York, but I could only work through telephone calls and correspondence. The composers thought they knew better. I had been there when we were shooting the scenes with the bass drum and I knew how effective it was, that we didn't need any melody line.

That's another subject completely. Melody lines can easily ruin the sequence. It's very difficult and you must stay with the composer and the musician to be able to avoid having him upset your basic intent. The music was written in New York and I was in California. It would just get completely out of hand, and we'd lose control.

DOWD: What kind of musical accompaniment did you have with the other scenes?

VIDOR: I learned from Griffith that the thematic melody and the other music written for The Great Love was made up from the songs and cheers used in World War I. There's a slight ironic touch about it, but that's what they were doing, and that's what we used.

DOWD: I wanted to ask you about the famous assistant director and the straight line in Texas that became a crooked line.

VIDOR: Well, I had the idea that to have an absolute straight line bumper to bumper with trucks, each jammed with men, would look great. In other words, two hundred trucks and four thousand men. I sent down an assistant because I was starting La Bohème and I didn't have the time in between pictures to shoot it myself.

I had David Howard go down there and line all this up. I would do rough drawings of what I wanted and he was supposed to execute them the way they had been drawn. He went down there and started getting drunk with the Army officers. No, I take that back. He would have drinks with them and get very palsy-walsy. The generals and the other officers talked him out of having a straight line, even though that was how it had been done in France during the war. How stupid can you be?

Anyway, they talked him out of the straight line and got him to make a big zig-zag shape. He sent all of the footage back and I started looking at it the night it arrived. Thalberg said, "Be sure to call me when you get through." I looked at the film and saw all of this zig-zag stuff with hundreds of men and trucks and everything, and then I called my assistant at four o'clock in the morning and he asked, "Well?" I said, "Not so well." There were some interesting scenes, but it certainly wasn't a straight line. He said, "What are you going to do about it?" I said, "I want to leave for San Antonio tomorrow night."

I left while he was still down there and I had to go out to Fort Sam Houston and talk to the generals. I said to them, "You didn"t do the straight line." One of the generals nearly jumped through the ceiling. He said, "I was in France and we're not going to do the straight line. It was not done that way, and it won't be done like that now. Besides, it's twenty-five miles out to the straight section of road." I just stood there, and a few days later we wound up shooting on the straight road twenty-five miles away. They had to pull out all of the troops and trucks again.

DOWD: How many men were involved in this?

VIDOR: Four thousand United States Army soldiers, and no extras.

DOWD: I saw a still in your portfolio the other day of a scene taken at MGM in which you are surrounded by those generals. They came to visit you at the studio afterwards?

VIDOR: Yes. They all came out to tell me how it was exactly the same in the film as it was in France. The funny thing was that we argued during the shooting so much, but after the film came out, the War Department told people that if they wanted to see what it was like in France during the war, they should see The Big Parade. After my experience with the technical directors the Army furnished, I never again had any use for technical directors. I showed them all the footage from the Signal Corps films that had the straight line formations, and they told me it never could have happened.

Speaking of that, we also had use of that footage, all eight thousand feet of it. It showed all of the cannons being loaded, the anti-aircraft guns, and lots of artillery fire. This stuff would be too difficult to stage, so we used the footage. We also had a shot where a cannon knocked a plane down. We had full use of whatever we wanted from that material. We had real Germans in the picture, all dressed in proper uniforms and fully armed. Some of the extras we used later on got to talking and found out that they had been in the same places during the war. Some of the German extras had even been firing on the men who were fighting on the Allied side. They would come up to me in pairs and tell me, "We were right in opposite places in line!"

DOWD: It must have been a parallel like in the foxhole scene, no real animosity between them when it comes down to it.

VIDOR: There never is any animosity between them. When it comes right down to it, when you put it down to the ordinary man, there is no animosity at all. There's not going to be animosity directed toward some young German fellow just because he happened to be born in Germany and then was drafted. He might be a school teacher, an accountant, or even a screen actor. You can't pull animosity down to two individuals facing each other. That's what the picture says. Up until this picture that type of scene never happened. I think five years later All Quiet on the Western Front had a lot of that, although that is about Germans.

DOWD: I think the same things happen between the German men and the Allies. You spoke about a field that had been wired for explosions that the men had to walk across. Can you tell us about that?

VIDOR: This is how you stage a scene with a barrage going on. You take a field like a tennis court and mark off zones. You put a lot of explosives that are controlled from a keyboard so that they can be set off by sections. There were actually such things as walking barrages during the war. They were planned so that artillery fired right ahead of the troops and cleared out everything in their way.

We set these things off from the keyboard, and the men had to stay up all night connecting the wires. It was a cold night and they started to drink, and eventually got the wires mixed up. The next morning we came in to shoot the scene. When we set off the charges, they exploded in the wrong areas, right in the middle of the men. It could have been very serious, but we had taken the precaution to sift the dirt over the charges so that no rocks could be sent flying through the air and accidentally hit someone. No one was hurt, but the explosions went off right underneath the men.

DOWD: How many cameras were there on this film?

VIDOR: I can't say definitely. In silent films if we were going to shoot a big scene, we'd pull out four or five cameras, and I know in some cases we had as many as ten.

DOWD: Kevin Brownlow mentioned something about the Akeley camera.

VIDOR: The Akeley camera was the equivalent of today's hand-held camera. It was developed for shooting wild animals. For a while we had it on a tripod, but the way in which the eyepiece was designed and constructed and the ease with which it cranked made it easy for picking it up and following movement.

DOWD: So you were using some of these even back then?

VIDOR: Yes, we always had it around when we thought we might need a shot of that type.

DOWD: The sets are very nice, too. The set of the town after the explosion, and the hospital ward were especially good.

VIDOR: That was a combination of painting and construction. The lower part of the set is real, and the upper part was all painted. We had a man named Warren Newcombe who did those shots, and we always called that a Newcombe Shot. You designed the set, and then turned it over to him and he painted the top of it for you. That way you could paint whatever you needed if you wanted to shoot above the heads of the actors.

DOWD: Is it true that after the film was initially released you had to cut 800 feet so they could get in another show?

VIDOR: Yes. There was 12,800 feet in the cut when it opened in the Egyptian Theatre in Hollywood. They wanted to take out 800 feet so that they could get in another show every day. In Hollywood and New York it was running as a reserved seat performance, but around the country, they wanted to get in as many performances as possible. They thought that 800 feet could be lost without hurting anything.

They had given Farnham, the title writer, the job of shortening it when I was working on <u>La Bohème</u>. He had gone through and cut out laughs and very important scenes. He just didn't know how to do it. I had to go down to the trash and pull out all the pieces he had cut out. He had probably not been to the previews and had not seen what had gone over well. I put up a big complaint and Thalberg told me, "All right, you can put that material back in, but I wish you would cut 800 feet somewhere."

I was directing <u>La Bohème</u> during the day, but at night I set up a cutting room in my home and went through the film carefully, looking at each splice and took a foot and a half before and after each splice. I did this so that the 800 feet came out, but did not affect the picture. In fact, people used to laugh at a certain point when Renée Adorée grabs his leg, and we just took out a few frames each night until the laugh wasn't there from the audience. Then we knew that we had taken out too much.

DOWD: How was its run in New York?

VIDOR: The film opened up in New York at the Astor Theatre on Broadway. There was a big sign up on the front of the theatre and it played to standing room only crowds for two years. It took in a million dollars at the one theatre, which was very good business in those days. It also had similar runs in Hollywood for six months.

Eighteen men would stand backstage with bugles and little wagons with iron in them making noise like real battle sounds. They also had tremendous ten-foot metal drums to give the sound effects for the big explosions. The theatre would shake, and the pit of your stomach would go in. I remember the orchestra came in and played for the first hour, and then the organist would take over. They had signal lamps out from someplace, one to blow the bugle, and one to cue the big explosions. I'll tell you, even though the picture was old stuff to me, to sit there and have those terrific explosions going off was really frightening. It really affected you.

DOWD: What was the premiere like?

VIDOR: I was at the premiere in Hollywood at the Egyptian Theatre. The theatre is set back away from Hollywood Boulevard. This area was lined with marines and flags. I think we got out of the car and were immediately accompanied by soldiers on all sides.

DOWD: That seems very ironic.

VIDOR: It was a new movement about honesty in war.

DOWD: Did you know it was going to be so good?

VIDOR: Yes, from the very beginning. Although at first we had different ideas about how the story would end up. First we started out with a different ending about the French girl. I think there was an ending that Stallings wrote where the other brother came over and said, "Poor Jim," or something like that. He was living with the French girl at the time. Then Jim went over and saw the brother who was prosperous and said, "Poor Bob," or whatever his name was. I thought it was just an opportunity to take full advantage of, and that's what we did.

DOWD: It really made a big difference in your career, didn't it?

VIDOR: Yes. Although I had gotten offers from the first pictures I made, this stuck me up into a very important top-director category. Had I wanted to, I could have really cashed in and set up my own company, but I had had the experience of running my own studio, and I didn't want the responsibility of studio operation, watching the box-office results, advertising, all of that. I didn't want any of that.

I lost a fortune by selling the percentage that I had in The Big Parade. They did all kinds of things to get it away from me and they succeeded. I was making La Bohème and it was turned over to a lawyer to handle it for me. Later on I heard that the lawyer had accepted a big bonus for selling me out. It even got into Congress, and they tried to prevent me from talking about it by paying me off again. I didn't talk too much about it. I didn't want to ruin my life, but my twenty-five percent interest would have really been a fortune. Maybe it's good that I didn't get it, though.

DOWD: What were the locations for the film?

VIDOR: The shellhole scenes were on the backlot of MGM. We used Clover Field near Santa Monica for the walking barrage scenes. When they put on gas masks and go into the woods we used a little patch of trees in Griffith Park. We used that same patch over and over again from every angle possible. I think they didn't have the eucalyptus trees in France, but those trees in Griffith Park probably looked something like the ones they had over there. After all, a tree is a tree, and we just couldn't go anyplace else to do it.

When I did see the actual location of the battle in France, I was glad I filmed it the way I did. It's much more barren than I thought. We shot the French house material in the studio in the French village. We shot the going-away scene with the trucks and the girl in Griffith Park. It rained one day, and I kept right on shooting in the rain. The next day it was sunny, so we had to wet everything down to make it look as if it had just rained, so that it all matched.

DOWD: One scene was filmed in Westwood, right?

VIDOR: The end of the picture with the two women plowing on top of the hill, where Adorée and Gilbert had been, that was right in the heart of Westwood, which was pretty much a barley field then. There was nothing but trees and hillsides. We had the plow and oxen up there for the filming. When the airplanes swoop down on the machine guns and the columns of marching men -- that whole scene was suggested by William Wellman. He had witnessed that in France and actually had been a part of it. He was a flyer, and he told me that the wheels of the planes had actually touched the helmets of some of the ground troops. I think we were able to do that in the scenes we shot.

DOWD: Were these Army pilots, or were they stunt pilots?

VIDOR: They were stunt pilots. The timing was very difficult without walkie-talkies. The planes had to leave Clover Field and swoop down on these marching men just in front of the camera and the right distance away from the set-up. It was very difficult to figure how long it would take and you didn't want to do it too many times. It was pretty dangerous. We had the planes about eight feet above the camera, and if they misjudged it at all, they would have hit somebody.

DOWD: How long did the film take to shoot?

VIDOR: Not very long. I'll guess and say it was about ten weeks.

DOWD: It looks like a much longer schedule.

VIDOR: Yes, it does. But actually in the going-away scene with the trucks and all the men running around, they were doing things like running in back of the camera, and going back into frame. We only had three trucks, and not too many extras. They'd make a circle and go back around the camera and go through the frame again. The most people we had at any given time was about 300. It actually looks like a much bigger picture, but we were able to do it on a slightly smaller scale. You would just watch the composition and maximize all your trucks and extras and everything, and it would come out looking pretty good.

DOWD: Do you conceive of there being a relationship between the three parts of your trilogy: wheat, war, and steel?

VIDOR: No, I don't think so, except for the fact that they all have possibilities for epic quality. We used the word "epic" a lot in moviemaking. They were subjects big enough to make big films about. Wheat was a big item in North American life, as well as steel. War had not been explored yet from the realistic GI viewpoint. It was more based on songs like Over There and songs of that sort.

DOWD: How did you meet Laurence Stallings?

VIDOR: I was reading synopses from the scenario department at MGM. They were all starting to sound alike. You always had minor reactions to just reading the synopses. I have always been plagued by the fact that I am a slow, laborious reader. I can't help but film the story in my head as I go along.

While I was reading all of these synopses, Thalberg went to New York, and I was to keep him informed as to what was going on. I was looking for a realistic treatment of war. Running in New York at that time was a play called What Price Glory? Thalberg sent me to see this play, and sent for Laurence Stallings and signed him up. Stallings had written a story called The Big Parade for a magazine. Stallings went on to write four or five treatments that were the basis for the film. Thalberg then had him come out to meet me, and he arrived and I read the five ideas.

He was a difficult man with a lot of energy, but he was very articulate. He had played football once, and had spent time as a newspaper man. He had lost a leg in the war, and had a mechanical leg to replace it, and at times he went around without it. I tried to pin him down to work on the script. He wasn't the type of man you could pin down, and at the time he was making the most of his visit to Hollywood.

If you stuck with him long enough, you picked up incidents and moods and atmosphere. I went with him when he went back to New York on the train. In New York we'd go to parties and to lunch at the Algonquin, the famous round table luncheon with all of those great writers. He talked a lot about his experiences, and he'd written a book called Plumes that dealt with his experiences when he lost his leg. I had a writing assistant with me named Harry Behn. After all of this, we came back to Hollywood and started to write the script.

DOWD: Do you think it was conceived of by you, or was it Stallings's anti-war story?

VIDOR: It just was a story that cut out all the bunk, all the fantasies and insincerities about the war. It happened to be the way we both wrote.

DOWD: Was this the first time you worked with John Arnold, the cameraman?

VIDOR: I'm not certain, but I think it was. Later on he became head of the camera department at MGM.

DOWD: There is a still that I found that shows (Hendrik) Sartov at the camera. Was he also working on this?

VIDOR: No, I think that was during a retake of the ending. By that time I was also working on La Bohème. After we completed the picture, we thought we'd better recast the people in the American home life, the family. After the studio saw the cut, they said, "My God, this is such a terrific picture, it should have the best actors you can get." Part of that sentimentality is due to Mr. Mayer wanting more material with the mother. They thought that the last scene didn't live up to the rest of the picture. So, I reshot the beginning and end, changed the casting for the family, and that was that.

DOWD: Claire McDowell plays the mother. She had been in Jack Knife Man and Love Never Dies, where she played the part of a young woman. Jack Knife Man was only six years before The Big Parade, yet here she is playing the part of an old lady.

VIDOR: She was not terribly old, but she had grayed her hair a little bit. She was one of my favorites, so I used her whenever I could. She was outstanding, and goes back all the way to Griffith, Biograph, and all that. I probably liked her when I saw her in those early films.

The other thing I wanted to mention about the ending was that when I shot Gilbert with his leg off, Mayer heard about it and was shocked that I was going to make their big romantic star a one-legged man. He insisted that I shoot the scene with him limping on a wounded leg, rather than an amputated leg. I remember it was a Sunday and I was aware that it was a terrible waste of time, but I had to shoot all of those scenes with him limping, rather than with a leg missing.

DOWD: But you didn't have them printed, did you?

VIDOR: No. The assistant cameraman always said, "What takes should we print?" I said, "None." They had never known of anyone doing this. Here we were shooting, and I kept on saying, "None." But we had to make the negative, that was the main thing. It was a safeguard that he wanted, and so I did it, but we never printed any of it. We just fed the negative to the lab.

DOWD: For La Bohème, you chose Lillian Gish to play the lead. Was this the first film she did after seeing The Big Parade?

VIDOR: Yes. They signed her to make pictures, and then brought her out to the studio to screen several films for her. When they screened the going-away scene from The Big Parade, she said, "Don't go any further. That's the director I must have for La Bohème.

She had it written into her contract that she could rehearse before the picture, just as she had with Griffith. When I talked with her for the first time, we discussed the method of rehearsing she had done with Griffith. I had wondered about it, and questioned lots of actors who had worked with him, and I was eager to try it. In La Bohème we had made some sets, just some rough flats put up to indicate windows and doorways, and she came along and said, "No, that's not the way we do it. We must have nothing on the stage at all." So we moved from the stage to a big lawn area.

I guess the theory was that while you were unencumbered with materials and physical objects, you performed better. For me, it didn't work. I had always done so much visualization up to that point, especially while I was working on the script. I thought it was a lot easier than moving actors and sets around when you started to shoot.

During these rehearsals, Lillian would be running around combing her hair, looking out the window, or something, and I would have to ask the script girl, "What is she doing now?" After about two or three days we abandoned it. She realized that it wasn't the way I thought or worked, so she was agreeable to dropping it.

DOWD: I know you admired Griffith a great deal. How did you feel about directing the great Griffith star?

VIDOR: I admired her, and she had been an actress I had almost been in love with through seeing all her films and performances. This was a tremendous thrill for me. You might say La Bohème was a little out of my element at that time, having never before been to the opera or to Europe. I was in a strange environment, but nevertheless it was a great thrill to direct her. She seemed to be such a beautiful actress, and she had wonderful expressive pantomime, and she had all of the Griffith training.

DOWD: She exerted an influence on every member of the cast in all aspects of production, didn't she?

VIDOR: Yes. She was especially determined about photography. This was an important thing to her. She knew about the cameraman, Hendrik Sartov, and I guess he came into the picture because of her. I don't know whether he'd worked for Griffith, but she'd known him in New York. They had a good rapport between the two of them as far as photography went. Sometimes he would place her in the frame as if she were posing for a portrait. She'd go through an entire scene without turning her head. This was a bit of an obstacle at first, but later on it loosened up a bit.

I had an assistant by the name of Robert Florey. He was a technical assistant, and later on became a director. He was very helpful, and we tried to get a poetic quality in the exteriors. I even thought the set of the garret was very exciting.

Lillian's theory of a love story was that they shouldn't kiss or touch at all. She thought that would make it more exciting, if they never culminated the story by touching. That was her theory, and we ended up doing it her way. When we showed the whole picture to Louis Mayer, he said, "I was expecting a great love story, and they never even kissed in the picture!" Well, after that we went back and spent a couple of days putting in love scenes in which they touched and kissed. Lillian was a real pro, and she was a wonderful woman. She entered into the new version of the script with complete enthusiasm, and was very convincing.

DOWD: You directed her in another picture, too.

VIDOR: She was in Duel in the Sun later on. We remained good friends, and we thought a lot of each other.

DOWD: In this film there were flashbacks that occurred near the end.

VIDOR: You see, I also used those in The Crowd. I was using that technique quite a bit. It still is good. In the case of La Bohème the flashbacks were used to show what someone was thinking about, what was uppermost in their minds. It's a natural expression in films. In fact, they couldn't buy the rights to the original opera, but the flashbacks helped tell the story, and we took a lot of material from a book called La vie de la bohème by André Murger.

I always felt strange about doing a film based on an opera, especially when you couldn't use the opera. I thought the film should be redone when sound came in, using the music from the opera production. Even so, my feelings at the time were that we shouldn't be dictated by other media, whether it was opera, theatre, or literature. I remember I felt we were blazing new paths, and I felt that we had to have the courage to be original about it. I think this was a good pioneering feeling with a new art.

DOWD: It's certainly a beautiful film to look at. I'm sure the original print must have been lovely.

VIDOR: Yes. We had some beautiful black-and-white photography. I don't think anything can top it as far as the beauty of Cedric Gibbons's setting and the poetic feeling of the rooms, and even the street scenes of Paris are great. I thought that with the big success of the long goodbye scene from The Big Parade, something similar might work in the streets of Paris.

Musically I was trying to do something with the struggle. That suffered from the bad print we viewed last night, because it turned out to be an exciting sequence, and there was even one scene missing, where she was picked up by a bunch of travelers and tossed about. Her body was thin and frail, and they sort of tossed this dying girl into the air, jumping around her and laughing, without knowing how ill she really was. It was quite astonishing, and I have no idea why it wasn't in the print we viewed. I would think they would leave it in the negative. I didn't miss anything else, though.

DOWD: How did it feel to see the dying scene, after all these years of not having seen the picture?

VIDOR: I thought it looked absolutely convincing. She looked really dead. There is no movement of breath, her eyes, or her mouth. I have never seen a picture of somebody looking dead right away, but her performance sure convinced me.

DOWD: Did you do that in one take?

VIDOR: Yes, we did. In the earlier part of the film her face is round and healthy, and during the course of the story she gets progressively long and thin, with her cheeks sunken. In preparation Lillian Gish stuffed cotton in her mouth, and did not drink any liquids for three days before we shot that scene. It looks absolutely astounding. This was also some hypnotic influence she had over her body. When it came time for her to die, she threw herself into the dying so much that it's about as close to dying as you can get without actually doing it.

DOWD: That was early method acting.

VIDOR: Yes.

IV

DOWD: Let's move on to The Crowd. How did you go about shooting and casting this film?

VIDOR: Well, in working on the story, I couldn't help but draw up an image of what the main character should look like. I was talking to someone on the MGM lot one day when a group of extras walked by, and one crazy fellow walked between us. I caught a quick glimpse of his profile and said, "That's the image I've been thinking about."

I chased this guy onto a bus on Washington Boulevard. I grabbed him and said, "What's your name? Would you like to come out tomorrow and see me? My name is Vidor." He said, "Okay, okay," but he never came back the next day. So, I went through all the extras on the lot until someone could give me his name, James Murray. When I got that, I called him and paid him to come down and make a test. When he came down, he said, "Oh, I didn't believe you back there on the street. I thought it was a gag or something." We made a test, and he was so good in the test, I gave him the part.

I also used Eleanor Boardman, who I was married to at the time. MGM was pretty liberal about letting me do this film, and casting it the way I did, with an extra in the lead role. I thought that if I put a star into that part, they would never believe that he was the common, unknown man who was losing his identity in the crowd. He had to be a man who was constantly trying, but never quite "making it."

DOWD: Were you influenced by German films of this era?

VIDOR: Yes, German films and art. At that time, the Germans were doing paintings with tilted tables, and they weren't in true perspective with the rest of the set. They were doing things in forced perspective. Some of the German films started with boom shots following people through streets for long stretches of time.

DOWD: How did you do the stairway scene?

VIDOR: It was just a stock stairway that was on the lot. We found it somewhere in a storage room. We set it on a bare stage, and then the backing represented the ceiling. You see, it would have very complicated and costly to build an actual ceiling and walls which you couldn't light anyway. In cooperation with the art department we developed this idea of just painting a flat to the side of the studio wall, painting the ceiling and the sides of the corridor in forced perspective. The whole set was very effective and cost practically nothing.

DOWD: What about the building when the camera climbs up the side and then goes into the office?

VIDOR: In order to do that scene, we had to build a miniature building lying flat on the ground. It was about twelve or thirteen feet long. At the top we had a sky backing. The camera was on a bridge type of thing with wheels so that you could look up at this building and see the height of it. Then we would move the bridge with the camera on it, and the wheels moved along the floor of the stage. As you'd come to the window you wanted to show, the camera tilted down. I think you could do it today with zoom lenses, or a helicopter.

DOWD: What were the locations you used for this film?

VIDOR: We had no process backgrounds, so we went to Niagara Falls. In those days, if you wanted something like Niagara Falls in the background, you simply went to Niagara Falls. I worked out a system to get a shot of people on the streets of New York. We put a cameraman inside three or four packing cases on a pushcart on the sidewalk. We cut a hole in the side of one of the boxes for the lens and shot real people along the street. It looked as if it was four packing cases piled on top of the cart, but we were able to fit the cameraman and his camera inside.

There are some other shots we were able to get on location with a camera truck. We used all sorts of signals and chalk marks to get these candid shots. We worked out a system of rehearsing without anyone knowing about it.

Between the shots I'd lean against the truck and talk to the cameraman inside. We were also beginning to work without a lot of makeup, so the actors weren't that noticeable.

DOWD: So the people on the street never even knew you were there?

VIDOR: No.

DOWD: Did you shoot in Coney Island?

VIDOR: Yes, I think we did some of the long shots there. For the close-ups we went to Ocean Park. Even so, we shot all over the streets of New York during the film.

DOWD: How did you shoot in the apartment with all the trains going by?

VIDOR: I remember looking for the location. We set up a few lights, and shot it in a real apartment. The actors don't really work in that scene, they just look off at it. It wasn't that hard.

DOWD: Although the film itself seems very realistic and natural, the construction of the scenes is very precise. The script must have been very tight.

VIDOR: Yes, I was trying for a certain mood. I think that is why the Italians picked up neo-realism. It is realistic, and yet it is affected by an artistic feeling so that the realism never completely takes over.

I think this film accomplishes that as much as any film I know of. It has an artistic feeling as far as precision goes, and yet it uses realism as a catalyst.

DOWD: How did you conceive of the individual relating to the crowd? This seems to be a major theme in some of your best films like Street Scene, The Crowd, and The Big Parade.

VIDOR: I didn't go for the unusual situation as a rule. My feelings were more inclined to pull somebody out of the usual and show his drama of life. You felt more of a relation to him that way, more identification. I wanted to say that this was an ordinary fellow, and this was a drama of an ordinary man. I had very distinct feelings about that. I had the distinct feeling that some pictures were made where the characters were so remote from the average man that he couldn't identify with them. That's why I saw this as just one of the mob -- this man was just one of the group.

DOWD: Do you think that the mass of humanity tends to swallow the individual? Some of the titles are especially pessimistic, such as, "The crowd laughs with you only for a day."

VIDOR: I don't think I wrote that title. It sounds like one of those philosophical tangents that title writers squeezed into the film. I'm not cynical about the crowd, I'm just trying to say that everyone of this crowd has the same sort of drama going on. I was trying to say that if you take an individual today and dig into his life, you're going to have a good story with drama. I was trying to dig in, get under the surface and find the drama. John Sims's life was certainly dramatic to him, and if you have the one protagonist's viewpoint, you have a chance to make the audience see that or feel that.

I've articulated this in recent years in my own thinking, and I had a feel for it back then, too. This is the solipsistic idea that nothing exists outside of one's own consciousness. I had more of a feeling for this than any other director. I used the leading character all through the story. You have a hard time finding any scenes in The Crowd that Murray's not in, or any scenes in The Big Parade that Gilbert's not in. They're all subjective viewpoints of the lives they lead, and that's the basis for the feelings about the story. I wasn't trying to force any particular philosophy, I was just trying to follow that line.

DOWD: So it's not a question of pessimism or optimism, it's a matter of there being an interesting story in every person.

VIDOR: Yes, and you have the chance to make it go whichever way you want. If you want it on that level, you can keep it there, or if you want to take it further, you can do that.

DOWD: There are certain parallels in The Crowd. When Murray is standing on the deck of the boat and he sees New York City as he is arriving there, I thought of your early days and how you came to Hollywood, wanting to "make" it.

VIDOR: Well, looking back I suppose I had an individualistic viewpoint to express, which pulled me along through that story. I know people today who don't have an individualistic approach. They just go along with the way the average man goes. They don't want to get out of that conditioned rut.

DOWD: The character in the film seems to be quite imaginative and inventive. However, he is stuck in this horrible routine at the office.

VIDOR: Once he answers an ad in the paper for a prize. Thousands of people could have answered the same ad. It's just a spurt of inventiveness. I would believe that he had some initiative if he quit his job and took a big gamble and was daring enough to say, "I'm going into the advertising business," but he doesn't do that. He just spends his money right away. He's stuck with a routine.

DOWD: You said that the "Months, endless months" title was not one of your titles.

VIDOR: No, it wasn't. That must have been something from one of those philosophical title writers again.

DOWD: What about the title in The Crowd which says, "You never know what the opposition is until you step outside the crowd"? Is that one of yours?

VIDOR: I might have suggested it, but it sounds more like a title writer to me. Title writers came on and got paid lots of money to write titles and get philosophical. I don't know what the title means. I guess you could say that it takes daring, initiative, and courage to get out of step with the crowd. It takes responsibility. Making your own world is a big responsibility. A lot of people try it, but fail. Most people just go along with it.

DOWD: That's what Murray does in the film.

VIDOR: Yes, he just goes along with the stream.

DOWD: I think the parting scene at the end is remarkably well shot and edited. It seems very modern and almost revolutionary to have her standing there in a medium shot just before each of the cuts. She starts to walk towards the camera, and towards him at the same time, and then it cuts to a title and she's saying something like "Your dinner is in the oven," and they cut to him, and he looks very sad, and then you cut back to her, and she moves forward again from the same position. I think you do this about four times. She is standing in the same place, and yet you know she is trying to move towards him.

VIDOR: Yes, that one sequence looks like I had a different approach than in some of the others. It looks as if I had given it some extra consideration.

DOWD: The film seems to be very episodic, very clean in that way, almost like chapters in a book.

VIDOR: That was the way it was thought up. When you sit down to write it, you put down all of these things you want in it.

DOWD: Did you conceive of this film with a musical accompaniment?

VIDOR: Yes, Tchaikovsky's Sixth symphony, the Pathétique. I remember when we were talking about it at my house in Beverly Hills, there was an old phonograph playing. I was playing some music conducted by Leopold Stokowski.

I would play those records and it seemed to fit the story somehow or another. I have the record on tape now, a new one, and I hear it today just how it sounded back then. It still suggests how I felt about the whole picture.

DOWD: Did you have musicians playing the theme when you were shooting?

VIDOR: Yes, somewhat. We only had a funny little violin and an organ and they couldn't play very well. I think that was the first time that I took a phonograph and actually played the record on the set.

DOWD: Were you using the metronome?

VIDOR: No, I don't think so. I may have used the organist or violinist to play at different tempos to control the actors' pacing.

DOWD: In The Crowd I noticed a tremendous amount of care taken in details and small gestures. You seem to have found just the essential details in everyday life.

VIDOR: The Big Parade had a lot of success with the details of the soldiers fighting during the war, and with this picture I was thinking about details of American life -- the leaky toilet, the kids going to the bathroom on the beach. I was thinking of that in the form of realistic scenes. That was the mood of the picture, the challenge to see if you could observe it enough.

DOWD: The thing I like best about this film was the way that none of the characters in the story seem to have any malice towards one another. I think this is very characteristic of your best films. There is no desire for revenge, none of the perverted aspects of the personalities that you find in von Stroheim's films.

VIDOR: You know, villains are few and far between. The drama of life is not dependent on villains. They don't have to be present to have a story. Divorce, tragedy, sadness, and illness are not dependent on villains. They get melodramatic when villains are introduced like Simon Legree in Uncle Tom's

<u>Cabin</u>. That was a fictionalized character. It's almost funny to have a character with boots, the whip, and the big moustache. I let someone else play with the villains. I have never had any villains in my life, and they're something I wouldn't know too much about.

DOWD: There is a scene where Murray comes home drunk and Eleanor Boardman is lying in bed. I think most directors would have used that as an occasion for a big fight. Instead, she just says, "I think I understand you." That was a nice touch.

VIDOR: I think I pulled that right out of my own experience with Eleanor. I think she said that to me once, and I wanted to communicate or preserve it.

DOWD: What were some of the improvised parts of the film? Was the rocking gesture Eleanor goes through thought up beforehand, or was it improvised?

VIDOR: I don't remember where I first saw an actress touch her stomach in relation to pregnancy. It might have been on the New York stage. I remember thinking that if she could hold her stomach in a certain way, it would indicate that she was pregnant. It was a way of caressing the womb. I remember thinking that one day I would use that gesture in a film.

Also, in silent films the actors would be able to reach a real virtuoso performance if they were allowed to improvise with the camera grinding away. I remember having seen Charles Ray doing this sort of thing in love stories years before.

That was all done in one close shot. I had the feeling that I could just do the whole thing in a close shot that stood by itself, with no cuts at all.

DOWD: Eleanor Boardman seems to have that power as an actress. She has tremendous presence.

VIDOR: I was interested in her as an actress, especially in this picture, and I wanted to get a good performance from her. She was the type of actress that if you didn't take the care to bring it out of her, she could just as soon go through it and mean nothing at all, just a walk-through performance. Jennifer Jones was the same way.

DOWD: Do you think you could do a remake of The Crowd today?

VIDOR: Yes, absolutely. I worked on a film project called Mr. and Mrs. Bo Jo Jones. It was a book I worked on with Sam Goldwyn Jr. for six or eight months a few years ago, and I had a very distinctive idea to make The Crowd in today's terms with a young married couple. She would get pregnant before they were married, but Sam Goldwyn Jr. wanted to change it because he thought it was corny. I thought it was wonderful, but I just couldn't get the point across. The writer we had working on it did three scripts which were all rejected by me, and then by Sam Goldwyn Jr. I just couldn't get it through their heads that my idea wasn't corny.

DOWD: I would think that American cinema needs films like that desperately.

VIDOR: It really does. They're real and they touch a responsive chord. They would have scenes where they faced the problems of today. It is a good human story, where young people get a good look at themselves. But that's the way it goes.

DOWD: Did you have much of a budget on The Crowd?

VIDOR: I would say we had about four or five hundred thousand. We had a delay of working with seven possible endings, and that cost a little, and then they had to make up their minds on how to release it. That type of thing has gone on for years.

DOWD: You had an Academy Award nomination for The Crowd, didn't you?

VIDOR: Yes, I did.

DOWD: For some reason it seems like the Crowd had been hidden for years. Many film buffs have never seen it.

VIDOR: Yes, I know. For a long time MGM wouldn't let it out. They didn't have the distribution they have now. The picture itself did get a nomination, and I got an honorable mention. A picture called Two Arabian Knights won that year. Back then there were five people who would end any kind of a tie. They were Louis B. Mayer, Douglas Fairbanks, Joe Schenck, Mary Pickford, and Sid Grauman. They sat up all night and Sid Grauman called me up and said, "I held out until five o'clock for The Crowd, but it didn't get it." The reason was that Mayer did not want to vote for one of his own films. Such a change from the way things are today.

DOWD: Even so, it has long been considered a classic.

VIDOR: Last year DeSica threw his arms around me and said, "Oh, The Crowd, The Crowd! That was what inspired me for The Bicycle Thief."

DOWD: How did the assignment to do Show People come to you? Did it come from Hearst himself?

VIDOR: They had bought a story. I think it was called Polly Preferred. We used to read these plays, and it was just impossible to film them. They bought this one, however, and that became the assignment. Instead of trying to adapt the play, we just started writing a whole new story. In this case, we did use the name Polly. The play was called Polly Preferred, but it had nothing to do with the film. It wasn't even about Hollywood. The play was about a girl going to New York to go on the stage.

The relationship between Mayer and Hearst was very close and powerful at the time. The pressure would be put on Mayer at the request of Hearst. I still had Stallings as an idea man. We started with an idea that this actress eventually became the Marquise de la Falaise de la Coudray, but she was hit in the face with a pie, and that brought her back to her senses. The pie was the symbol we used to bring her back to the ground.

After we got the whole script and story planned, Hearst read it and saw how Marion Davies would get hit in the face with a pie, and he was adamant that it be changed. Mayer called me in and asked me if it wouldn't be just as well if a stairway collapsed underneath her and slid her into a pool. I fought for the pie because it was a symbol. There was nothing like the custard pie as a symbol of the Mack Sennett comedies. We finally called a conference and I walked up and down and I argued and explained why I wanted the pie. At the end Hearst said, "Well, King's right, but I'm right too, because I'm not going to have my Marion hit in the face with a pie." He was determined, so we settled with a bottle of water in the face.

Even after that, we had to get rid of him. We had to work out a plot to have the Examiner say there was an important conference and get him called from the set where we were working. The Examiner did that, and he left. When he was gone, we got out a strong hose and nozzle and squirted Marion in the face with it instead of the pie.

DOWD: Is it true that you took a pie in the face during the story conference with Mayer and Hearst?

VIDOR: No, I've never heard that before. We did get some good advice from Buster Keaton about pie throwing, though. He told us, "Above all other things, don't anticipate. You can't anticipate getting hit with the pie. You have to turn into it unexpectedly." There is a certain technique of how to take one and how to receive one. It must always be a custard pie, too. That sticks to the face better. You have to turn away from something and then go right into the pie. That's what we wanted Marion to do in the picture. She was supposed to be waving goodbye to somebody when she turns around and gets hit with the pie.

DOWD: What was Marion's initial reaction to this scene?

VIDOR: She would do anything I told her. It was Hearst who put a negative view of it into her mind. Usually she'd do anything the script called for, anything I asked her to do.

DOWD: You talked before about a button Hearst was wearing on his pocket during the story conference. What was it?

VIDOR: It wasn't a button. When we had this conference, it was in Paul Bern's tiny little office. It was really between me and Hearst, with Mayer and Bern also present. When I was walking up and down the floor arguing my side of the question, I looked in Hearst's pocket and there was a folded copy of the Los Angeles Examiner sticking out. The part I could see had some colossal headline such as, "Hearst wants Coolidge to Serve Second Term," or something like that which indicated the power he held in those days. I got sort of shaky and thought, What chance does a young fellow like me have with a guy like Hearst?

DOWD: You used the Sennett Studios to film the story, and you also used some of the Sennett comedians. Were they largely out of work by that time?

VIDOR: Yes. The Sennett comedians had already finished their work quite a few years before.

DOWD: You originally cast Murray for the part that William Haines eventually took, right?

VIDOR: Yes.

DOWD: Where was the casting office set located?

VIDOR: That was an actual office at MGM, I think.

DOWD: Was that the scene where Elinor Glyn meets Lew Cody?

VIDOR: Yes. That was the executive studio office. We arranged it so that you could see the exterior of the studio out the window. We had all kinds of things going on outside the window, and it looked very realistic.

DOWD: How were you able to achieve the extreme depth of field that you see in that scene? There's a fire going on outside the window, and yet it is very brightly lit inside.

VIDOR: That was done by building up a very strong series of lights. The cameraman had to stop the lens down, which gives you greater depth of field.

DOWD: Do you remember how you convinced Chaplin to do the autograph scene?

VIDOR: Chaplin and Marion were very good friends. I remember we all used to go out to the (Hearst) ranch together and have parties. There was not much convincing to do. The power of the Hearst press at that time was so great that all he had to do was ask someone, and they would do it. Chaplin remained very independent, however, especially in his relationship with Marion. I think Hearst got a little jealous of him at times. Anyway, all it amounted to was a question of asking Chaplin to do it, and he agreed.

DOWD: Could you identify the man who was with him in that scene?

VIDOR: Yes, that was Harry Crocker. Harry Crocker was from the very well known family from San Francisco, the one that owned Crocker Citizens Bank. He was always sort of a playboy, and later was given a column of his own in the Examiner. When Hearst was away he jumped in and managed things for Hearst. He was also very close to Marion. I knew him well, and I had him in scenes in The Big Parade. He was always at the ranch and did more or less the same thing with Charlie. I'm sure he's in Limelight. He could do lots of funny gags and acts. I remember him eating records and even doing a little act about Napoleon. He was a fixture in the Hearst group.

DOWD: In Show People you seem to be satirizing your own career, especially your work at Metro. The Imperial Russian costumes are from His Hour and you are satirizing The Big Parade at the end. What motivated you to do this?

VIDOR: Humor played a big part in our early lives. We were not making the films for immortality, we were making them somewhat for ourselves. We were thinking of giving the people we knew an inside joke. We certainly weren't making this picture for reviews. Our pictures were made just for the moment, and I thought I would do things that would give my friends a laugh when they saw them.

DOWD: In Show People there's a moment when they are trying to get Marion to cry. Someone comes in and says, "Your father is starving to death," and she begins to laugh. That is somewhat like the story you told me about Eleanor Boardman.

VIDOR: Yes. Eleanor told me a story about Rupert Hughes getting her in back of a set once and pleading with her to cry, telling her that her mother had been in an automobile accident. Then she broke out laughing and told him that she hated her mother, and that was the last thing on earth that would make her cry. I thought that was very humorous and I used it in the film.

DOWD: What about Gilbert? Did he ever react to the obvious satire of himself in this film?

VIDOR: Well, he had a great sense of humor. When he saw the film he said, "You son-of-a-bitch! I'll get even with you!" We were a close-knit group -- it was always free, easy, and fun.

DOWD: How did you decide what bits people would do at the star's luncheon sequence?

VIDOR: Well, I knew that Douglas Fairbanks did these things at the dinner table. I went around and talked to each one, and asked the others what they would like to do. Mostly it was Douglas doing his stunts at the table.

DOWD: In your book there is also a picture of a scene from Show People that is not in the film. It is the scene where Garbo is imitating herself. That must have been cut out because it has never been in any print I have seen.

VIDOR: Yes, it's too bad they cut it out. I rather liked it myself.

DOWD: Do you remember any other scenes you did for Show People that were not in the final picture?

VIDOR: No. Everything else was included in the picture.

DOWD: This is your last silent film and it seems sad because you were really at the height of the silent gag. Did you have any feelings about this? Show People is a bit prophetic because most of the people in this film would make very few films again, yet here they are at the height of their fame and stardom.

VIDOR: Well, we used them because they were the top names at the time. Louella Parsons and Marion Davies could just about ask anybody to come in and be in the picture, and they'd come. That's what happened.

DOWD: Did anyone ever talk to you about basing films on Show People later on, like Singin' in the Rain?

VIDOR: No, but I thought it would make a marvelous musical.

DOWD: Red Golden was your assistant on this film, wasn't he?

VIDOR: Yes, and he was playing the part of the assistant in the film also. When the company is shooting out there at the river, he points out Marion Davies to Marion Davies in the film, and then grabs her. I thought that it would be amusing to have Marion Davies looking at Marion Davies in the film.

DOWD: You have a story about the first dramatic director we see in the film.

VIDOR: He was a comedy director. He started out as a trained actor at the Sennett Studios and later became a motorcycle cop. One time I was going to the Rose Bowl and I saw him directing traffic out in the middle of the street. I leaned out the window and saw that it was Harry Gribbon. Well, I always gave jobs to Harry and the part in that film was one he did for me.

        There's another thing about directors in that picture. The director chews the end of a handkerchief. This was patterned after John Ford. Years later Ford said to me, "You son-of-a-bitch! That was me!" Then there is the director who is making the screen test. When he starts to have difficulties, he takes the back of his hand and hits his ear. This was a mannerism from Jack Conway. All these guys would see this in the film and know I had satirized all of them.

DOWD: Were the cops in the film actually Keystone Cops?

VIDOR: Yes. You can't actually get people and teach them those kinds of gags. We just put in an order for a certain number of Keystone Cops, and they already knew how to jump around and do all of the things we wanted them to do.

DOWD: When Billy and Peggy are watching the preview in the theatre, there is a man sitting next to his mother who says, "I'll bring that girl over to the studio in the morning." Was this a takeoff on Mayer or Thalberg?

VIDOR: No, because he was the casting director at the other studio. I vaguely remember that we were satirizing someone, but I don't remember who. The fellow looks a little like Goldwyn, but he's a casting director, not a producer.

DOWD: Who was the melodeon player in the film?

VIDOR: I thought it was Sam Musenheimer and I knew he wrote the very popular song "Whispering," but I recently saw a copy of that song and the author's name was different. It is the same man, though.

DOWD: Was the pool the real Sennett pool?

VIDOR: Yes. The Sennett studio was almost completely vacant. When we rented it out there were sets still standing, and the pool was one of them. It was used when they wanted a grand lady, a pompous character they usually had in their films, to fall into the pool. If I had the film to do over again, I would have used much more of the studio. I didn't know that it would be completely torn down.

DOWD: When Marion Davies meets Peggy Pepper, where are the dressing rooms? At Metro?

VIDOR: Yes.

DOWD: The Harry Gribbon character really was based on Sennett himself, wasn't it?

VIDOR: No. These were directors like McCarey, Capra, and the Keystone directors. The way they told stories was the way they spoke, and they all spoke in broad pantomime. They had everything down in gestures. They talked differently from the dramatic directors. I worked on some of those Sennett comedies as an assistant, and that was where I started to see some of those things.

DOWD: There is also a scene where they are out in the park shooting, and the stunt double jumps into the water. Was that a glass shot?

VIDOR: No. I think that was done out at Paramount, or Lasky's place on Barham Boulevard, near Warner. They had a lake and a pond out there. I think we might have built a projecting rock if it wasn't already there. There may be one shot that was done with glass. If you had to have a castle or something, you could always paint it in with a glass shot. Painting always meant a stationary camera. We would paint the sky or a building in, but we couldn't tilt or pan the camera then. On this picture there was just one glass shot.

DOWD: Was the orchestra the actual Marion Davies orchestra?

VIDOR: Yes, it was four piece orchestra. They had a bass, a cello, and two violins. These fellows would have a steady job doing this during the daytime, and at night they'd write music on the side. Many of them turned out to be good composers.

DOWD: When she comes in to do her scene, she sees a dramatic scene going on in the other set, and runs through the back of the set and ruins the take.

VIDOR: I was always running up against this because my voice wasn't very loud. Robert Leonard and Orson Welles both had loud voices, which helped them. Since there wasn't any sound recording going on, the company shooting right next to you would often be much louder than you. I used to carry a megaphone all the time. The actors didn't like it, and it wasn't good to speak to them through the megaphones, so I sometimes went right up to them and gave them instructions. I couldn't sit near the camera like the other directors.

DOWD: In the film there is a scene where they are trying to get Marion Davies to cry, and when they finally succeed, they have to run back to the camera to get it on film as quickly as possible. Did that ever happen?

VIDOR: Yes, only we would run out of film. The cameraman wouldn't tell you that you were just about to run out of film. You would spend all this time trying to get the actress into the right mood, succeed, but when you went back to the camera and said, "Take it!" you'd be out of film. By that time the actress would be finished crying, and you would have to start all over again.

DOWD: In the last scene where you are directing what looks like The Big Parade, you are talking to Marion Davies and in the background we can see both Gordon Avil and John Arnold. Who was shooting the film if both of them were in the film itself?

VIDOR: It was probably Clyde de Vinna. MGM had a lot of cameramen, and if you needed an extra crew for a couple of hours, you could get them easily. It was also a chance to give some other cameraman a trial run.

DOWD: Was Gordon Avil the assistant cameraman on this film?

VIDOR: I think he was more or less the camera operator.

DOWD: Was it after this that you got him a position as a full-time cameraman?

VIDOR: I liked him so much that I gave him the chance to be first cameraman after that. I liked his personality and I thought he was worthy of it.

DOWD: Marion Davies is really a fine comedienne and I think she has been forgotten by a lot of people. What did you think when you saw the Susan Alexander character in <u>Citizen Kane</u>? Why do you think she was portrayed that way?

VIDOR: There was the usual ignorance of people not knowing anything about the real characters. It goes on today, the vicious attack of dramatizing and distorting things to the point of accomplishing sensationality, and I knew then that they didn't really know her. She was very thoughtful, very kind, and very generous. I don't know what motivates people to distort or downgrade somebody. I never remember seeing her dramatic pictures, although I've heard they weren't good. In any case, she was a delightful comedienne.

DOWD: In <u>Show People</u> she seems to be a woman totally without any pretentions.

VIDOR: She had none at all. She was always kidding herself, and even those around her.

V

DOWD: Would you describe how you got the idea to make Hallelujah?

VIDOR: In Texas and Arkansas I was constantly with the Negro people and had a very large appreciation of them. Our family employed one Negro woman, and my father had mostly black men working in his sawmills. I saw very much of them as a group. I was very impressed with their music, their feelings, their attitude toward life, their feelings about religion, and their feelings about sex and humor. As long as I can remember I wanted to make a film about them.

This one Negro woman was in our family for years. When she died I had a big desire to dedicate a picture to her. I didn't put the title down anywhere, but it was always in my mind. I listed all of these things that I remembered, things that were marvelous to photograph and make into a film, but the studio kept turning the idea down. They didn't want to make a film with all blacks in the cast.

I went to Europe in 1928 with The Crowd, and in Paris I read in Variety magazine that sound was taking over the motion picture business. I took an early boat home and stopped in New York and visited Schenck, who was the president of Metro-Goldwyn-Mayer Pictures Corp. I told him all of the things I wanted to do, and brought along a list of scenes. They still were skeptical and didn't want to go for it. Finally on the second day I came back and said, "You know you have to pay me. I have a contract for each picture, but I'll draw no salary, and throw my own money in with yours."

The first estimate for the budget at that time was around $350,000, and I had a contract for $100,000 per film. I alone would be putting up around a third of the budget. His reply was, "Well, if you think like that, I'll let you make a picture about <u>whores.</u>" The fact that I was willing to risk my own salary in the investment was what got to him. The great advantage then was that they didn't have to buy a play or a book for the story; I simply had to present the ideas to make the film.

So, I came back to California and worked on the story and script. I would say six weeks was all it took to get the screenplay together. It probably took longer to see Thalberg about it than it did to write the script. I went to Chicago and New York to find the cast, and then from New York I went on to Memphis. It was difficult there because the blacks weren't allowed in the dining rooms of the hotel. We had to rent a special hotel to do all the casting work.

DOWD: How did you cast the individual members?

VIDOR: In Chicago we went to Negro Baptist churches, listening to the choirs and talking to the people. They had to be able to sing well because we intended to use their actual voices. We also went to Negro nightclubs, always looking for people to cast.

I saw a man standing on a street corner in Chicago and thought he was a fine type for the father, the minister father. I don't think we picked up any more people there. Then we moved on to New York, rented a hall, and sent out word that we were looking for Negro people from the stage and choruses.

We found Nina Mae McKinney there, the girl who played the lead. She was third from the right in the chorus in the play <u>Blackbirds of 1929.</u> Once we found her, it didn't take very long to decide she was the one for the part. I had Paul Robeson in mind to play the lead, and when it came time to make the film, he was not available. I think he was in a play and couldn't leave it. Daniel Haynes was the understudy for the leading Negro actor in <u>Show Boat</u>, so we got him. The woman who played the mother was a musician who had been in plays. The other girl, Victoria Spivey, had made records before. She played the sister.

We still didn't have the young brothers, but the older brother was cast in New York. For the three young boys called Sears, Roebuck, and Poe, we picked up the actors in the Peabody Hotel in Memphis. When I was still searching, we saw these three boys come in and dance on the floor for contributions of dimes and quarters. We signed them up and put them in the picture. We picked up two or three other people down there, too.

We shot a month or so in Memphis and then did the swamp scene in Arkansas. We would go across on a ferryboat to the cotton fields. Some of the street scenes with the children were also shot in Memphis.

DOWD: Did any one of your characters ever act in a film before?

VIDOR: No, I don't think so.

DOWD: Was this your first sound film?

VIDOR: Yes. You know, at that time they would make a film with 50 percent sound. You used to have signs outside theatres that would say "Eighty percent sound!" We decided to make it a sound film, but we didn't have any sound equipment on location. So, I had this terrible problem. How were we going to have the action running at a set speed throughout the entire picture? If you shot a scene over two or three days, you had to remember the exact speed that the actors were singing at so that you could duplicate your shots from take to take. There was no portable sound equipment then. We had absolutely no sound during the whole six weeks of shooting, but finally we put the whole thing together.

DOWD: How much of the actual picture was shot on location?

VIDOR: I'd say about half of it. On location we stayed at the Peabody Hotel and went out from there each day. We went all around Memphis, and did a little filming in Arkansas.

DOWD: Was the original title Negro Story?

VIDOR: That wasn't a real title. I think it was just a working title that we used for reference. We never intended to call it that.

DOWD: Can you tell us something about the improvisations in that picture?

VIDOR: Looking at the film today, I see a lot of it. You see, the Negro actors all understood this, and were able to do it. We were still writing scripts in titles. When we were writing the script, we didn't know whether it was going to have sound or not, so the dialogue lines were all written in title form. There were very few of them. In silent pictures the idea had been to have as few of them as possible.

When you got to a dialogue scene there would be no dialogue written out for it. So, with the spirit of the actors we would do off-the-cuff dialogue and make it up as we went along. It took quite a while to get over the silent technique. The first scene was a crap game taking place on the docks. This had to be ad-libbed -- there was nothing in the way of dialogue written for it. We would have certain key lines in mind to set the pattern for the scene, but that was it. We were not thinking in words yet.

DOWD: Did you have a special rapport with the actors?

VIDOR: Yes, very much so. They knew that I understood the spirit of what we were doing. The relationship was absolutely friendly, close and very understanding. I respected them and they respected me. We got along fine. We never even had a single quarrel about anything.

DOWD: Nina Mae McKinney really gives a beautiful performance in this film. Could you talk a bit about directing her?

VIDOR: Well, it took no great effort to bring it out. She just had it, whatever you wanted. Whatever you visualized, she could do it. If you have bad actors, you work like the devil to get an acceptable performance out of them. If you have a very good actor, you start where the bad actor leaves off. The same amount of time and effort is spent in just improving what a good actor can do, or adding to it. That's the difference between an interesting performance and a dull performance.

In the case of the father who was not a good actor, we used every possible trick. When he's looking up at the sky, we had big cue cards with his lines written on them. You were sweating everything to get a scene that was acceptable, as against Nina, who was full of life, full of expression, and just a joy to work with. Someone like her inspires a director.

DOWD: Can you sense a good actor or a bad actor right away?

VIDOR: I can spot them on the first day of shooting. I made the tremendous error twice of being fooled by a test, because they'll put a great deal of effort into a day of testing which will never be duplicated again. I've had a couple of occasions where the end of the first day came, and I said, "Oh boy, I've made a mistake in casting this actor."

I played the guitar and sang spirituals as far back as I can remember, and I just seemed to have a natural affinity for this type of thing, which helped me very much in selecting the cast. I knew and loved all of the spiritual music. In my home town of Galveston you could hear them down on the docks, pushing cotton bales around and singing songs, or even a melody without any words, just made up as they went along. I had the idea that we could express the feelings with a melody instead of dialogue. Melody is not quite the right word, but it was a sort of wailing type of thing. I planned scenes where we would write the music out of the mood of the scene, out of what we were trying to say.

We always had a group of singers standing by on the sidelines to assist, and I had a Negro woman who was a musical director working for us. Her name was Eva Jessye, and within ten or fifteen minutes she could work out a musical arrangement with her people so that we could say exactly what we wanted to say in each scene with the music. We did that about half a dozen times. They'd just come back, and one would start to wail, and the others would pick up at that point. Then the girl would say something like, "Deke is gone," and by the time you got the word "gone" out, the others would come right in and start to wail, "Oh, poor Deke, he's never going to come back," or something like that. From that you go right into a song, a musical expression of what they're feeling. The others pick it up, and you're on your way.

DOWD: Could you talk about Thalberg's role in the production and post-production?

VIDOR: I must hand it to Thalberg and the others for giving me the permission to do the film. With Thalberg we just had one talk: "What writer do you want?" or "Who do you want to work with?" Then you didn't see him again until you finished the script. He was a very busy man, getting out fifty-two pictures a year. He would look at the rushes, I suppose. Near the end of the picture he had the idea that he wanted to put in Irving Berlin music. I know that the singing waiters was an outgrowth of that, in addition to the song at the cotton gin in the beginning.

DOWD: Was that "End of the Road"?

VIDOR: Yes, "End of the Road" was Berlin's. He might have written it for the film. We wanted a song for the homecoming where the character is out of prison and on his way home. I suppose instead of getting somebody on the lot to do it, Thalberg wanted Berlin to write the song, but I was against it because it seemed to have a Tin Pan Alley popular Broadway sound to it that I didn't want. To this day it disturbs me.

DOWD: Let's talk a little bit about the scene where Daniel sings "Express to Hell."

VIDOR: I had gone to preachings in the South, and to implement this idea, they did a lot of black recordings on discs for me to listen to. I got hold of these and could listen to them over and over again. I had recordings of the best black preachers in the South.

The shooting of that scene was done on the MGM lot. I remember distinctly the cutter going absolutely mad as he was trying to synchronize the soundtrack and the picture. It must have been shot without synchronization. The sermon was designed from our knowledge of the ministers and their style and form.

DOWD: Could you talk about the baptism sequence? You said once that you deliberately didn't use any close shots until that scene. Why?

VIDOR: Going back, a lot of pictures like Joan of Arc were all done in close shots. I had the idea that in the use of these close shots, long shots, and medium shots, and all kinds of shots, that you should hold off on the big close shots until you really had to have them. I don't even think I used them in that sequence. I intended to hold off until the shouting came. That's where they all go around to the watering trough outside, and the bucket is thrown in the person's face.

I had attended the same thing when I was only ten or twelve years old. You can imagine the impression that the baptism had on me. There'd been about three or four of us white people there just inside the doorway watching all this going on. The people would go into hysterics and have to be escorted out. This was just something I could never forget. I saved the close shots until then, the big close-ups where I thought they would really mean something at the time. Sometimes they were used so much in film that they didn't have any meaning.

DOWD: In the scene where Deke leaves with the girl, and she seduces him and follows him out of the house, you tried to make the scene build.

VIDOR: Yes. Did you notice the tempo dropped down when the girl came back? This was to try to reach the point of ecstasy. The whole idea of the scene was to build to a point where he'd forget he was a preacher and just give in to the girl again. It's the sex and religion theme going through the whole thing. The ecstasy arrived at such a high pitch with the lack of inhibition. This was all part of that religious expression and it fit in with being seduced by the girl. He left forever, just ran out the door and that was it. He left everything, career, family, and the rest of his home life. In one version of the scene, the girl got on the train and hid in the baggage car, where the donkey was and after that the mother went in and whipped her. We took that scene out before the picture was released.

DOWD: Which girl was that, Nina Mae?

VIDOR: Yes. I don't remember how the scene ended. There doesn't seem to be any gap, but we may have taken it out before the picture was finally edited. These scenes really are the heart of the Negro character, and we tried to preserve the purity of the ethnic quality of the Negro without interference from the vaudeville stage, or Tin Pan Alley, or even Broadway.

DOWD: Can you explain where the donkey came from?

VIDOR: There was a line in the script that said, "You can't make a silk purse out of a sow's ear." The property man saw that line and thought that he better take along a sow's ear. We had a donkey in Memphis and then we wanted to add some shots in Los Angeles a month later. When the donkey arrived in the morning, there was one ear missing. One ear had been cut off. You can't have a donkey with two long ears in Memphis, and then show him later with only one ear. The property man came to the rescue with the sow's ear. He taped it to the donkey's ear and smeared it with makeup. That's how we were able to have the donkey.

DOWD: What were the difficulties you had in distributing this film?

VIDOR: Although the southern people are supposed to express more racial prejudice, they nevertheless understand the Negroes more, and I had the feeling that the film would show all over the South. I went to New York and saw the man who did all the bookings and said, "Have you seen Hallelujah?" He said at first that he had, and then later on he admitted that he had never seen it. That could have been one of our first problems. Then he called his secretary and asked her how she had liked it. She said, "I don't know what it's all about." That was the reason they had not booked it up until that point.

There just happened to be a man from Jacksonville, Florida in the office. He came in, said he'd heard the conversation, and said he might look at it and book it. This man said he would like to see it and I said, "I'll tell you what I'll do. I don't know what picture you're playing now, but I'll bet $3,000 that this picture will draw more than your current picture." So, he took the offer and booked it. It actually did make him more money than he was making with the original picture.

In Chicago they sent me to have a special preview showing, and we had all the film critics in the projection room and showed them the film. They wrote the reviews and then some fellow with a little theatre on a side street booked the picture and had a black-tie opening. He had a great attendance. The big problem with booking the picture was that people were afraid of filling the entire audience with blacks. This was the old complaint that we had right from the beginning.

I don't know whether it ever got into the profit-making category or not, but the first budget that we started out with was around $120,000. Irving Thalberg took three or four months to look it over after I finished it. Then he flew in actors and actresses from all over the country, with all expenses paid, while he did post-production on the film. He added Berlin's songs then. This resulted in the picture costing nearly $500,000. That money was wasted. I got a statement recently for the first time in at least twenty years, giving me some payment on my salary for the picture.

DOWD: Were you in any way blacklisted, or was there a stigma attached to your career after making this film?

VIDOR: No, because the critics were just marvelous about it. Goldwyn said he would have given $2 million for it, and I could have made a profit right there. I could have made at least $1 million on it. I tried and tried to make other black pictures. I even took a job directing with a black theatre in New York. Laurence Stallings had written a play and he wanted me to do it. I tried to, but it caused such an uproar that I was forced to quit. I was constantly trying to get another good black in the theatre or film.

DOWD: Do you remember the name of the play that you were to direct for Stallings?

VIDOR: No, but it was a musical, too. If I hadn't been doing Solomon and Sheba, I would have had the job of directing Porgy and Bess. As far as musicals were concerned, I did "Over the Rainbow" for The Wizard of Oz. I always wanted to do musicals, but they took me as a dramatic director more than a musical director. It's just one of those things in Hollywood.

DOWD: Who was the second assistant director on Hallelujah?

VIDOR: There was a Negro bootblack at the studio. He had a stand set up and we called him Slickum. We made him second assistant director in charge of the Negro cast. In other words, he lived in the Negro hotel, traveled with the cast, and generally looked after them. He also acted in some of the scenes. He's now a minister.

DOWD: There is a title at the beginning of the film that says, "Dialogue by Ranson Rineact." Who was he?

VIDOR: I don't know. MGM had people under contract, and if you would send the script to them, they would suggest two lines, and then you'd later find their name up there on the titles. For years and years I fought people getting credit this way. I thought that this was a sin, especially since these people would later get jobs from these credits.

DOWD: How did you feel about sound at this time?

VIDOR: It was generally thought that with gestures, the meaning was more abstract in the acting. They could be taken in different ways by different people in the audience. Let's take that crap game, which was the first scene I shot for the film. In silent pictures it could be taken that they were betting five or ten dollars, or even five or ten cents. It was wide open, but with sound I realized that I suddenly had to pin the exact figure down. This is generally what you were faced with. We were going from an abstract, impressionistic mood, to saying things in exact terms.

It took years to get back to having pictures that left some things unsaid. In a silent film you couldn't leave to get popcorn because you might miss something. The minute sound came in you could get up, walk around, maybe go out and buy some ice cream, and you could still hear the sound track and you wouldn't miss anything.

You see, they jumped right in and bought a lot of plays for the first sound films. They were all simple, and they had people seated on couches with just line after line of dialogue. I had a feeling that eventually they'd wake up and find their error, and get them moving again. Fortunately in Hallelujah it was all movement. It was designed that way. Most directors were pretty sad about what had happened. We were all sort of shocked that it came right at the time it did. We felt we were just being able to find out what the medium was all about, what it could do, and we felt that we were just getting a grasp on it.

DOWD: In terms of your career, do you think that the advent of sound was a dividing point?

VIDOR: No, I don't. I couldn't have had a more colorful, moving film than Hallelujah. I don't think sound was a turning point for me, but it was a turning point for Griffith.

DOWD: Do you remember talking to Sergei Eisentein about Hallelujah?

VIDOR: No doubt I probably had him come out and have lunch with me and so forth. I remember specifically one evening when he brought Old and New and showed it. I had other contacts with him that I've forgotten, but he must have come out to the studio. It was quite an attraction for people to come on the set and watch a scene being done. Scott Fitzgerald and Eisenstein both came out.

DOWD: Can you recognize definite philosophical changes in yourself?

VIDOR: Yes, definitely.

DOWD: I know a lot of directors like Ford and Hawks have directed the same picture more than once. You never did that, did you?

VIDOR: I always tried to move along. I think the reason why I haven't done more pictures is that as long as you believe in good and evil, you can have these two forces working. As time went by, I just began to believe in one force. It may look like evil, but it wasn't. Therefore, you have cut out all the conflict. My growth has led me to become less aware of the drama in things.

DOWD: Let's move on to the other sound films. Tell me about the improvisation in the script of Not So Dumb.

VIDOR: I think that any changes we did in the play were probably done in the writing of the script. It was natural of me to take advantage of anything that might occur on the set, in the rehearsal, or in the shooting. Certainly when you had a humorous character like Don Stewart, or Marion Davies, they might say anything. Elliot Nugent had written a very successful play with James Thurber, The Male Animal. Anyway, with this kind of team, anything was possible.

DOWD: They played that game where the script writer, Franklin Pangborn, makes up a story for a film to be called Sin. They make several comments satirizing screenwriters, and someone says, "He even makes love in subtitles." Were you trying to satirize a certain type of film, or a certain type of script writer in that?

VIDOR: I'd have to research this to be able to answer that correctly. It's right in line with the way I thought at the time, the way I still think today. Certainly I originated this when George Kaufman and Marc Connelly wrote it. I would really have to get out the play and have a look at it to see how much of this was in the original play.

DOWD: There was one change that Hearst insisted upon, where Gordy and Dulcy were not married. Is that right?

VIDOR: Yes, I'm sure of that. He didn't want Marion playing a married woman. He feared that this would put her in some kind of category, and he wanted her to remain youthful. I'm certain of this because it's natural that the play would be about a married couple.

DOWD: Why didn't you make another film with Marion Davies?

VIDOR: I remember having a feeling that I didn't want to make too many of this type of picture because you became a different class of director. At that time you were put into different categories if you made certain tpes of films, whether they were dramas or comedies, or adventure or whatever. I didn't want to be put into those types of categories, so I moved on to other things. I wanted to be considered a director of unusual or important films, so I had to watch that I didn't become known as just a light comedy director.

I remember requesting that I didn't want to do any more Marion Davies pictures for a while, even though I did agree to go on the set of The Red Mill, a film that was being directed by Roscoe Arbuckle under the name of William Goodrich, just to help out a bit. It was in the middle of that film, and they asked me to go and sit there every day and watch it, and make sure that they didn't get too far away from the script. I did that out of friendship more than anything.

DOWD: That was a Marion Davies picture?

VIDOR: Yes.

DOWD: There is a title on the film (Not So Dumb) that reads, "Dialogue by Edwin Justus Mayer." Who was he?

VIDOR: He was another successful New York playwright. The Firebrand was one of his very good plays. He was an excellent writer, and had done quite a few successful plays. I don't remember his work on this film, but he did do a couple of films with me.

DOWD: How was Donald Ogden Stewart cast in the film?

VIDOR: He was always around when we were making The Big Parade, and he was a close friend of John Gilbert. We always played tennis together at my house on Sundays. He probably asked to do the part. It was so close to what he was like in real life, and he knew the character from the play so well, I let him do it.

DOWD: This film was released both as a silent picture and a sound picture because some theatres were not yet equipped for sound. Kevin Brownlow saw the silent version in England, and thought that it drags terribly because all of the gags are sound gags.

VIDOR: I never would have done it as a silent film because of that. Some of the dialogue Marion Davies speaks reminds me a lot of the lines from The Patsy -- those crazy lines that don't make any sense.

Aside from that, our general goal was to get it away from the stuffy action the play contained, and get the characters moving around the set. That was our idea. The way it came out sounding like The Patsy evolved like that. We wanted the character to come off sounding like a "dulcy" instead of a patsy. At that time there was a word called "dulcyisms" that referred to that. They were natural to Marion and fit her speaking pattern very well. That's how the idea of the Dulcy character came about, as well as the sound gags.

As far as the sound went, there was a general feeling going around that people were going to have a terrible time making the change from silent actor to sound actor. If the voice matched the image, then there was no problem. When people with high-pitched voices were cast as heroes and suddenly had to speak into a microphone, it could be a disaster. However, a lot of actors had the right abilities, the right rhythm for talking pictures.

DOWD: From this picture you went on to make Billy the Kid. How did that come about?

VIDOR: I read The Saga of Billy the Kid, by Walter Noble Burns since I was searching for a Western to do. I became interested in the character because of the tie-in between the gentleness and destructive anger that co-existed within this man. The combination was a new character for films. It appealed to me very much. I tried for three or four years to get an approval for this story.

Finally, one or two other people came along and wanted to do it, and Thalberg remembered that I had been trying to promote it for years. He told me if I would use Johnny Mack Brown, I could do the film. I didn't think that Brown was ideal for the part, but I wanted to do it, and I was afraid that if I didn't do it, somebody else would. I didn't think that Brown had the violent look of a killer. He had been a big football star in Alabama and played in the Rose Bowl one year. He was an end, and when you went to see him play, you could hear him running down the sidelines calling to the quarterback, "Here I am, Poolie," waving his arms up and down. The studio thought he had the potential to be a Western star, and I believe he was a good athlete. He did all of the stunts himself, even jumping on the horse and riding backwards, which is terribly difficult.

DOWD: Who would you rather have cast in that part?

VIDOR: Well, Cagney was quite young and I thought about using him. However, I was always trying to pick a face out of the crowd -- I was trying to get someone who had not been established yet. Alan Ladd had the gentle, frightened character who could turn into a violent killer in a flash. He did that in Shane. I would have rather discovered someone who thought in that manner. He would be more believable. You would think then that you were seeing the real Billy the Kid, rather than somebody who had been established in other roles, or who had been a football star. That was the ideal casting I was thinking about, but I had to abandon all of those thoughts when they told me I was to use Johnny Mack Brown.

DOWD: You also said you would have rather had someone else for the part of Pat Garrett, right?

VIDOR: Yes. When you read the story, you get a much different impression of the character than Wallace Beery. Here again, I was learning a big lesson, which had occurred on many films before. Was it better to have an individual like Wallace

Beery, a definite personality, or should I follow the character exactly the way the writer had written it?

The real character Pat Garrett would not come through as definitely and strongly as a man like Wallace Beery. The Beery character dominates the part. In seeing the picture again, I felt a little of that coming through. I don't feel Beery would have ever taken the secondary position the script called for. You can't picture Beery being in any kind of secondary position. If you picked up a more indefinite personality and developed him, then the villainous sheriff could have developed differently, perhaps as a friend to the main character.

Again, I suppose Irving Thalberg and the executives at MGM were looking for box-office appeal. They were trying to sell the picture. It was always a battle between names and personalities to get the film sold.

DOWD: Was Helen Hayes cast in the film?

VIDOR: Yes, she was suggested for the film. It's a rather sad story. Helen Hayes and Charlie MacArthur were good friends of mine, and we discussed the different possibilities I had in casting. Later on she told me that I had said that she wasn't good-looking enough, that she wasn't beautiful enough for the part. Thalberg must have made this up to defend himself for not giving her the part. We discussed her and chose someone else. We made a bad choice because we were halfway through the picture with another girl, and discovered that she just couldn't act at all. Afterwards, I thought I had been quite stupid not to use Helen. The picture would have been much better.

DOWD: Gordon Avil shot this film in both 35mm and 70mm.

VIDOR: Yes. The 70mm had a feeling of depth and stereoscopic reality, and really showed the Grand Canyon very well. Both cameras were right alongside each other when we filmed. This difference proved to me the great value of 70mm, the great potential it had. In the rushes, we'd run the 70mm stuff first, and then we'd look at the 35mm. The difference was tremendous. There was just no comparison. The 70mm film seemed to see around each object. This sold me forever on wide screen films.

We had to make both versions because there were only twelve theatres in the country that could run the wide screen material. There was only one such theatre in Los Angeles at the time. The picture opened here in 70mm, and it was just beautiful. I thought that this was the way that all scenic films would go eventually. Later on I was told that the Schenck brothers had gotten together and decided to withhold the wide screen format because most theatres and exhibitors were still paying for the installation of the new sound equipment, and they thought that to have them re-tool again would be too much.

DOWD: How did the fact that you were shooting in two formats at one time affect the way you shot?

VIDOR: I discovered that you must shoot the angles just the same, no matter what width film you were using. You had to shoot the angles for accent and feeling. My first impression was that we would have to stage things differently for each camera. You'd have the principal action going on in the center of the wide screen, and being as wide as a proscenium stage, you'd have atmosphere and incidental action going on off to the right and left. Well, to cover such a shot we would shoot it only once in 70mm, and then the 35mm camera would continue to take these incidental action shots from the left and right of center screen.

At first I thought that we would lessen the set-ups by one-third. When I took up wide screen direction again later on, I began to think that it wasn't a question of size or width, but that it was a question of emphasis, especially at the time I was doing War and Peace. So, eventually it didn't really lessen the set-ups that much at all.

DOWD: What were the locations you used for the 70mm shots?

VIDOR: I went all over the western part of the country looking for the right locations. I used the Grand Canyon, and Zion National Park. We were also very close to Monument

Valley. For some of the shots I was looking for something like the scenes from The Covered Wagon.

The problem I had on some of these locations was the fact that I wanted large, sweeping shots to use for the wide screen. We had to carry these cameras all the way up to the top of some of those mountains. I had Boy Scouts stationed along the way, and they were supposed to signal my messages with flags down to the actors. Almost always they ended up jumbling the message up so that I had to run up and down the hill to get things straightened out. Later on in one lcation we discovered that the forest rangers had a phone installed at the top of the mountain, so I was able to talk to the rest of the crew by phone.

DOWD: Didn't you make an exact reproduction of the Lincoln County Courthouse?

VIDOR: Yes, not only the County Courthouse, but the entire street was built from photos we found of the town. The street is just the way those early photographs looked. We might have used our imagination for the Tunston House, and the bar, but everything else is very realistic.

DOWD: Was all of this constructed out in the San Fernando Valley?

VIDOR: Yes, it was built against the hills on the other side of the valley.

DOWD: Did you use any sky backdrops in this film? The clouds all look so real and fluffy.

VIDOR: We were shooting a lot in Gallup, New Mexico. The skies there are wonderful, and we were able to get a lot of good footage there. We didn't use backdrops. They usually had beautiful thunderhead clouds, and that's one of the reasons we always wanted to go out there to shoot. In fact, Kit Carson's cave is near Gallup somewhere.

DOWD: This was where Johnny Mack Brown was supposed to be starving to death?

VIDOR: Yes, this was the cave where he was finally captured. Kit Carson was supposed to have hidden out there.

DOWD: The lighting in the cave scenes was beautiful.

VIDOR: Yes, I like it very much. Even so, whenever I see it I get sick because of something I remember. When we were shooting there, I told the crew that we needed a dead horse out near the mouth of the cave, and the property man and the assistant director had forgotten to bring the dead horse we had arranged for. I was up in the top part of the cave yelling, "Where's the dead horse?" Unbelievably, they brought out some old Indian horse and hit it over the head to kill it. I could hear the blows way up inside the cave. They were killing it right there for the shot. I'll never forget the sound echoing through the cave. I look at the film and see the dead horse lying there, and it makes me sick. Even at that time I got sick, and I was very angry with my assistant director for doing it.

DOWD: How did you do the scene where all the horses are running in the beginning?

VIDOR: There was a herd of wild horses there, I think. We staked out the camera position and had the cowboys chase the wild horses around for the shot. That's about all there was to it.

DOWD: Was there much improvisation in terms of the dialogue?

VIDOR: Yes. I had Stallings with me on the set in the studio. I can recognize some of this in the dialogue. It looks like there was quite a bit of that going on. Stallings was a good dialogue man. He had written a lot of plays, and had a good ear for it. We would do a little experimentation on the set, and he would throw out some very good incidental dialogue.

DOWD: What do you think of the Western as a genre?

VIDOR: Well, one thing I always had to fight was that I was more interested in the photography than anything else. At least this was one of my biggest interests, and I thought that we could always get great scenic stuff in these pictures. I wasn't around the same area where Ford shot in Monument Valley, but I had the idea that if the picture had lots of great scenery, it would go a long way. In addition to the scenery, the Western was a chance to take people in cities, the ones who were sitting in the theatres, and allow them to experience all these great open spaces and vistas. The Western permitted this. Those were my main interests with the Westerns.

DOWD: Did William S. Hart come out to visit you?

VIDOR: Yes. He claimed he owned Billy the Kid's revolver, and he brought it out. I suppose the publicity man arranged for his visit, and he only stayed an hour or so. Perhaps he stayed for lunch, I'm not sure.

DOWD: You're in the film yourself, aren't you?

VIDOR: I think so. It was in that scene where Billy is looking for somebody in the bar, and there is a man sitting there with his hat pulled down over his eyes. I used to do that occasionally.

DOWD: Going back to that one scene in the cave, I think it is the most beautiful sequence in the film. The camera follows him very closely and then he goes outside and you have this tremendous long shot of all the people, the men who have tracked him down. They are on their way up.

VIDOR: Yes, I like it. I don't know whether this is the place to talk about it or not, but with the big screen image, you were just thinking in terms of much bigger scenes and shots. This is another reason why Hollywood studios are not being used as much as previously. The wide screen format needs big shots like that one. Before this came in, you would build something on the backlot because it was just a little square picture. Now you can't do that. People want to see the real places depicted in the picture. You can't fake these things so easily. You want to take advantage of magnificent views because of this wide film.

DOWD: Was Mitchell's original 70mm camera very bulky?

VIDOR: It looked just like the 35mm camera, but it was much wider and much heavier. One of the things that used to happen was that all cameras used to jam up now and then. When this 70mm film buckled inside the camera, it would take you half an hour just to pull all the film out. The great thing about the MGM system was that the negative was all shot on 70mm, but it was then reduced to 35mm for the prints. The discovery was that if you reduced the film down to 35mm, it would then stand the enlargement just as if it were really 70mm.

VI

DOWD: You moved from MGM to Goldwyn to make
Street Scene. How did that come about?

VIDOR: Goldwyn had tried to get me to work for him
years before. I don't remember the exact circumstances, but
getting the assignment to do Street Scene was quite a prize. It
was a well-written, well-constructed play by Elmer Rice. It
was certainly above the ordinary play in scope and meaning. I
had seen the play a couple of times, and liked it. I thought it
was fine material for a film.

DOWD: How did the casting work out?

VIDOR: The play was running for a few weeks in downtown Los Angeles, and although we didn't use the two leads,
we did use most of the others. Whoever did the casting of the
play had done a very good job. Estelle Taylor, Buster Collier
Jr. and Sylvia Sidney were not in the play, but we used them
for the picture. They were used in order to put together a
regular motion picture cast.

DOWD: How did you decide to accept the conventions of
the original play? By this I mean using just the street set.

VIDOR: Well, I have always had a very distinct feeling
that when anyone wrote a good play, book, or anything, they
were inspired and they moved along with that inspiration. I
have always respected this inspiration, and I think it gives a
unity to the piece itself, a certain unity that you don't want to
tamper with. I'm always reluctant, and very careful not to
upset the entire package that inspires the writer.

I wanted to try to not get away from that one facade. In the theatre all the audience saw was a sidewalk. They didn't even see the street. I hoped I could enlarge it to include scenes in the street, and further down the block. My first thought on this was of a fly. I thought, to a fly, a face is a complete landscape, with valleys, hills, and all sorts of things. This caused me to think that if we treated the front of the building like a face, a camera would move around like a fly moved around, and that would give me enough compositions and movement for the picture.

I had many copies of the house made, and I tried to make each set-up look different. I also worked out a system with the camera following anyone going out of a door, then picking up the next actor and the next extra just entering through the same door. This gave a flow to it, and it was challenging to see how much movement we could put in one static set in front of the building. I think it worked out. I think the constant change of composition makes it very interesting.

DOWD: Richard Day, who also did all of the sets on the rest of your Goldwyn films, constructed the set for Street Scene. How was this done?

VIDOR: The set was built on the backlot. Instead of building a whole New York block, we put the house at one end of a half-block, and then built another house, identical to the first, at the other end of the street. This way, when we were shooting on one house, the other house could be prepared for the next shot. We could shoot half a block in either direction, so it worked out fairly well. Also, this enabled us to have high platforms and special shots worked out on one house while we were shooting at the other house, and everything would be ready for the next shot when we needed it.

DOWD: How did you choose Alfred Newman to do the score?

VIDOR: Newman was under contract to Goldwyn, and was right there on the Goldwyn lot. I got him by way of doing a Goldwyn picture. Usually, a composer doesn't come in until after the picture is finished. In this case he didn't have anything to do, and he was available. He spent a lot of time on the set, and became very familiar with what I was trying to do. We would talk about music as the shooting moved along. This never happened to me anywhere else, except for Hallelujah.

DOWD: Is there any documentary footage in Street Scene? Or was it all shot completely on the set?

VIDOR: I think we had some second unit stuff done in New York. There were one or two combination shots that contained partly New York and Los Angeles studio shots.

DOWD: I know we saw a print that doesn't do justice to the lighting in this film. Both Street Scene and Hallelujah are very dark films. Was that a deliberate decision?

VIDOR: No, the first half of the film is a night scene. I don't remember it as being too somber. It has controlled lighting, but I don't think of it as being dark.

DOWD: The theme of Street Scene is one of foreboding. It's a fatalistic film. You can tell from the beginning of the picture that something is going to happen. There's an ominous quality about it.

VIDOR: Yes, that's true. That is all due to Elmer Rice. I didn't originate any of the story. Some of the scenes are mine, but the story is basically his.

DOWD: There were some shots, especially at the beginning, that are very typical of your films. The sequential nature of the shots and the way they establish a certain atmosphere are evident. For instance, those long traveling shots with a different person in each window is one of them.   Did you notice that in your own work?

VIDOR: Yes, that's all mine. That was simply a result of trying to use film to its fullest extent. I was trying to embellish the film with a few silent movie techniques. That comes from my desire to establish more atmosphere. In the play there was a thing about a boy trying to learn to ride a bicycle. We shot this and at the end of each act, he can ride the bicycle a little more. In the end you see him riding down the street on his bike.

DOWD: Could you talk a little bit about the crowd scene where Sylvia Sidney returns home after the murder?

VIDOR: When I was watching it the other night, I recalled that instead of letting the assistant director tell the extras what to do, I worked with each one of them myself. I think we had extras very close to the main characters. Instead of just treating them as a mob, I gave them individual things to do and also controlled the action to the point where it would enhance or point to the principals, instead of distracting from them. I was conscious of the flow that I could control, and the benefit I would have of making everything enhance the main characters. Instead of treating them like pasteboard cut-outs, we treated them like individuals.

DOWD: The long musical interlude in the middle of the film is very unusual for a sound picture. Did you use this to adhere to the act structure of the play?

VIDOR: Yes, definitely. It was not to separate them, but it was to blend the acts, and give it a feeling of smoothness. There is a value to the act structure where you have first, second, and third acts. I was always thinking of this in terms of cinematography, too. It is a transition between acts, and yet it must also separate the moods.

DOWD: Do you think you could have turned Street Scene into a film if you had been offered the script during the silent era?

VIDOR: No, I don't think I would have accepted Street Scene as a silent film. There is a lot of movement there, but I think the script really uses dialogue and sound well to convey the story. It is best to have sound for this type of picture.

DOWD: The sound effects are fantastic. It was a tremendously expressive soundtrack of city noise.

VIDOR: We were thinking about that very much in those days. I was conscious of making the most use of sound. Some of us hadn't been too happy about the transition to sound, but we were trying to take full advantage of the sound. We were very conscious about using the sound creatively and imaginatively.

DOWD: I noticed the similarity in the tracks of <u>Street Scene</u> and <u>Hallelujah</u> in the street merchants who were selling their products. Is that the kind of approach you were using in <u>Hallelujah</u> -- where someone is talking, and then the talk becomes music?

VIDOR: I think that's just a natural extension in the context of the film. I was embellishing the mood and atmosphere. The film called for that, and I think I was just extending the obvious.

DOWD: I like the way you set up the shots when somebody goes out and walks down the street. You do that without cutting. How did you manage shots like that with those big cameras and sound equipment?

VIDOR: By then we were out of the "ice boxes," which gave us a lot more freedom. We also had cameras down in a hole in the ground for some shots. They weren't so cumbersome that you couldn't put them wherever you wanted to. I suppose sometimes we'd take all the big covers off, or maybe we'd shoot it with a wild camera and put in the sound later. I determined that I would not be limited by the bulk or clumsiness of the cameras.

DOWD: All the films that you made during the thirties are either films about marriage, Westerns, or similar topics, with the exception of <u>Street Scene</u> and <u>Our Daily Bread</u>. Why didn't you make any gangster films? Were you at all tempted by the crime of the thirties?

VIDOR: No. I wasn't thinking about gangsters much. I was leaving those to someone else to do. I suppose I had a certain romanticism and sentimentality that was evident. I wasn't offered any of those gangster films, and I don't think anyone ever considered me as a director for those pictures.

124

DOWD: Is there some element of Galveston in Street Scene?

VIDOR: I definitely could feel the same atmosphere. In Galveston you could get several different families living on one block, but in New York they could all be living in the same tenement house. I have to say that it is Elmer Rice's creation. I was very impressed with his work, and I identified with it to some extent. I could feel that atmosphere as I directed it, and in that way I suppose you could say that some feelings of Galveston are in the film. They're my own.

DOWD: Do you think Street Scene is in any way dated?

VIDOR: No, I really don't. I believe that things should have a time and quality of their own. It's like Shakespeare, although I'm not trying to compare myself to him. The good writing of any era doesn't seem to date. It's just the cheap, insincere work that becomes dated. Technically, the photography is not dated. I thought Gregg Toland photographed it, but on the screen it gave credit to George Barnes. Both of these cameramen knew everything the cameramen of today know. They were able to do those scenes as well as anyone around today could. I don't think the acting is dated, so there's really no reason for the film to be dated.

DOWD: If you were to do a remake of Street Scene today, what would it be like?

VIDOR: I've never thought of doing it any other way. Lester Cowan told me a couple of years ago about the idea of remaking it in Puerto Rico, and I didn't know what he was talking about. In San Juan, how are you going to get Jews, Swedes, Hungarians, and all those other nationalities? This type of film is what we used to call a "Grand Hotel story." We brought all these different families together in a New York tenement house. You would put them all together in this house, mix them up, and see what came out. We said just about everything we wanted to say with this type of film, so I really can't think about doing it over again.

DOWD: Does this film express a personal view of yours?

VIDOR: If I were going to write something similar today, I would write something else. I would put it into a different place. I would do it about a different subject, and would get the intent, the motivation, the raison d'être to be something else. I would do it in a more contemporary way. That way it would be more of a personal statement. But you see, by doing all of that, you would be changing the whole thing entirely, so it's really hard to say. I prefer to let the film stand on its own.

DOWD: The Champ was photographed by Gordon Avil and written by Frances Marion. How did this picture get started?

VIDOR: There was a comedy director by the name of Charles Reisner. He had a child named Dink, who was quite a character. He probably told the original idea of the story to Frances Marion, who sold the story to the studio. Leonard Praskins wrote the script. The similarity between this picture and Stella Dallas is very strong. Gordon Avil had been camera operator on quite a few pictures of mine, and I gave him his first assignment as cinematographer. We worked well together.

DOWD: When we talked about Jack Knife Man you spoke about how difficult it was to direct the child. You seem to have drawn a wonderful performance from Jackie Cooper in The Champ.

VIDOR: The boy in Jack Knife Man was just pulled out of a group of children. Jackie Cooper had made Skippy with Norman Taurog. He is an absolutely wonderful performer. He knew what he was doing. All you had to do was set the mood and tell a little bit about the story, and then tell him exactly what you wanted him to do.

When we got down to the end of the picture, he had to have this very hysterical sobbing scene. I wanted to achieve something a little beyond fake acting. I wanted to really feel it. We did many things to get him to really feel the emotion. He and Red Golden were good friends, so I told

Jackie that I was going to fire Red. We even told him that his mother was being taken to the hospital. I'm sure he didn't believe these stories, but he was enough of an actor to understand what we were doing, and he went along with it. Pretty soon he swung into it and became hysterical, and started to throw a tantrum. The result was great. He was a very good actor, and a joy to work with.

DOWD: There is a scene where he steals some gum and cigarettes while he is waiting to see his mother. He is also singing a song. When we were watching it, you said that it was off the cuff. How much of that scene was improvised?

VIDOR: All of it. In the script, it simply said that he went to the door and waited until someone came out. So, all of the little things that he did while he was waiting were made up on the spot.

DOWD: This was still one of your first sound pictures. Did you find improvisation harder to do with sound?

VIDOR: Only as far as the actors having to learn some lines. Wallace Beery was improvising a little. Quite a few lines were all off the cuff. It seemed to work pretty well.

DOWD: You said once before that you tried to alternate between making artistic pictures and commercial pictures.

VIDOR: Yes. I had a feeling at that time that if I just made the films I wanted to, I would be classified as an artistic director, and wouldn't have the professional power that I wanted. They would say that I was an artistic director, and that I just made artistic pictures. If I made two or three box-office successes, that would keep my name up and show them that I was able to make successful films.

Sometimes the pictures I made as non-commercial ventures turned out to be more successful than the ones I started as commercial pictures. An interesting thing is that when I left MGM and later returned, the studio manager came to me and complimented me and wanted to give me a job because of two films I had made as artistic projects. They were still making lots of money. He didn't mention The Champ, but that was a big success.

DOWD: What was the story about driving past the Chinese Theatre at eleven o'clock each night?

VIDOR: It was simply the fact that everybody could go and have a good cry that marked the success of The Champ. I found out that Grauman's Chinese Theatre let out at that time each night, and those were the days when I was seeing a lot of Chaplin. We used to spend a lot of time on Hollywood Boulevard. We usually had dinner at Musso and Frank's and then we would walk the length of Hollywood Boulevard. I always timed it so that we would be walking past the theatre when The Champ was getting out. I would watch the people come out with their handkerchiefs in their hands, wiping their eyes. This was a great joy to me. I'd go by about every three nights to see this.

DOWD: Where was the house where Jackie Cooper goes to meet Irene Rich?

VIDOR: That was Marion Davies' bungalow. It was a big house that they called her "dressing room." It had a dining room, kitchen, living room, and a bedroom upstairs. It was later moved to Warner Bros. when Marion started working there. We used the back entrance to the house.

DOWD: Beery did not use a double for the fight scene, did he?

VIDOR: No, not at first. The way it worked out was that he told me he would do the role if it didn't require any fighting. But then the more we worked on that scene, the more he ended up doing. He was supposed to just do the scenes where he would get up off the ground, and we were going to use doubles for the long shots. But in looking at it now, it looks as if he did the entire thing himself.

          The day we were to shoot those scenes, I saw him standing around with several beautiful girls who were working on the lot. I said to the assistant director, "See those girls? After he leaves them, get them to come over and sit on the set when he does the scene." They showed up for the scene, and when it was time to do the fight scene, I said, "All right, bring on the doubles." Beery stood up and said, "What do you mean? I do all my own fighting!" That's how he ended up doing so much of that.

DOWD: He seemed to hesitate halfway through his lines. Was that something he did on purpose?

VIDOR: He was probably one of those actors who don't want to appear to learn their lines too well or too exactly. I don't think he'd ever speak a line exactly as it was written unless it was right in line with his character. He wanted to be crude and mumbling a bit. He was not thinking in the exact words the character was supposed to be speaking with. As far as I was concerned, I didn't care if he spoke the exact words, as long as he put across the feeling of the scene. I like an actor to adapt things to his own character and way of speaking.

DOWD: There was a shot where the punching bag goes through the window. How was that done?

VIDOR: That was done with a thread. We suspended the bag by a thread so that if you hit it hard enough, the thread would break. Then it was just a question of making a number of takes to get it to hit the window properly. We had a special effects man taking care of that. You would just say to him, "I want the punching bag to go flying through the window," and it would be his job to see that it was done properly.

DOWD: As in your other sound films, the fact that you had all that equipment to deal with didn't seem to stop you from moving the camera around.

VIDOR: When we were running the silent films, faces were always in profile. We called these fifty-fifty shots. In this film you began to see people's backs. I also noticed that we were using quite a bit of panning and perambulating. This was just at the beginning of the era when we could move all that stuff around. The cameras were still noisy, and sometimes you had to do a re-take because of camera noise. Sometimes you could see some obvious places where the camera had to stop moving. This was obvious in the cell scene. You couldn't get the camera into small places. However, we were able to put the camera tripod on a dolly, and then move the whole thing around the floor. This was what we called a perambulating shot. I liked to move the camera around, and I used a lot of this in The Champ.

DOWD: From Hallelujah on, it seems like your films get darker. Were you conscious of this?

VIDOR: I knew that as we depended on dialogue more and more, we could have the faces more in shadows and we could pay more attention to effect lighting. With sound, you were not completely dependent on facial expressions to tell the story. I realized that I could do a whole scene in the dark if I really wanted to. It freed the lighting to help establish more of the mood.

———————

DOWD: Bird of Paradise was your first film with Selznick as your producer. Did Mayer lend you to him?

VIDOR: Yes. Selznick was married to Irene Mayer. He had been given the big job of running the RKO studio when he was very young. He became head of production there, and asked me to come over and make Bird of Paradise, which was a very well-known play at the time. I believe Lenore Ulric starred in the stage version. I was given the play to read, and it was very badly written. I read one act one night, and went back the next day and said; "I just can't read it, David. I'll never make this picture if I have to read this entire play the way it is written." I was interested in the South Seas theme, though, and still wanted to do the film.

Selznick said, "I don't care if you make the play or not, just as long as you have the girl jumping into the volcano somewhere in the story." He wanted the basic story of the American boy and the native girl who fell in love. "If you give me three good love scenes, as there were in The Big Parade, you can do whatever you want." We kept the basic theme the same, but after that it was my job to originate three unusual love scenes.

I was a little disappointed with what I got on the underwater love scenes. I had an idea to try to make a back light out of the bubbles. I had a boat then, and we could fish at night, and I had seen the phosphorescent light that some fish have. I thought if we could have a back light in a similar way, we could have a great love scene under the water. The other idea I had was to have a bed of rose leaves under a roof of big ferns. I suppose the third idea was the orange juice idea, where she feeds him from her own lips, sucking the orange and then giving him the orange.

We had to leave for Honolulu on a certain date, and we were supposed to write the script on the way over. I took a writer along on the ship, but the seas were so rough, we didn't get any work done during the trip. We arrived on location with no script whatsoever. The rest of the company was due to arrive in about a week. We had to write the script while we were looking for other locations. So, we went around asking people what they did, and what the native customs were. There is one scene in the picture where they are sliding down the hill on the leaf of a plant. They break it off and sit on it, and slide down the hill. That's one of the scenes we picked up from the natives.

When we first got there, there were no palm trees, so we had to have the telephone company move them down to where we were going to shoot. Then a tremendous storm blew all the leaves off the trees. The men had to crawl back up and nail them on. It also rained the entire time we were there. I think we had about three or four clear days the whole time. So, we finally came back to California and went to Catalina and shot the rest of the stuff there.

DOWD: The titles list three fine cameramen. Did you actually use all three?

VIDOR: I think (Clyde) de Vinna was one of them. He was a specialist on exteriors and titles. He knew filters, and he knew how to make skies dark, and how to change tones. He also had been to the South Seas before. Eddie Cronjager was the head cameraman. I can't remember who the other one was.

DOWD: Was it Lucien Andriot?

VIDOR: Yes. Maybe we did some re-takes with Lucien.

DOWD: You must have used a tremendous number of lights in Hawaii. Didn't you have problems getting electricity in some of those rural areas?

VIDOR: We had a truck. I remember I wanted to go with very portable equipment. I had dreamed of having it all contained in one station wagon. When we actually started to shoot this, we ended up with generator trucks, a sound truck, a prop truck, and an electrical truck. Instead of just moving into some remote area, by the time we got all of the cars, buses, and trucks in, it would all be trampled down to nothing. That was a big problem. I had a hope of having everything small, as small as the equipment is today. But back then, I had ten trucks. They had to be brought over and unloaded by crane, and when you went into the jungle, you always had the problem of how to get the trucks in to the shooting location. I was trying to fight this tendency, but I just couldn't lick it that time.

DOWD: Did you say that Busby Berkeley choreographed the dance scene?

VIDOR: Yes. We were shooting in the backlot at RKO then. It was the same lot where they shot Gone With the Wind, about a half mile back of the MGM studio on Washington Boulevard. We also made Duel in the Sun there. I did not see his name in the credits, but he did work on it. I guess he was with RKO at the time, but I'm not sure.

DOWD: Did you have an orchestra along, too?

VIDOR: No. Max Steiner from the music department probably made the music beforehand, and then played it back during the shooting.

DOWD: Did you have any censorship problems about Dolores Del Rio not wearing a top in the dance scene?

VIDOR: Not that I remember. Selznick was not a fellow to be easily put down in matters like these. He went to New York to get permission to use the word "damn" in Gone With the Wind. I know he had to be very careful in shooting that scene. The lei was covering her breast, but I don't think we had any other problems.

DOWD: How did you shoot the underwater scene?

VIDOR: There was some tank around Hollywood that was especially equipped for that type of shooting.

DOWD: It is a beautifully photographed film. One really has the feeling of an exotic South Seas island.

VIDOR: We knew the locations were there, and we utilized them to the best of our ability. I was very much in the romantic mood at the time. I figured that if we had enough exotic, romantic locations, that would be all we needed.

DOWD: The film also bears a certain resemblance to Wild Oranges.

VIDOR: Yes, it does. It had lots of photographic atmosphere.

DOWD: Did you have any trouble shooting the scene with the giant turtle?

VIDOR: We had a running gag that whenever we didn't know what to do, we should go and shoot a couple of shots with the turtle. We had a real turtle, and fake one as a back-up. We also had turtles that were pulled along by wires buried underground. In looking at it, it looked as if we were working with a real turtle all the time. We didn't have any flapping legs arranged, but we could shoot some scenes of Joel McCrea riding it as it went along.

DOWD: Dolores Del Rio's difficulty with the language, and the scenes that are built around communication between them are very reminiscent of The Big Parade.

VIDOR: Yes. With The Big Parade I found that we could do pantomime scenes because you are legitimately using the technique, since the two characters cannot communicate by words. It was a great facility in making pantomime legitimate and I was still striving to do that, and was thinking in those terms when I made this picture. It just seems to make for good scenes between men and women.

DOWD: How was Dolores Del Rio able to keep up with speaking in Hawaiian? Was that difficult to direct someone speaking a language neither you nor she understood?

VIDOR: We had to break it down into phrases and when you do that, it is easier to put them back together to form sentences, so it wasn't all that hard.

VII

DOWD: Cynara was the second of four films you did for Goldwyn Studios. There seems to be a definite similarity in your Goldwyn films. What makes that so, and what do you think the similarity is?

VIDOR: I think Goldwyn was always striving for very high quality. He went for the best writers, and aimed as high as he possibly could. I think that had something to do with his background. I suppose all of his films had a certain slickness. He had Richard Day, one of the best art directors, Gregg Toland, one of the best cameramen, and had writers like Thornton Wilder and Sidney Howard. William Wyler also directed for him. There was an air of perfection around the studio.

DOWD: This was a Frances Marion screenplay. Was she around at the time of the shooting?

VIDOR: Goldwyn hardly made a picture without going through her first. He had great faith in everything she did. She didn't come to the studio at all. All the scripts and paperwork were sent directly to her home. She didn't have any contact with the actual production. I think Frances came in for a run-through once. This was not typical of all the pictures she worked on, though I suppose she worked a great deal on Stella Dallas. Goldwyn would let the script go through her hands first, and she would do such a good job that she would eventually be entitled to a credit.

DOWD: It seems as if you had really perfected your sound cutting technique, because it flows much more smoothly than Street Scene.

VIDOR: It was a stage play, and we didn't stray too far from that basic form. The whole point at that time was to figure out how to make a film from a stage play without losing that continuous flow. It was a question of making some of the things that were talked about in the play visual, to communicate them by pictures. It sometimes ended up that you only needed about a half of the original dialogue that was necessary to tell the story in a theatre. When you told it with certain camera movements and expressions, you didn't have to talk so much about it.

DOWD: You seem to have a certain fondness for including movies within your movies. In <u>Cynara</u> there is a scene from a Chaplin movie. Do you remember how that came about?

VIDOR: Chaplin and Goldwyn were part of United Artists, and in a way, they were friends. The business association was rather close. I imagine Goldwyn managed to get the film through that channel. It was rather difficult to get one of Chaplin's films, or even a clip from one of them. He watched them very closely, more so than anyone else. I was quite surprised myself to see that it got into the film. I didn't think it would happen.

DOWD: Was this the first time Phyllis Barry ever acted in a film?

VIDOR: Yes. I learned another lesson from this. In seeing it again, I didn't feel as let down as I did the first time. I particularly leaned toward the unknown young girl because this part seemed to call for that. We made tests, and I can't remember how many we did. The problem is that a girl, an aspiring actress, will give quite a bit of effort in a test, as much as Lillian Gish would give you every day for the duration of the picture. You see the test, are quite surprised, and you put her in the part because she seemed to work so hard. Later on you see that they never give you that same amount of energy during the rest of the picture. I had this happen to me twice. However, in seeing it again, I thought that she was absolutely competent, pleasant, and right for the part.

DOWD: Was Ronald Colman's speech during the swimming contest scene improvised?

VIDOR: I had a feeling that it was improvised as I watched it again. There wasn't so much improvisation going on at that time. Dialogue was a new thing, and we were not yet so free and expert with it. If you got on the set and found out that what had been written was inadequate, you would quickly knock out a speech right on the spot that seemed to do the trick. That was what the scene we saw looked like. I could only prove it by finding an old script and checking it.

I think one of the reasons I agreed to do the film was the fact that I would have an opportunity to work with Colman. It certainly was not difficult to get good performances out of all of the actors in that picture. They were just good actors.

DOWD: I noticed in the script there was an ambiguity in the motivation. You never quite figure out what people are thinking.

VIDOR: In running through all these films, I see a reflection of my own character and attitude. Conditioned thinking tried to freeze everything like love and romance into a set category, with set responses. I know that my life work has been to upset this tradition.

The guy is in love with his wife, but is he a dirty bastard for being in love with the other girl? Of course not. He's attracted to her, and she fills a need. He respects the girl, likes her, and feels a certain amount of tenderness toward her. It's a real theme of love being universal, and not being confined to one person. If someone has love in their heart, they can love a hundred people, or even a thousand. Or, it can only be two or four.

DOWD: I think you made some really terrific films about marriage during this period. The honesty at the end of the film was very unusual, although The Crowd, Stella Dallas, and Wedding Night are all very good films about marriage.

VIDOR: It is really a problem of our lives. It should be treated honestly and sincerely. My attitudes are that it is still a puzzling situation. No other contracts are absolutely binding, and neither is the marriage contract. It is an interesting subject, and it can't be ignored in our daily life.

DOWD: There is a perfectly wonderful cut in this film. It happens when he is in the cab coming home, after he has met the girl. She has given him her address on a piece of paper, and he says there is only one woman in his life and rips up the pieces of paper and throws them out the window. The paper flutters in the air, and then you cut to St. Mark's Square in Venice, with all of the pigeons flying up into the air, just like the pieces of paper.

VIDOR: I get a kick out of that now. We were working with abstract forms like these pieces of paper flying through the air, and the pigeons. What better dissolve or cut than to tie those two shots together? This is pure cinema.

DOWD: There is another good cut in Cynara when Colman is sitting in his study, after he has found out that the girl has committed suicide. He says, "Oh no," and starts pounding on the desk. Then it dissolves into the judge pounding on the gavel.

VIDOR: I particularly liked that myself. I remember Lubitsch doing it one time. I tried to get a visual segue through the abstract design and movement into the next scene.

DOWD: Let's talk about The Stranger's Return. Were you the one who chose to make the film from the story?

VIDOR: I don't remember exactly, but I was aware that the writer, Phil Stong, having written State Fair, was a man who had a feeling for the Midwest. I knew he had a feeling for the country and the people. There was a writer by the name of Lucien Hubbard who was also a producer. I think that's who actually discovered the story. That's also why he was the producer on the film. I always felt you didn't have to upset the novel too much if you were going to make a film out of it. You wanted to stick closely to the book if you wanted to retain the original feeling.

I always favored getting the original author to work on the script because he was the one who best knew what he was writing about. He had a feeling for the people, the atmosphere, and the characters. It was a strange experience when I had to get Phil Stong to write some additional sequences, and he would leave out or spoil the original feeling of a sequence. He had a very bright wife, and I got the feeling that she had helped him write the book. He started working on the script and did two or three drafts, and when I saw that it was completely changing the story, I asked him, "Who wrote this book, you or your wife?" He would say, "What?" I would say, "You left out the main part of the scene!" I didn't think it was possible for a fellow who had written the book to forget some of the key scenes. He was changing the story more than some studio writers would.

DOWD: William Daniels was Garbo's first cameraman, and he was the cameraman on this film.

VIDOR: Yes. Garbo had first choice in getting Daniels. If she was going to make a picture, there was no chance of anyone else getting him. He was a pleasant, charming man, and a wonderful cameraman. He was delightful to work with. I put in a request for him, and she did not happen to be using him at the time, so I got him. I considered myself very lucky to have him. He was very helpful and easy to discuss things with.

DOWD: This picture did not have expensive sets or big productions, yet you had an outstanding cast. Were you able to choose who you wanted in your films at this point?

VIDOR: Pretty much. It was a cooperative thing then. You would go down a list of a half-dozen people, usually starting with the studio's stock company. (Lionel) Barrymore was under contract as one of the actors, but I don't think Miriam Hopkins was. She was working with Lubitsch around that time, so I probably got her from Paramount on loan. I don't remember the details, but if you saw eye to eye with the producer, he would do all that he could to get everyone you wanted. In this case, we sent Miriam Hopkins the script, and then we got together and read it. Nobody was supposed to know that we were trying to negotiate for her, but when I saw the copy of the script I had sent her, the last page had the inscription, "King, if there's any changes you would like to make, I'd be happy to do them for you." Lubitsch had found out after all.

DOWD: When we were watching it last night you said you shot it in Chino.

VIDOR: Yes, that's where we shot it. This was about the closest farm country you could get in Los Angeles. We stayed at an abandoned country club. It was about an hour or so from Los Angeles, so instead of going back and forth each day, we decided just to stay out there.

          We had constant trouble with the sound on that picture. I think we had to do a lot of the sound over. We didn't have directional mikes in those days, and they would have helped us a lot. I worked with an art director on that picture by the name of Doris. I don't remember what her last name was, but she later went on to do layouts for Disney. I had been looking for a certain type of architecture, and I was inspired by several paintings by Grant Wood. We built some of the buildings out there in Chino.

DOWD: The script is very subtle. There are so many things that could have been hammered into the audience, but you didn't let them get that big.

VIDOR: I was just thinking about that. It was interesting to me to see how we treated the wife, who was sort of a negative character. We never shot a close-up of her through the entire film. That way she was never emphasized. We were shooting close shots of the other characters like Franchot Tone and Miriam Hopkins, but there are none of the wife. The camera technique becomes very important there. By using that technique we were able to make her fade away.

DOWD: You see her and you hear her, and you think about her, but she never really means that much to you.

VIDOR: You never see her long enough to have her mean much.

DOWD: It is easier to walk away from somebody who is as negative as that. However, it didn't foreshadow the ending. There is also a lovely shot of the threshing machines. Did you have a hard time finding those?

VIDOR: I don't think we had to look too hard. We were not trying to dig up old, outdated equipment. We just wanted active, current machines.

DOWD: In this film there is an eye towards the accuracy of the atmosphere. The whole montage of farming life was very nice.

VIDOR: The farm has always been my favorite atmosphere. It's proven by the fact that I now live on one. I used to be kidded a lot about some of the symbolism I used with the plow turning over the earth. It meant a new cycle of life, a new generation. There was a quality of metaphor.

DOWD: The ending is really very complex because the girl from the city now goes to work on the land. The farmer goes to the other world.

VIDOR: That type of thing was indigenous to the rest of the story. I thought it was the right sort of ending.

DOWD: What was the story about Barrymore on location that you were going to tell?

VIDOR: One day Barrymore asked if he could get off early because he had some very important business he had to attend to. I didn't know what it was, but we arranged to shoot his stuff early and let him go. When we finished work, we went into town to do something. We were driving along the street in this tiny town and found a group of fellows sitting outside of a drugstore on a bench. One of the fellows was Barrymore. He was wearing the fake beard that he was supposed to wear on the picture. He never did explain what he was doing. It was probably that he wanted to go to town and see whether they could detect whether or not he was an actor.

DOWD: Was he an easy person to direct?

VIDOR: Yes, he was. He had a slight gruffness and he grumbled and grunted and said all kinds of things, but underneath he was a very good actor. He was always on the job, and if someone else didn't know their lines or fooled around too much, he would get after them because he had directed a lot before his work on this film.

DOWD: Where did you experience his work before you were making this film?

VIDOR: He was on <u>Hallelujah</u> as a dialogue director for a day or two. The black people would hide from him because he was always talking to them about voice delivery and the finer aspects of acting.

In any case, he was an interesting man to work with. One time we were in the country club eating breakfast. His sister had given him a car that he was fond of. He was telling everyone about it, how beautifully it was made, how well it performed, all of that. Someone asked him what the name of the car was, but he couldn't remember it. He could only remember that the name started with a "B." People from all over the dining room were calling out names like Buick, but none of them were right. He jumped up right in the middle of his meal, went to the phone and called his nearest relative, John Barrymore, in Beverly Hills. He talked to him, but <u>he</u> couldn't think of the name either.

Then he called his sister Ethel in New York. She was in a play at the Court Theatre at the time. He got her apartment, then he got in touch with the theatre. She was on stage at the time, and they would not disturb her. He finally gave up on her, and then came back to the table and sat there, still trying to think of the name of the car. People were still calling out names as they thought of them, but nothing was close to the name he was looking for.

Finally, he jumped up, threw down his knife and fork, and said, "Give me the fire department in Rye, New York." He got the fire department and told them, "This is Lionel Barrymore in Chino, California, and my sister gave you an automobile, and you made a fire engine out of it. What's the name of it?" They told him, and he hung up and came back smiling. He announced that the name of the car was Bentley and he then sat down and was able to finish his meal in peace.

DOWD: In the film there is a reference to the Barrymores. I think it must have been a joke of yours. It is where Franchot Tone and Miriam Hopkins are discussing the plays they have seen, and then someone mentions Ethel Barrymore.

VIDOR: That sounds like one of my tricks. I did that with Marion Davies in the other film. I was always interested in the difference between reality and fantasy. This pulls it into a reality, and yet it's a fantasy at the same time.

DOWD: There was a scene about the dog in the church. I thought that went over very well.

VIDOR: Yes, I liked that too because we didn't make a real gag out of it. Capra would have kept that going. He would have made a big gag out of it. Chaplin would have had the dog get up and the tail would begin to keep time to the music. I liked the fact that I just had him walk in and sit down. That is all the comment it is worth.

DOWD: You said that you thought a love scene was cut out of the picture.

VIDOR: Certainly it was cut out of the print we saw. Going back to the love scenes in The Big Parade and Bird of Paradise, I was thinking of ways to have love scenes played out in unusual ways. I was amazed that the scene wasn't in the film because it was mainly what I remembered about the whole film. It was a love scene that took place in a pile of hay on the ground. I missed some other scenes that I know I shot of the girl, where we see her deeper feeling for the farm and the country. There's a moment where Barrymore realizes the feeling the girl has for the land, and that she would grow to have a great reverence for it.

DOWD: There is a well done editing job where Miriam Hopkins tells Franchot Tone that she loves him, and suddenly you hear this horrible laughing, and you cut from that to

Beulah Bondi standing right there in front of them, and we see that she is the one who is laughing. I thought that was a striking moment.

VIDOR: We were aware of the effectiveness in cutting and editing. It seemed to work out very dramatically, especially after all this time. You had a certain feeling that the actual cutting was helping the scene.

DOWD: What about the scene where the women are all yakking away, and Barrymore is making those horrible faces? What was he really doing?

VIDOR: He was imitating them. I would guess that I saw him doing that in the rehearsal, and I said, "We must have that put into the scene." He liked to play the irritable fellow. That is why he is so good in this part.

DOWD: There is a line at the end that I think Miriam Hopkins says: "Sometimes we are entitled to all we can get out of life." That sounds very much like something out of Street Scene.

VIDOR: Philosophically, the emphasis is all on duty and obligation, and nobody has the courage to say, "This is what I'd like to do." It is always the dichotomy of conflicting forces, the dichotomy of following something from a vague sense of duty, or else being honest and true with yourself. These things weren't clear to me during this film, although I was going through psychoanalysis five or six times a week back in Los Angeles. I do not remember if I wrote that line or not. At least it is a thing that might show through in a number of my pictures.

DOWD: That must have been a big thing for you to go into Los Angeles for psychoanalysis every day when you were making the film.

VIDOR: No, I did not go in from Chino. I probably couldn't go during the actual shooting. I stopped the visits during the shooting, although I may have gone in a few times on the weekends. The romance I had with Miriam Hopkins broke me up and left me with a terrible torch.

DOWD: Both this film and <u>Our Daily Bread</u> are about the same sort of thing.

VIDOR: Yes, they are. I told you earlier that I always favored stories about farming country.

DOWD: Did you say that you got the idea for <u>Our Daily Bread</u> from <u>Reader's Digest</u>?

VIDOR: Yes. I had a strong feeling about what was going on in the country at that time. Milk trucks were being over-turned, and Hoovervilles were springing up all over. I read an article in <u>Reader's Digest</u> that claimed that we would all have to go cooperative, and cut out the use of money. There were barter theatres that were running in the South where they brought produce to exchange for their tickets. The article was just a few pages long, but I bought the rights anyway. It was more or less a good examination of the economics of the time. After that we started to write the story.

DOWD: Did you write this with Elizabeth (Hill)'s help?

VIDOR: Yes, she was my wife, but she had been a writer on a lot of my scripts.

DOWD: Was Irving Thalberg the first person you took it to?

VIDOR: Yes. I remember getting him to read it, and he liked it and said it was darned interesting, but he didn't think he could approve it for the studio.

At that time they were into the glamour cycle, and Thalberg said it was just too bad that he couldn't approve it. I was very close to Chaplin at that time, and I told him about it. He said he could get me a release with United Artists to do it. I tried various ways to get the money together, and I talked to a couple of banks. Finally, I had to take what stock and real estate I owned and borrow the money myself.

I borrowed from a special company that dealt with motion picture loans. It cost roughly a hundred thousand dollars to make the film. I dismissed the sound truck during the last week of shooting so that I could finish the picture. These shots had to do with the digging of the ditch, and the flood scene where the water comes flowing down. Dismissing the sound gave me an added budget of one hundred dollars per day. I shot it silent, and put the sound in later. The orchestra music, the sound effects, and all other sound cost me around twenty-five thousand. Actually, the picture cost one hundred and twenty-five thousand.

DOWD: Did you make your money back on this picture?

VIDOR: Yes, I got my money back to pay back the loan. I don't know how much more I got out of it. I would think a little bit here and there, but not very much.

DOWD: Was it United Artists who finally released it?

VIDOR: Yes. They released it, but they did not do a very good job when it came to advertising and publicity. Anyway, it got good reviews and there was a wonderful excitement about it. After United Artists stopped distributing it, another company stepped in and took over.

DOWD: The characters are John and Mary Sims. These were also the same names of the people who played in The Crowd.

VIDOR: Yes.

DOWD: Did you see this as a continuation of The Crowd?

VIDOR: Yes, the same people under different economic conditions. It was the "average man" idea. The Crowd shows a member of the mob, and this man is also one of the mob.

DOWD: You had James Murray in mind for the lead, didn't you?

VIDOR: Yes. I talked with him in a Hollywood bar and told him that I had a story I would give him if he would lay off the booze for a while. He said, "Screw it, the hell with you." I said, "O.K., Jimmy, screw you!" and walked out and left him sitting there. He was too far gone to play the part anyway, so I got somebody else who looked like him.

DOWD: You also used a couple of people who had been in your films before. They were Sidney Bracey and John Qualen.

VIDOR: Yes. We were limited, and could not pay anybody over a few hundred dollars. You could get a good character actor for three or four hundred at that time. This was a weekly salary, and probably the leads would be stretched to four or five hundred dollars. That was all we could pay.

DOWD: Where was the film shot?

VIDOR: For interiors, we worked out of the Goldwyn Studio on Santa Monica Boulevard. The exteriors were done on a rented golf course in Tarzana. That town was named by Edgar Rice Burroughs, the man who created Tarzan. He lived there. They had a golf course that had folded, so we rented that. The golf course was in an area with a lot of shrubbery, and it had an old house sitting in the middle of the land. There was no source of water, so we had to bring in a tank every time a shot needed water in the picture. We had a tank of water pumped down the hill when we wanted to fill the ditch.

DOWD: I noticed that you used diagonal lights in this film.

VIDOR: They were in vogue then.

DOWD: Were you at all influenced by Sunrise during the making of this film?

VIDOR: I don't think so, although I was certainly influenced personally by Sunrise. The only one that could have been an influence in Our Daily Bread was a Russian film. I think it was called Turksib or The Earth Thirsts. I saw it just a short while before I started production. I think it only had a flute and a bass fiddle for the music.

DOWD: Could you talk about the final sequence with the metronome and the drums?

VIDOR: I was taken up with the metronome rhythm, the controlled rhythm. I had done it as early as marking metronome scores for Three Wise Fools. In Our Daily Bread I decided to think in terms of the musical climax in the picture and orchestration. I tried to do that in The Big Parade, to have it so exact that the orchestration would fit and would be absolutely synchronized with the picture. That is, building to a climax, and then tapering off with a couple of scenes. To me, this is the ideal form, especially for an ending.

I dismissed the sound equipment at the end of the shooting, and used the metronome. Later, of course, I would have done it to a music track played back during the shooting. Anyway, we put a metronome on a tripod so that it would support it in a level way, and then had an assistant stand by with a bass drum to beat out the four-four rhythm.

There were two or three reasons for doing this. One was for the music, and one was for increasing the tempo gradually through each successive shot. If you shot without this pattern, and without the metronome, you wouldn't know if the men were digging faster or slower than in any of the other shots. I wanted control, and I wanted each scene to speed up a little bit from the scene before it. We undercranked the cameras a little bit to help out for that. We laid it out so that the picks came on beats one and three and the shovels came down on two and four. They were instructed to step sideways on the beat, and they conformed to that.

DOWD: When the water finally hits the field, there were people somersaulting all over the place.

VIDOR: Yes, that was to express ecstasy. When they were jumping up and down, we used to call them pratfalls. We hired fellows who had worked for Mack Sennett in the silent comedies, and they knew how to do all of that to express joy physically.

DOWD: I noticed that in the end of Hallelujah, a little boy is doing cartwheels.

VIDOR: Yes, that's right. It's a good bodily expression to communicate joy and happiness.

DOWD:　　　　What was the atmosphere like on the set of Our
Daily Bread?

VIDOR:　　　　We lived in a trailer right down there in
Tarzana. It was a wonderful atmosphere. You got to know the
people and they were all very enthusiastic and helpful. That is
why it looks as if they are working so hard to dig the ditch.
They were all enthused about the project. I would say that
most of them were employed because we knew them from
other pictures.

DOWD:　　　　Joseph Mankiewicz has a credit for this picture.
What did he do?

VIDOR:　　　　He didn't do anything more than just take the
script and go over it. At that time dialogue was thought to be
some sort of magic. It was a hangover from the theatre. It
was called dialogue writing, not script writing. If someone read
the script, and they could not think of anything else to say,
they would comment that the dialogue might be improved.
That's what Mankiewicz did. It became a regular cliché to tell
someone that the dialogue could be improved.

DOWD:　　　　What did he write?

VIDOR:　　　　I don't know, but we weren't enthused about
everything he wrote. We might have kept a few lines.

DOWD:　　　　One of the most depressing scenes in the film is
a scene where they are lining up, and each one is telling what
he does, and you come to the end of the line and the guy says,
"I'm the undertaker." Addison Richards was just terrific in that
scene.

VIDOR:　　　　They giggle at him now. Maybe he was too
tough. I thought he was a good actor in that part. I like that
finish, and the designing of that scene. I guess that brings up
the thought that even undertakers are required in every group
of people.

DOWD:　　　　There is also the violinist. I think the scene
where he is playing on the hills is the most beautiful scene.
What was the inspiration for that?

Vidor, King Vidor's

Kate (Wallis) Vidor, King Vidor's mother.

VIDOR: I don't know. It's hard to tell, because it was a conglomerate of everybody who was working there. My wife worked closely with me on that, as did Ralph Slosser, my assistant director. I would have to say that it was the product of a group of people, not just myself or anyone else.

DOWD: Was there any blacklisting after this film?

VIDOR: Perhaps only from the direction of Hearst. Although I had made a few successful pictures with Marion Davies, they remained loyal to my former wife Eleanor and not to me.

DOWD: You took this film to Europe almost immediately. What was the reaction there?

VIDOR: I think we had a press preview in London. I think the publicity man for the picture came along on that trip. I remember when we got to Paris, the headline in the Paris paper said, "King Vidor prefers food to sex." It was a big headline stuck up in the window of a shop on the Champs Elysées. Sex was supposed to be the biggest theme for pictures, and I was talking about the idea that being able to eat came first for people, and sex was second.

DOWD: I imagine the reaction to that was sensational.

VIDOR: Yes, but that was the theme I believed in. I was half laughing because all the movies they were making were about sex. I remember being in England, and realizing that the same thing was happening there. In any case, the publicity certainly didn't hurt the picture.

DOWD: Do you think people liked it?

VIDOR: I think so. Usually I got better press releases and reactions in Paris and London than I ever got in America.

DOWD: You've been showing this film on the college circuit. What has the general reaction been?

VIDOR: I have found that the kids of college age really react beautifully to this film. I chose it for the Directors

Series for the Academy to talk about, and I found terrific interest in it. In fact, I found it had more interest than The Big Parade because we had such an amazing lesson in anti-war feelings, and The Big Parade was rather mild in its anti-war lesson. Our Daily Bread doesn't seem dated at all. I have shown it in Houston, in New York, and in Madison, Wisconsin, and I always end up talking about it more than any other film.

DOWD: To me it is one of the few films where you feel a kind of exhilaration in knowing that people could really live that way.

VIDOR: It glorifies the earth, and growing things in general. It glorifies helping each other. It gets away from all of the complications of money exchange, middlemen and competition. Those values are just as valid today.

DOWD: I know when you showed it at the Museum, there was one line in there that got howls -- when they were trying to decide how they were going to be ruled.

VIDOR: They were talking about democracy. I like that line, too. I think it was, "We don't have to have a democracy, we have to have a sacred covenant," and someone else says, "That is how we got into this mess in the first place." The whole idea of living communally seems to have come back into its own now. That accounts for at least some of the picture's popularity.

DOWD: What about the rights to the picture?

VIDOR: I still own all the rights.

Charles She
father.

King Vidor, about three ye

King Vidor, about three years old, Galveston, Texas.

Charles Shelton Vidor, King Vidor's
father.

Kate (Wallis) Vidor, King Vidor's
mother.

Publicity still from The Intrigue, (1916). King had a featured role (left), while Florence Vidor had a bit part (second from right).

King Vidor directing Gordon Griffith and Ruth Hampton in a scene from The Lost Lie (1918), one of the shorts in the Judge Brown series.

King Vidor on the set of <u>Three Wise Fools</u> (1923) with the future
Mrs. King Vidor, Eleanor Boardman.

Directing Florence Vidor and Clyde Fillmore in <u>The Real Adventure</u>
(1922). Clyde Barnes is behind the camera; the remaining are
unidentified.

TEMPO 70

<u>SCENE 286 F - INT. FINDLEY'S ROOM</u>

     Findley finishes lighting his pipe, takes off
his other shoe and throws it to the floor.

<u>SCENE 286 G - INT. SIDNEY'S ROOM</u>   TEMPO 40

     Sidney shows slight relief and quietly exits
out of door to hall.

<u>SCENE 286 H - INT. HALLWAY BY SIDNEY'S DOOR.</u>   TEMPO 00

     Sidney quietly tiptoes out into hall and
closes door after her. She stops as she hears
three old men winding watches.

Script sample from <u>Three Wise Fools</u> showing King Vidor's use of
metronomic beats.

King Vidor with Laurette Taylor, star of
Peg o' My Heart (1923).

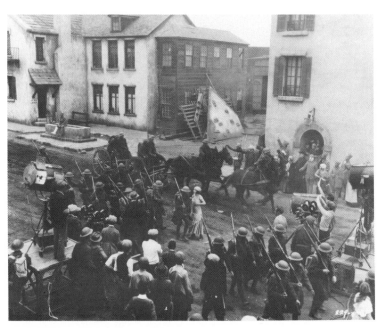

Production still from The Big Parade (1925).

King Vidor with Marion Davies, on the set of <u>The Patsy</u> (1928).

James Murray and King Vidor on the set of The Crowd (1928).

The famous studio lunch scene from Show People (1928). King (in foreground with light jacket) directs (left to right) Polly Moran, Dorothy Sebastian, Louella Parsons, Estelle Taylor, Claire Windsor, Aileen Pringle, Karl Dane, George K. Arthur, Leatrice Joy, Renée Adorée, Rod La Rocque, Mae Murray, John Gilbert, Norma Talmadge, Douglas Fairbanks Sr., Marion Davies, and William S. Hart.

King Vidor (w/megaphone) directing the baptism scene in Hallelujah (1929).

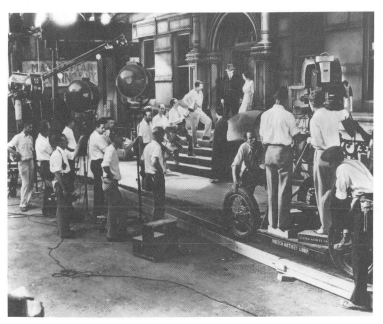

Production still from Street Scene (1931) with Joan Qualen and Sylvia Sidney.

King Vidor weds Eleanor Boardman (1926). Front row, L to R: Louis B. Mayer, Rupert Hughes; Second row, L to R: Samuel Goldwyn, Irving Thalberg, King, Eleanor Boardman, Marion Davies, Sylvia Thalberg, Edith Mayer, Marion Davies's mother; Third row, L to R: Elinor Glyn, unidentified, John Gilbert, Marion Davies's sister, Irene Mayer, unidentified, Marion Davies's father; man in rear with glasses: George Jomier (French teacher), to his left: William Haines. The remaining are unidentified.

King Vidor (left) with Karen Morley and Tom Keene, Our Daily Bread (1934).

With Elizabeth (Betty) Hill, the third Mrs. King Vidor, on location during <u>Northwest Passage</u> (1940).

Gregory Peck, King Vidor, and Jennifer Jones, on the set of <u>Duel in the Sun</u> (1946).

King Vidor (left) with writer Ayn Rand and Gary Cooper during production of The Fountainhead (1949).

Directing Tyrone Power in Solomon and Sheba (1959). During production, Power suffered a heart attack, died, and was replaced by Yul Brynner.

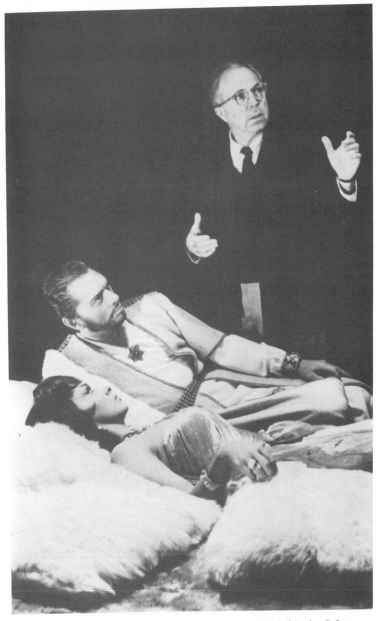

King Vidor directs Yul Brynner and Gina Lollobrigida in Solomon and Sheba (1960).

Preparing a spectacular shot from <u>Solomon and Sheba</u> (1960). Yul Brynner is at far right, mid-photo, with beard.

King Vidor's Willow Creek Ranch, Paso Robles, California.

King Vidor's Beverly Hills guest house/office/editing room (c.1974).

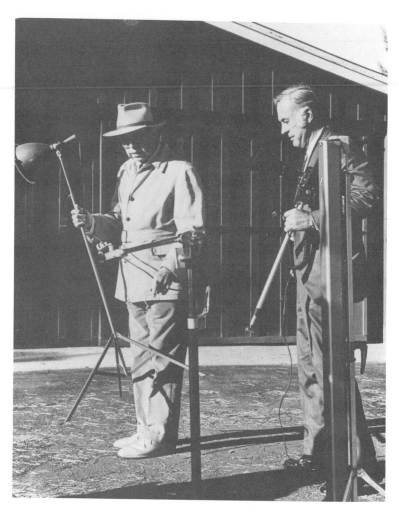

Preparing a set-up during the filming of the documentary Truth and Illusion (1977).

VIII

DOWD: Let's talk about <u>Wedding Night</u>. Do you remember seeing the first treatment?

VIDOR: Yes. When you say first treatment, I think I remember that I read a treatment that had the names in it. I don't think they used Scott Fitzgerald's name exactly, though. Studios at that time had legal departments and were always worrying about being sued if a film was too real, and I imagine they changed the names in the pictures a little more back then. As far as I was concerned, my knowing Scott Fitzgerald helped. Certainly I can see it in my direction of Gary Cooper. There's a certain lightness, a certain smartness, cleverness, trying very often to say something unusual, trying to make the most out of life, yet still somewhat shy. As I saw the film the other night, I know I was thinking about having Gary Cooper actually play Scott Fitzgerald.

DOWD: Were you the one who chose Gary Cooper for the part?

VIDOR: I'm not sure how that came about. I may have been thinking about him for the part, and the studio may have brought him in. I can't remember.

DOWD: What was the incident on the first day of shooting?

VIDOR: At that time we were very conscious of the dialogue. This attitude was set by Capra's film <u>It Happened One Night</u>. I started to work with the two characters. Gary began to stutter and stammer and interrupt himself. He spoke very slowly at times and he was also having trouble just remembering his lines. He just was not used to memorizing and having to speak dialogue.

151

I had to use a technique of letting him say a couple of lines, and then cutting to the other person he was playing the scene with. The next day I went to the rushes at noon, and here was this wonderful screen personality. Everything else was forgotten. He was a fellow that just charmed you up there on the screen. Looking at the film now, it seems as if he speaks with a certain amount of smoothness.

I suppose I was being pressured by Goldwyn. I remember Selznick once said, "When you get all through having them play a scene as fast as they can, do one for me that is twenty-five percent faster!" I think I was being harassed by Goldwyn for the same thing. They were fearful about any kind of slow pace in their films. I suppose Gary was a little nervous that first day of shooting, and that may have been one of the problems. I felt like a dentist pulling syllables out of Anna Sten's mouth. I would have my wife or another person working with me sit in the sound booth and just listen to see if the words were coming out fast enough. In the finished film they certainly seem to be fast enough.

DOWD: You said once that you thought Gary Cooper was one of the greatest screen personalities of all time. What would you say are the qualities that make him this?

VIDOR: One very important thing was his way of moving, the way he walked. Gary had wonderful movements. I think one time by the fountain in the picture he had a rather stiff leg of some sort. He'd been thrown by a horse and had hurt his leg, but even so, he still had this great way of moving, and it came across well on the screen. That is in addition to his looks, his concentration, and his strength.

DOWD: Cooper would seem to be your type of actor. Yet you directed him in only one other film. Did you have any other projects in mind for Cooper?

VIDOR: I don't remember specifically. I worked on a story for about ten years, The Milly Story, and I thought he would be ideal for that. I noticed in this film that whatever went through his mind registered beautifully on his face. That was my type of actor. A lot of people say that you can't photograph thought, but you certainly can if you have a Gary Cooper.

DOWD: Gregg Toland shot this film. Could you talk a little bit about what it was like to work with him?

VIDOR: My complaint with cameramen was always that they used too many lights. I had "Keep it simple!" stenciled on things all over the studio at Goldwyn. It was painted on ladders and boxes and platforms. I had a feeling that everything we had done was far too complicated, too involved. Gregg Toland was a man who naturally lit the scenes with few lights, maybe only two or three, instead of twenty or thirty. This appealed to me. If I wanted to move the camera over five inches to the left, he rigged up a thing where you could slide the camera without having to disturb the lighting. Any other cameraman would be brokenhearted after spending an hour to light something. I think simplicity is the hardest thing to achieve with any work of art.

DOWD: Was this Walter Brennan's first film?

VIDOR: Yes. The woman in the casting office came to me and said, "I have a most interesting actor who you may want to use. He just came into the office." I talked to him and I jumped at the chance. He was just wonderful to talk to. He later told me that I had given him his first chance in films.

DOWD: Did you ever talk to Scott Fitzgerald about Wedding Night after it was made?

VIDOR: I don't remember that I did.

DOWD: This film was made in 1935, the same year Hollywood was making lots of sophisticated comedies about marriage. Wedding Night is a very stark portrayal of marriage. I think it was quite unusual for a picture of its era.

VIDOR: At the time, I was in a postion to add my own contribution and my own individuality to the film. It was probably bought with the idea of making another It Happened One Night, which had done very well at the box office. But when I came onto the picture, I started to think of comparing it with my other films, and stopped comparing it to Capra's films. I wanted to have the opportunity to put some of my own feelings and individuality into it. The picture, as far as marriage, romance, and all that is concerned, is full of my own beliefs and convictions. The writer on this film, Edith Fitzgerald, spent a lot of time with me in preparing the script. We were good friends, so I was able to slant and control certain treatments in the script.

DOWD: In the beginning of your copy of Taps and Reveille there is a note from Fitzgerald saying that you were the model for one of the characters in Crazy Sundays. Do you recall the incident at the party that he wrote about in that book?

VIDOR: Yes. I was living on Tower Road then, and I was married to Eleanor, but we were quarreling and disagreeing about many things at that time. I had asked Scott to come up and spend Sunday with us, and he arrived at the house just before noon. Eleanor, having known him for a while, didn't mind exposing what was going on and confided in him. She was outspoken. Eleanor talked to him all day long about our problems. Later on we all went to Thalberg's house for dinner or something. Scott went back the following week and wrote Crazy Sundays.

DOWD: In the Margolies article, he mentioned the fact that you and he had spoken about doing a film together. I think it was to be about Napoleon. Was this true?

VIDOR: I think we did talk about it.

DOWD: Do you remember any of the details?

VIDOR: He gave me a book called A Hundred Days. I don't know what story we were going to do, but we certainly talked about doing a picture like that. With a writer, a director is always looking for stories, so that type of collaboration would be normal.

DOWD: Did you see him later on in his life?

VIDOR: You know, I went with Sheila Graham myself, and even announced at one time that we were going to be married. I went with her for a month or so, just before she met Scott. That probably was the reason we didn't see each other after that.

DOWD: How do you see the relationship between the character Gary Cooper plays, and Fitzgerald himself?

VIDOR: I was particularly struck by the similarity between the two. Cooper reminded me of the way Scott used to ask surprisingly psychological questions about the person to whom he was talking. They were surprising because they penetrated beyond the usual conversation. They seemed to go right to the point. He was interested in probing a little deeper than polite conversation. He had the courage to ask what he wanted to know. Cooper did the same thing.

DOWD: Would you talk about Goldwyn's inability to understand the construction of Wedding Night?

VIDOR: Goldwyn was a very strange, unusual, complex man. Culturally he aimed at the highest level, but as a person he had great trouble in understanding some of the simplest things. In Wedding Night we had a situation where Cooper had met the farm girl who lived nearby, and she was going to be an inspiration for the novel he was writing. He was talking to her, finding out about her life, and this would be the basis of the novel. There was something in the picture that collapsed the time element so that the second scene between them looked like it happened the next morning. In the third scene, he was having her read some of the book, and from the dialogue it appeared that the book was finished. At that point Cooper says something like, "You were my big inspiration for this book."

I tried to explain to Goldwyn that a man couldn't write a novel in one night. I told him, "The girl couldn't be the whole inspiration for the book, the passage of time was too brief." He just couldn't understand what I was talking about. I would explain to him over and over, and try to diagram it, and he just could not understand me. He said, "King, I don't know what the hell you're talking about." The only thing to do was go ahead and shoot the scene and show it to him on the screen. It was only after we did that that he understood that what he wanted to do just wouldn't work.

He used to do that to other directors, too. I remember Ford, Wyler, and Hawks all had the same problem. You had to shoot it, then show it to him, and then he'd catch on. After this, we put in some things, made some additions, and changed the dialogue a bit to clarify that the sequence with the girl actually took place over a period of at least two months.

DOWD: What was the story about Goldwyn coming on the set during the shooting?

VIDOR: One day I was sitting with Gary Cooper and rehearsing, trying to get him to put all he could into the scene, when Goldwyn walked onto the set. He watched for a few moments, but he was a very impatient fellow. He came over to see me and said, "Would you mind if I talk to them?" I said, "Go ahead." He sat down and gave a short talk, then he got up, turned around, and said, "I just want to say one last thing: If this isn't the greatest love scene ever put on the screen, the whole goddam picture will go right up out of the sewer." With that, he turned away and ran off the stage. There was a pause while he left, and then Cooper turned to me and said, "Did he say what I think he said?" I answered, "He most certainly did." Gary started to roll on the floor, laughing. We all got so silly afterwards that we couldn't do any more shooting that day.

DOWD: So Red the Rose was your next picture. Douglas MacLean is listed as the producer on this picture. Was this the same MacLean who was in court with William Desmond Taylor?

VIDOR: Yes. Paramount had bought the story, and he was assigned to produce it. I think that was when I went over there and worked with Lubitsch, who was then head of production at Paramount. Lubitsch and my agent talked it over, and gave me the assignment. MacLean had been an actor and a light comedian for Ince and he was quite a large star in his time. After he became too old to be a star, he became a producer. We got a very good film out of it, no matter how it was made up or arranged. The story was from a book by Stark Young, who was a Southerner. I was also from the South, and I knew a bit about that type of tradition. I see lots of dialogue in this picture that I recognize as Stallings's.

DOWD: You can recognize all of them. His touches are very much in the Southern atmosphere. Did you cast Margaret Sullavan?

VIDOR: I don't remember how this was done, but I know she was one of my favorite actresses. I certainly was pleased with her. I was very much moved by her reading of one of those scenes when I saw the film.

DOWD: When you rehearsed for this film, would you rehearse one actor at a time, or would you get all of the actors together?

VIDOR: We got as many together as possible. In a lot of pictures you could never get them all together. On this film most of them were on salary from the start. If you didn't do this, you would never be able to get them for rehearsal. I never did much rehearsal, but it was an opportunity for the actors to have a chance to free their characterizations and a chance for me to talk to them at length about their parts. We didn't just walk around the set, we sat at a table and read lines. It was just like a stage play.

DOWD: Mrs. Vidor worked on this one, too.

VIDOR: Yes, she did as a matter of fact. If I had to leave for some reason, I left her to finish a shot. I forget which shots they were.

DOWD: Isn't she the one who discovered Bob Cummings?

VIDOR: Yes. She was working as an assistant to me. She saw actors and gave them a scene to see how they read it. She came into my office one day and said, "You must see this fellow. I think he is the man we are looking for." It turned out to be Robert Cummings.

DOWD: Was your family ever involved in the Civil War? Did you hear a lot of Civil War stories as a child?

VIDOR: Yes, I heard a lot of them. When I was a boy there was still a lot of the "damn yankee" feeling around. You could cheer the song "Dixie," but never "Yankee Doodle."

DOWD: The Randolph Scott character is somewhat like the lead character in The Big Parade in that he doesn't want to go to war.

VIDOR: Yes, he is against war. I don't know whether we originated that or whether it was in the book. We still have the original book. I was always trying to get a crack at war in every film.

DOWD: There is that great reunion scene at the end which is like The Big Parade. Were you the one who thought of the bit about the father with the hats before he goes off to war? That sounds like your humor.

VIDOR: Yes, it does, but it could have been Stallings. We might have even written that right on the set. It would be interesting to get the script and see how it was written.

DOWD: The script gets very complex when Johnny Downs switches the jackets. That was a very complex situation.

VIDOR: Yes. So many of my films go through what I call "death pains" to get them ended. Many films go beyond the point where they should finish. However, I think we were able to end this one in the right place, thanks to that little bit of writing.

DOWD: How did you determine how this would end?

VIDOR: There is a logical place for every ending. I think it is important to end films where they should end, and not let them go through the pain of ending themselves, or trying to end themselves.

DOWD: Randolph Scott was certainly good-looking in this film.

VIDOR: Yes, he was. It was in the era in which most leading men were good-looking. Today, none of them are good-looking. Margaret Sullavan was also good-looking. She was a magnificently sensitive actress. She had good voice control, and that talent touches me. I thought Janet Beecher was a very good actress. I didn't realize how good she was until now.

DOWD: Certainly they're irreplaceable. You went on to make another film at Paramount, The Texas Rangers. Who handled your move to Paramount at that time?

VIDOR: Myron Selznick was my agent then. I remember once he became very upset with me because I had told someone how fast and economically I was able to shoot a film. I guess he didn't want anyone else to know. When he found out I had talked to someone about this, he became livid. His face became red, and the veins in his neck stood out. After a barrage of names had been thrown at me, he said, "If you ever mention how inexpensively you can shoot a film again, I'll never represent you again."

I started Texas Rangers after So Red the Rose. I had heard the typical Texas Rangers stories as a kid, about their bravery and effectiveness, and I'm quite sure that I was the one who motivated the script. We didn't have a story, but we had a book with a lot of facts about them. I sat down with my wife Elizabeth and Louis Stevens, and together we wrote the story.

We were writing it for Cooper, who was the top box-office actor at the time. We cast Jack Oakie for the part of Wahoo, but Cooper's manager didn't want Gary to work with Oakie, and pulled Cooper out. He thought Oakie had too many stunts, too many tricks of acting, and would dominate Cooper's slow, easy manner. Fred MacMurray was under contract at Paramount at that time, but he hadn't been established as a Western star or a cowboy hero as Cooper had. He got busy and practiced riding for a month or so before we started.

DOWD: He had never ridden before?

VIDOR: That's right. He had played trombone in an orchestra when he was discovered, and I think he had only made one picture before this. He worked at the stables every day with the wrangler attached to the film, and came through as a darn good rider.

We shot this film up near Gallup, New Mexico. Then we worked in Santa Fe for a while at the Ranger headquarters there and in Santo Domingo, between Santa Fe and Taos. We built a couple of interiors up there so that we could work in bad weather. I remember that there were no booms out there on location. This was before the small, portable location equipment. For the last shot, I wanted to pull back away from the grave. The grip said, "I'll build a boom if you'll give me half a day." So, we built a boom out of telephone poles with a place for the camera at one end, countered by the other weight at the other end.

DOWD: You mentioned once that you built some sets on location, in one case so that you could shoot through a window to show the panorama of the landscape outside.

VIDOR: It was mainly the Indian village, I think. We used this as the headquarters for the Rangers. We could shoot the interior of the jail there, and have all the real action going on outside, instead of having a process background. I remember those sets were built right in the village. We could have all of the background action going on whenever we needed it.

We got three tribes of Indians in order to make up a tribe of five hundred. We had to set up three separate camps for them. They demanded that they all be kept apart, with different corrals and separate food. They had brought their own horses, and wanted to remain apart from each other.

DOWD: The confrontation scene between the Rangers and the Indians was the big battle of the picture.

VIDOR: Yes. We didn't do much rehearsal on that one. There wasn't much to rehearse. A battle scene is the most difficult scene to prepare. You can diagram it for the groups involved on-camera, but that's about it. My method was to plan it out on paper, and then bring in the guys who were going to participate, pretty much the way the Army operates. I remember confining the fights to a closed area so that we could cover them with the cameras adequately.

This battle didn't seem to be too distinctly choreographed. It seemed to be just a helter-skelter type of fight. We usually asked for volunteers to do falls. A certain number of them are going to get shot and fall off horses, and a certain number are going to get hit with guns -- you just have to assign a number of men for each stunt. It was very dangerous to fall off a horse in that scene. You ran a tremendous risk of being run over by the rest of the horses.

DOWD: Was the Running W used on this film?

VIDOR: Yes, I know it was done. It was illegal as far as the SPCA was concerned, but I remember specifically that it was done. It may have been that it had not been outlawed yet, but it certainly has been illegal for several years now. This was where you put a wire rig on the horse to make him trip in a certain spot. I remember the special effects men were always using piano wire. They put two big stakes in the ground, one hundred feet or more away, and ran a line between them and the horse. When the horse ran to the end of the line, it would jerk both front feet back so that the horse would go down on his knees. That is why it was outlawed. The rider shoots through the air, so you know exactly what is going to happen. You can take close-ups because it happens exactly at the end of the wire. It probably hurt the horses, in fact it probably killed a lot of them. Now they train horses to fall by having the riders turn their heads when they want the horses to fall. It doesn't hurt them at all, and I have seen them do it over and over again with no ill effects.

DOWD: Do you remember some of the scenes Jack Oakie improvised?

VIDOR: He would not necessarily improvise whole scenes, only bits of scenes. He was always clowning around and always trying to make people laugh. Sometimes in a rehearsal you would see him clowning around and you would end up keeping the material in the scene. He could learn new scenes and new pages very quickly, almost as fast as they could be written. He had a photographic memory. It was an amazing ability, and I suppose this came from his theatre or vaudeville training.

DOWD: I read in Jean Cocteau's autobiography that he came to your set with Chaplin.

VIDOR: I think they spent half a day on the set. However, this was at the studio, not on location. Charlie phoned and asked if he could bring him out. He was fascinated by the studio. In Europe they work with very small studios, and after I did War and Peace, I just couldn't believe all of the departments they managed to squeeze into those small facilities. I worked in big studios in Hollywood, and after I came back from working in Europe, I realized for the first time how big they really were.

DOWD: There is a really nice stunt in this film during the cliff scene.

VIDOR: On any picture where I had a lot of action, I would go out with the cameraman and we would look for interesting bits of local scenery that could eventually be used in the film. I'm sure I ran across the tree and the cliff on one of these trips and realized that it must be in the film.

We always had stunt doubles who looked very much like the stars. After the stunts had been decided upon, we would meet with the stuntmen and figure out how much they would cost. The stuntmen would be there on a regular salary for just ordinary or fast riding, but for a dangerous thing of this sort, we would make a deal just for that one stunt. Some of them were seventy-five or a hundred dollars.

DOWD: Did you use cowboys to play the parts of the Rangers?

VIDOR: Yes, that was one idea I had. We picked real fellows and real wranglers because they didn't look like actors. We wanted real riders, and we wanted them to feel at home in the saddle. That had gone on since the beginning of Hollywood, though, so it was nothing new.

DOWD: There actually were real cowboys in Hollywood?

VIDOR: Yes. They used to ride up to the studio on their own horses. They had hitching posts outside the Lasky Studio on Vine Street, and they would ride in and sit around on the benches and talk all day.

DOWD: The first Ranger you see riding with Oakie in the film was a real cowboy, wasn't he?

VIDOR: Yes, his name was Frank Cordell. He probably had worked around in a lot of Western pictures before. They were usually told that there were no acting skills required, but I made actors out of them, including Cordell. They were always much more convincing than actors. I wanted to have real experienced, weather-beaten fellows without makeup.

DOWD: The shoot-out scene in the film looks a lot like the one in Duel in the Sun.

VIDOR: Yes, I was completely surprised. We didn't have any second unit directors on this that I know of, so I must have shot all of that.

DOWD: The photographer on this film was Eddie Cronjager. Was he known primarily as an outdoor photographer?

VIDOR: I think he was basically known as an exterior photographer. He also was the same man who shot Bird of Paradise. He was a specialist, and I remember that some women stars used to ask for him. I also noticed that he used a lot of filters. We did a lot of day-for-night shots in this film. At first, you never shot a night scene during the daytime. But by using proper filters, we began to do it more and more. I remember experimenting with filters and making tests and I think he was a big part of that. It was much better where you could see a little distance, rather than having just the foreground lit up when you shot night scenes. I'm sure this is the first picture where I did day-for-night. It was a great convenience.

DOWD: Who thought up the idea for the song, "I can't play my banjo with Susannah on my knee"?

VIDOR: I don't remember the original source of that song. Jack Oakie was a bad boy sometimes, and would stay out all night long. He had a bit of a drinking problem at the time, which he eventually dropped. One morning at the La Honda Hotel in Santa Fe, we were leaving to drive out to the location, and Jack was just coming in. We had to concoct a few hours worth of work while he could go up and take a shower and get dressed.

          The governor of New Mexico arrived and we rounded up a baseball game right in the village. I was made an honorary Indian chief and called Chief Look-For-The-Sun because I was always going around with a blue viewing glass seeing when the cloud cover was right for shooting. Anyway, we put on this big thing for the governor to take up the morning's visit.

DOWD: Did you have your own 16mm camera there?

VIDOR: Yes. I was doing some of my own experimenting with film while this was going on. It was basically color tests with the new film that was coming out. It's kind of faded now, and I am very glad that we shot the film itself in black-and-white.

DOWD: Stella Dallas was made at Goldwyn. Was this the last Goldwyn picture you made?

VIDOR: It probably was. The films I did there usually turned out pretty well, the stories were all tempting, and the casts were great, but after this picture I wrote myself a note that said, "No more Goldwyn pictures!" and put it in my desk drawer. He was a very difficult man to work with. For example, in Stella Dallas he came on the set and said, "You'll have to change your whole cast. The people are terrible, and we cannot make this picture." It was very painful.

DOWD: What was the story about the bicycle scene in this picture?

VIDOR: As time went on with sound pictures, we began to think, Couldn't we go back to some of the esthetics of silent pictures? The problem was that we would shoot a silent scene, and then as it got into the picture and it was being run, it would just come along all of a sudden without sound. They were meant to have sound accompaniment, but Goldwyn would never realize this during the rough cut screening. He would tell us to take those shots out.

To get around this, we had to get some music to go with those shots whenever they were shown to him. The bicycle scene was one of those. I liked it very much. The trouble was, to get it by Goldwyn, we had to get a record or something and play some music along with it whenever we showed it to him. The same shot without music would never be accepted by him.

He just didn't seem to have a grasp on what we were doing. The crazy thing was this would vary from time to time. When he stormed onto the set and demanded that the cast be fired, he completely upset all the actors and actresses, made me very mad, and then left. I couldn't do any more shooting that day, and when I got home I thought, What a fellow to work for! That night around midnight I got a call from him. He said, "King, I've just seen the rushes. Everything is wonderful. The people are great." I said, "Okay, Sam, thank you." He said, "Have a good sleep. Get a good rest. We'll see you tomorrow."

DOWD: You had a good cameraman on this picture, didn't you?

VIDOR: Yes, he was Rudolph Maté. He was excellent. He eventually went on to direct pictures for Columbia.

DOWD: This film, as are three out of the four pictures you made at Goldwyn, is about class differences. It was something you depicted very well. In the restaurant scene, you noticed almost immediately that the girls are of a different class than the men. In <u>Stella Dallas</u> there are a lot of subtle things that Barbara Stanwyck does, even at the beginning where she is successfully deceiving John Boles about her class in society. You depict that very well, but that was never a great concern of yours, was it?

VIDOR: No. In one way it is a class story. Goldwyn had made it before as a silent film, and it was very successful. He wanted to make it again as a sound film. It is a very successful type of picture. I realized that it would be a good picture very soon after we started. We had a good cast, great photography, and everything seemed to work well. I was enthused about the project, and one credit to Goldwyn was that he always mounted his projects with great people. I decided to give it a sense of reality -- I didn't want this to be just another superficial film. I believed it really could happen.

DOWD: Did you cast Barbara Stanwyck in the lead?

VIDOR: I don't remember exactly, but I don't think so.

DOWD: What did you think of her performance?

VIDOR: I thought it was wonderful. I don't know whether she was nominated for an Academy Award, but I think she should have been. It is very difficult with that sort of performance to keep from going overboard in getting funny and comical. She was such a good actress, and she has such an appealing voice and knows how to handle it. She seemed to get sympathy in spite of the broad strokes of her character.

DOWD: There seems to be a film within a film in Stella Dallas.

VIDOR: Yes, I don't remember what the other film was, but I think it was from an old Goldwyn picture. It could very well be the original version of Stella Dallas. The characters in the new version would really be going to see themselves in the old version.

DOWD: I thought the parting scene at the train and the ending were just beautiful. Do you remember anything about shooting these?

VIDOR: No, I don't. You can really ham it up on scenes like that, but I think they came off rather well, and we held ourselves in check.

DOWD: I have been noticing that you often include lines about movies and directors within your films. I noticed that after Stella comes out of seeing the film, which is probably the original version, she says to John Boles, "I wish I could be like people in the movies, well-bred and sophisticated." Of course, Show People is just loaded with lines like that.

VIDOR: Yes, also in Show People watching Bardelys the Magnificent we had the same type of situation. I was able to keep what I was doing in perspective. I have a little satirical feeling about the Hollywood people. They are probably the most misunderstood people in the world, and I was just trying to show them in some way.

DOWD: Did you do the cutting yourself on these Gold-wyn pictures?

VIDOR: Yes, I did. Sometimes they would fall into Goldwyn's hands, but he didn't really change them. He might have some objection to some part, or perhaps he would make some suggestions, but as far as the cutting went, I was in charge. He had some good editors working for him out there, and we worked together rather well.

The only thing I remember in this picture is that he called me up late one night and said, "You told me you were going to take close-ups, but you didn't take them!" I told him that they were there, and suggested that he might have turned away to talk to someone while they were projected during the rushes. He said, "Well, I didn't see them, and I was watching all the time!" All I could do was say, "Go watch them again!" That was the only problem I had. He frequently would turn away and talk for a long time while a picture was running, and he would often miss entire scenes.

Since editing is so close to writing and directing a film, instead of leaving it all to the editor, I would go along on every bit of editing that was done. At least I could try to put the picture together the way I wanted it. I tried to cut with the camera, as Jack Ford used to do. I didn't take a lot of extra shots. There weren't a lot of ways to put the picture together, except during battle scenes, where you had a lot of extra cameras and second units working. Most of the stuff where you had extra cameras going took a little longer to edit, but the parts shot with only one camera were easy to do. I would usually decide right there on the set what shot I was going to use, and I would not shoot the action for every scene in every type of shot -- long shot, medium shot, and close shot.

IX

DOWD: Did you find Thalberg easier to work with than Goldwyn?

VIDOR: Yes. Thalberg knew how to behave better. Also, he was making so many pictures that he didn't have time to interfere on any one picture too much. You had very little contact with Thalberg while you were making the picture.

DOWD: After returning to MGM, you made The Citadel. How did you get involved with this picture?

VIDOR: I probably told my agent that I would like to do that picture. When I got out to the studio, they were still trying to get Robert Donat to be in the film. He was making a lot of demands about stills and all kinds of things connected with the film. I didn't want to do my preparation work in England, I wanted to do that here, and arrive in England ready to go. I did some of the casting and interviewing here. I believe I talked to David Niven about the film before I left.

They went ahead and signed Donat anyway, and I did not meet him until after I arrived in England. He was supposed to be one of the biggest romantic stars at the time, and I was very surprised when I first met him. He was a very thin, stooped, meek man. He was like some bookkeeper, and he looked awful. He used to get sick between films, and I guess that was why he looked so bad. We met in a restaurant, and he came to my table and sat down. I noticed in the film, that he wore that Norfolk jacket with the padded sleeves. Once you know this, you can see that he really was very frail.

He was a wonderful man, though, and he couldn't have been a better friend and actor. He had his little idiosyncrasies, but he was such a great performer, I couldn't blame him at all. He couldn't have anybody in his eye line, for example. If he had to look in a certain direction, there couldn't be anyone in his line of sight.

He was also constantly working with makeup. His closest buddy on the crew was the makeup man. Together they would work out what makeup he should use. They used tiny bits of red under the nose and around the ears. He would do that after the camera was going, and I would have to stop the camera while he brought out his mirror and touched up his makeup. I said to him one day, "Bob, I can't help but think that you give a great performance, but what would it be like if you didn't have a mirror?" He had a good sense of humor.

He was the only actor I knew who actually went to look for locations and wanted to sit in on every story conference. He wanted to get in on all the atmosphere, not for controlling any of it, but just to absorb as much of it as possible, which I encouraged. When I went to Wales to look for locations and to photograph the sites, he went along and observed everything. We went into the mine shafts, and even went into some of the miners' homes, and Bob was right there all the time.

I want to say something about the script adaptation. The climax comes through his dishonest, insincere practices as a Harley Street physician practicing solely for the money, and as a result his closest friend, Danny, dies. In the book (by A.J. Cronin), this was a little tailor who lived in the neighborhood. We simply would have had to broaden the tailor and try to make him sympathetic. We wrestled with this thing for a couple of weeks in the studio at Culver City, and looked into the possibility of having the man be his best friend. Ralph Richardson was superb and he played Danny. I don't think I've ever made a picture that has had such great people in such small parts as this film.

DOWD: The cast of this film is absolutely fabulous. Emlyn Williams was a superb actor who played a small part, as did Francis Sullivan, Rex Harrison, Ralph Richardson, Rosalind Russell and even Donat. How was this all arranged during the casting?

VIDOR: At that time you could go into London and go to the theatre and see such people as Rex Harrison, who was playing in a show called <u>French Without Tears.</u> They were so dedicated to the theatre that they worked for hardly any salary at all. They were glad to pick up a few days of work on the film. I think Harrison worked for maybe three or four days at the most. Richardson was on much longer, and Sullivan worked for a few days, also. They were all glad to pick up the film work at the same time they were appearing on the stage. They were great, great actors.

DOWD: Victor Saville was the producer on the film, and Ben Goetz, the head of the studio. What was the relation between the two?

VIDOR: Saville was the one who found the book and took it to them. When I came into the picture, I was considered the producer. Goetz believed in the producer-director deal, and liked the power it gave to that one person. So, Saville ended up working on the casting, and helped on the settings, and I was made the producer-director. If there was ever a scene where Saville and I disagreed, I would just tell him to go ahead and shoot it his way. I knew he had been a director himself. When that came up, he would eventually say, "Go ahead and shoot it your way. There's no reason to shoot something that we disagree on." If there was an absolute impasse with Saville and myself, Goetz would side with me because he knew that I had the ultimate responsibility for the film.

This film reflects that kind of support, especially from the executive head of the studio. I think it reflects it more than any other film I've made because I can find no compromises in the casting or in the direction. There is no compromise at all, and it seems to be more finished in every way than any other picture I've made. It doesn't have the inherent problems that occur when a producer insists that you put something in a film. When that happens, a director tends to do it halfheartedly, and it will show up on the screen.

DOWD: Would you characterize Ben Goetz as the ideal producer?

VIDOR: He would be an ideal executive. He didn't interfere at all with the artistic part of the filmmaking, such as
the script or the editing.

DOWD: You had a very good cameraman on this film.

VIDOR: Yes, I had Harry Stradling. I think his photography is just beautiful in this film.

DOWD: What were the actual locations you used?

VIDOR: We went to Wales and shot process backgrounds
and some atmospheric shots. I don't think we used any actors
in these shots. The mine entrance was actually built on the
lot. I tried to close off a street near the studio, but I think we
ended up building the street on the lot. At the Korda studio,
Korda had just made a film called Knight Without Armour in
which Donat had played with Marlene Dietrich. They had these
wonderful night scenes with railroad trains coming in at a
station. I had seen this beautiful photography and I said,
"Wherever they did that shooting, I want to use it, too!"

It turned out that they shot it on the lot. They
still had the tracks and the railroad station set standing when
we moved in to use it. They also had a river going right
through the middle of the studio. It had swans and willows and
flowers and plants, and it looked great. They had built the
studio around an old house, and the river just happened to be
next to the house. The studio wasn't all that big, but it was
the location of the studio that made it so well suited for
production.

DOWD: Was A.J. Cronin there when you were shooting?

VIDOR: He came by and we had some stills taken with
him.

DOWD: Was he pleased with what was going on?

VIDOR: I think he was. He didn't talk much and he didn't
get enthused very easily.

DOWD: What was his reaction?

VIDOR: He was very quiet, and as far as I could see he was pleased. I think I told him why we made a change and he said it was a great improvement. It wasn't any big reaction, but he liked what we were doing with the script. He certainly liked the cast.

DOWD: How was Rosalind Russell cast? She is the only American in the film.

VIDOR: There was an English girl named Elisabeth Allen signed to play the part, but after I met her, I thought Rosalind would be much better. I told Goetz that I thought we should have Rosalind Russell in the part if we could somehow settle it with the other girl. They tried to do that, but they couldn't settle because it had already been announced in the press that she was going to play the part. The girl brought a lawsuit against them, and the studio lost. However, Goetz appealed the decision and won. His attitude was not so much that the casting for this part was so important, but that if this girl won, it would mean that you never would be able to change the casting in a film in England again. That was what Goetz was really worried about.

DOWD: While we were watching the film the other day, you pointed out two things. You mentioned the technicalities of the first examination that Dr. Manson, played by Donat, made.

VIDOR: Yes. While I was in England I suddenly discovered that the English are very technically conscious. They employed a young doctor to serve as technical director. The first thing I ran into was when Donat made an examination and the doctor stepped up and said, "You're doing it too quickly." I said, "Who is making the picture, you or me? I'm making it for the audiences, and you want to make it for other doctors. I have to make it the same way I see an examination from my own experience." He was offended because we wouldn't do it absolutely correctly. After it was shown, the rest of the doctors accepted it. I went to Goetz and said, "Take the doctor off the set. I don't want him."

When the actor was standing in front of the examining board after he has supposedly malpracticed with the American, the doctor said to me, "Nobody walks up and down in an English court." I said, "Well, he's going to walk up and down in this one. To begin with, it's an examining board of a bunch of doctors. It's not a court." That how I thought it should be, so the rest of the time he moved around. I'm sure that every doctor who has ever been on trial never sat the entire session through in his seat.

By then I was so tired of technical directors and assistants that it was just like a red flag in front of a bull whenever I saw one. If I absolutely had to find out something, I'd go and find out about it myself.

DOWD: I noticed that in this film you really direct animals well. There's a shot where Hawkins, Richardsons' dog, along with Richardson and Donat, are looking down at the sewer and then they look up and the dog seems to look just as intently as the other two. There is something funny about that shot, and also the way Richardson says to the dog, "Sit down, Hawkins!"

VIDOR: I found a long time ago in two-reelers that animals seemed to come off rather well. I was always using animals after that. I discovered early that should I ever use animals, I would have the best results if I treated them the same way I would treat any human actors. I was the boss, and they had to do a scene the way I wanted to do it. I think actors want to be told what they must do. They only object when the director doesn't tell them. They sort of flounder around if they don't know what they're doing. So, I would give the dog instructions, just like I would any other actor. It seemed to work well.

DOWD: Did you have any problems with the actors on this film?

VIDOR: No. It was just smooth sailing.

DOWD: How did you and Donat get along generally?

VIDOR: Very well, and he actually asked me to be the godfather and sponsor for his children, who were coming to America.

DOWD: There is a montage sequence in the film when they leave to go to England. It is a sequence that shows the unpaid bills, the empty appointment book, Rosalind Russell refusing a vacuum cleaner. It was very effective, and beautifully done.

VIDOR: This was an era in which we were very interested in montages. Different directors were doing different types of montages, and they were all experimenting a lot. Slavko Vorkapich was at MGM and used to do most of the studio montages, but I don't think he ever did any for me. Usually I would see a film and would realize that a lot could be told by a good montage. I would write my own montages. I didn't do all the dissolves and trick stuff myself, but I would write them out and work on them myself.

DOWD: Another scene that is terrific is the elevator scene. You see the backs of two men: one dressed very badly and the other tall, tailored, and elegant. The elevator doors open, they walk in, and the doors close behind them. When they turn around inside the elevator, we see that one of them is Rex Harrison.

VIDOR: This is a nice thing because it shows you what lenses and cameras can do. I am sure the elevator didn't move. It was one of the things I liked to do -- create the illusion without having anything move. The less you have to move, especially mechanically, the more fun it is to make the illusion carry onscreen.

DOWD: When Harrison turns around and faces Donat, he turns and says, "Scruffy, huh?" At this point Donat scratches himself. I thought that was fantastic.

VIDOR: I would tell an actor what to do as far as the camera movements were concerned and what to think about in a scene, and I used to talk quite a bit. But in addition to that, on Donat's wall was a chart of each scene, how he would dress for it, how he would play it, and the general feeling of the scene. This is something you cannot direct. You cannot make somebody do that. This is where the acting goes beyond that. He probably saw the word "scruffy" in the script and wrote in his notes to scratch his head. Then he would ask me, "How about if I scratch myself right at this point?" I would say, "Great, do it!" This is an explanation of achieving depth and philosophical meaning. This was what lay beyond the obvious. Donat knew exactly what was going on. You can see that in his performance, and it looks very good.

DOWD: It is the first time I've seen a film where I was able to like a character completely, even at the beginning, because he is really touching. I have never sensed that in a film before. He was an actor who could produce two genuine feelings and make them both seem real. You always get the feeling that someone is posing as the villain.

VIDOR: That is absolutely true. He was blocked and thwarted, and then had the opportunity of having money thrown at him. It is a classic form. He made you understand why he was accepting it.

DOWD: Richardson does two great drunk scenes. I'm sure they were one of the hardest things for him to do in the film.

VIDOR: Yes.

DOWD: Do you remember directing those?

VIDOR: I remember thinking that he must have had a past with a drunk, or else experienced it in some way. I think he did a bit of drinking himself in those days. It is kind of an easy scene to play, but a difficult one to play convincingly. There again, Richardson was just a superb actor. I saw Richardson recently in London. He was in a play, and had just won a Tony Award.

DOWD: There is another incredible moment of self-defeat on the screen, and I was wondering how it was done. After Danny has been killed, Rosalind Russell is in the hospital and says, "Is he all right?" You see Donat's back and he turns around and his eyes are filled with tears. I have never seen anyone look that genuinely distraught on screen. How did you shoot that?

VIDOR: I think most good actors can make tears come to their eyes fairly easily.

DOWD: Just like that?

VIDOR: I think most of them can do it, particularly a man like Donat. If he couldn't, we might blow menthol inhaler in his eyes just before we shot the scene.

DOWD: What kind of rehearsals did you have?

VIDOR: We didn't have a series of rehearsals. We rehearsed a sequence just before we shot it. I used to try to spend about half an hour at the end of the day rehearsing the next day's scenes. That way you could let your actors think it over before returning to the set. The cameraman could then see where all the actors were going to stand, and we would all be prepared. That is the ideal method that I found.

DOWD: Would you actually have them out on the set, or would you just explain to them what you were going to do?

VIDOR: I had them out on the set. I never had a chance to rehearse the whole picture. Street Scene was the only picture I was able to rehearse completely. During the rehearsals that we did manage, I would explain their parts and characters to them, and try to correct them during the reading. Some of the best actors can't do well when they read lines. I never had the great luxury of rehearsing all of my pictures completely.

DOWD: It must have been tremendously gratifying to have several actors respond as well as they did in this film.

VIDOR: It was heaven. There are always people who will want to argue with you rather than work on the picture. I'm not saying that all actors are obstinate, but lots of actors have to go through arguing, fighting, or just being convinced before they will do a scene. That's not so with a bunch of London pros. Our actors were doing stage performances every night, and working on the film during the day. To do all that, and still turn in such great performances takes a lot of talent. Under those conditions, you just don't have time to fool around. That was the case with Harrison. He had to finish the day's work at 1:30 sharp in order to catch the train into London so that he could get ready to make his appearance that night. They were all right there, pitching in and working right alongside us. They were truly great performers.

DOWD: Do you think there is a family tradition of great acting? Gielgud and Richardson came from families of actors.

VIDOR: Yes. In England, they shift from bit parts and leading parts, playing everything, and that is how they get all that great experience. They've had the chance to play all kinds of roles. Actors like Peter O'Toole can walk in and play a tremendous lead, but you should see what they've had to go through, the real great training they have beforehand. We simply don't have it in this country.

DOWD: How was Pare Lorentz involved in the film?

VIDOR: I took him along during the boat trip with me. We were able to talk about the script and the scenes. I paid his passage over and back, and I think he talks about it in his book. He was just crazy about the story. I think he contributed some things in those talks we had about the script. I couldn't put my finger on the exact details, but I know he did offer some suggestions.

DOWD: What happened after you finished the picture?

VIDOR: As soon as I finished The Citadel, Goetz offered me Goodbye Mr. Chips. It's hard to explain in today's light why I didn't take it, but at the time I was building a home back here in Los Angeles. I had been getting pictures of it while working in England, and I was anxious to come back and see it finished. At that time life was moving rapidly for me. I didn't want to stay for another picture. The same thing happened to me after War and Peace. Today it's different because you have jets to go back and forth on. Besides, the war was on its way. I had witnessed some of the blackouts in France.

DOWD: Your next picture, <u>Northwest Passage</u>, did not appear until February of 1940. Do you remember what you were doing between those two pictures?

VIDOR: The war had started, and I was working on getting my children back into the country. I had two young daughters in Europe, and that took about a month. Their mother followed later.

DOWD: When you came back from England, Thalberg had died. Was there a change in MGM without him?

VIDOR: Not a noticeable change. During his time at MGM, Thalberg pictures were subdivided among some of the other producers. After he died, they were just distributed a little more, and there was no one like him left to take such a great control of all the productions. Things went on much as before, but I still missed working with him.

DOWD: <u>Northwest Passage</u> was shot in color. What techniques were used in this type of photography?

VIDOR: I think they called it three-strip Technicolor. We had some problems with this because a second unit had gone up to Idaho and shot some material, and it would not match some of the stuff we shot later on. I'm not sure if they had used Technicolor film, but when we shot some things with Technicolor a little later, the two pieces of film didn't match up.

I was trying to make the uniforms for the picture blend into the scenery. We made lots of tests with this in mind. The reason for having them blend in with the background was that they would be more realistic, and they would not be so easily spotted by Indians. They had to blend in with the forest colors. When we made the tests, the greens came out very vividly. I complained to the people at Technicolor and they said, "Well, that's the green that Zanuck likes." It was a vivid Irish green, much greener than the costumes really were. Anyway, I persuaded them to mix up another shade of green for their dye transfer process.

I had another problem with the blue skies. The story is supposed to deal with all the hardships they had at that time, going through the swamps, and even living in the trees. Technicolor always went for the most vivid blue skies they could get. In trying to emphasize the difficulties they were living with, you couldn't show all these beautiful blue skies and wonderful scenery.

DOWD: There must have been tremendous difficulties with the cameras, which were very bulky. Did you go to Idaho with all of that equipment?

VIDOR: We had two trains loaded with equipment. In fact, thirty miles from Boise we had ninety boats, thirty or forty tents, Indian teepees, a full crew of carpenters, and all of the usual film production staff. I had gone into the project thinking that it would be the last of the big production expeditions, and it had grown even larger after our initial estimates were made. We took over a resort that was not in use.

Some of us had tick fever. Everyone was afraid that they would be bitten by ticks. I remember we used to come in at night and put a white sheet on the floor, undress on the white sheet, drop all the clothes on the floor and see if there were any ticks that showed up on the sheet. If you saw any, you would kill them. Then you would have to put on different clothes after you took a shower. Those were just some of the hardships we had on location. (Spencer) Tracy brought a doctor and a masseur. He was well taken care of. I guess in the long run it was more important that he remain well than anyone else.

DOWD: You recruited Indians, too?

VIDOR: We brought them down from Wyoming. I think they were from the Blackfoot Indian tribe. They had a separate village. We didn't have the same trouble that we had on the picture I had done in Arizona, Billy the Kid. They all lived in one village, and we had to feed and take care of them daily. There were no restaurants, so we had to cook for them in addition to building them a place to stay. They actually had their own little village. They were brought down roughly four or five hundred miles from where they lived, and that alone cost us a tremendous amount.

DOWD: Was this period the one in which you started to do some painting?

VIDOR: Yes. You see, for years we thought in terms of black and white. Suddenly we moved into color, and my color sense had been neglected all those years. I had heard of cool colors and warm colors, but I had to learn what they meant because I didn't want to depend on anybody to tell me all of that. I learned that greens, blues, reds, and a few other colors had a strong influence on the mood of a scene. I became interested in buying paintings and going to art galleries, but John Marquand gave me a set of paints and I sat down and started painting. That was where I learned the most. I started to paint pictures as soon as I knew I was going to do this film.

DOWD: I noticed in your paintings that you seem to paint in perspective quite a bit.

VIDOR: I studied up on perspective and that was about the only thing I knew. No one told me about the other techniques, and I had to discover them all myself. I wanted to learn to draw sets and camera set-ups, but I had difficulty with that. I never could express myself with a pencil.

I did attend a group painting session at Edgar Bergen's house a few times, but I really had no instruction. I knew a lot about composition from my work in black and white and this experience helped me quite a bit with my painting. I seemed to be influenced by Impressionism. I did a lot of work with forced perspective in my films, so this interest in art really did carry over into my pictures.

DOWD: Did you choose the book Northwest Passage was based on?

VIDOR: No. It had been in pre-production for quite a while before I started working on it. I brought Laurence Stallings with me. We went to work and very quickly we worked out a solution of how to do the story that contained Book I and Book II. Part two of the book was an examination of the disintegration of a man who had been built up into a strong heroic figure in the first part. I think I brought my wife Elizabeth into it as well. We all worked very rapidly on it.

Hunt Stromberg, the producer, didn't go for it, so he had a writer named Talbot Jennings come in and begin work.

At this time I had to bring the production up to the location because the water level of the lake where we were shooting was going down. We had to start filming right away. When I was leaving, Stromberg told me, "By the time you finish the first part of the picture, I'll have the second part sent up."

I did the entire picture in three months of work, and at the end of that time I still had not received the second part of the script. I called the studio and they said, "Come back." So, I loaded up the trains with all of our stuff and we came back.

When I saw the producer he said, "Keep the actors on salary. We'll have it in another week." They were sitting right where I had left them three months before. They were probably still working on the same line of dialogue. After another week no progress had been made, so the head of the studio said, "Take these people off salary."

I went to New York and started to work on something else. After I got to New York they called me up. Jack Conway had written a different ending to the story. We didn't have jet travel then, so I said, "Okay, let Conway shoot the tag," and left it at that. We never even got to the second half of the story.

DOWD: Was that to be a sequel film?

VIDOR: No, it was all to be one film.

DOWD: I noticed that there were specific lines in the film that pointed out that that might have been the way things were going with the production. One of the lines was, "I hope you never see me when I'm not a soldier," indicating his own knowledge of his vulnerability. He also seems to be a pathological type. I was waiting for this to develop.

VIDOR: Yes. Had I known we were not going to do the second part, I would have made the character go another way.

You've got to remember how long this fellow was isolated. He was just pulling himself together because he was going toward the bottom of the barrel through drinking and debts and general dissipation. Looking at it, I know now I would have had him turn out differently. I would have made the character stronger.

DOWD: I heard you say before that you don't like the idea of coming into a picture with some of the preparation already done. Did you feel this was a problem on Northwest Passage?

VIDOR: They want to hand you something in a hurry. I turned down both Gone With the Wind and Ben Hur for the same reason. They think you can do your work in a few weeks when some other director has had a year to prepare. I don't separate direction that way. I think the direction starts back when you start on the script. In this case, the only thing that had been done was the selection of the location. They may have already started to build some of the sets, I'm not sure.

DOWD: What was Stallings's specific contribution to this script? Did he go on location?

VIDOR: No, he didn't. He was off the picture and I don't think that Stromberg liked working with him. Stallings at the time was with MGM. He was a fellow who would come in and start a picture, but you could get his contribution in only two or three weeks. He was not the slow, plodding kind of worker. He was bouncy with ideas. He could get a whole story line and develop it in just a few days. Consequently, it was he and I who worked out the original story line for the script, but after a few weeks he was gone, and I left for production.

DOWD: Did you do the casting for the film?

VIDOR: Yes. I cast Walter Brennan and Bob Young. I don't know whether Tracy was lined up for it when I came on or not. I probably cast all of the parts except for Tracy.

DOWD: Did you have someone else in mind for Tracy's part?

VIDOR: No, I don't think so.

DOWD: The scene with the boats reminds me of the tempo and pacing of the water scene in <u>Our Daily Bread</u>. You seem to be able to build to a musical climax.

VIDOR: Yes, that was the way I was thinking.

DOWD: Were you using the metronome in that picture?

VIDOR: I don't think so, although we might have used it with the boats and the rowing. I rarely went on locations without taking the metronome, though.

DOWD: Were there any other directors who used the metronome?

VIDOR: I don't think anyone else did. This picture was basically an adventure story, and I wanted to make the most of this. Consequently I didn't make use of the metronome all that much. Years before, I had been on the Feather River in Northern California and I had seen the danger of working in a river. I think I was more concerned about the actual images on screen than the tempo.

I had almost lost one of my leading actors in <u>Love Never Dies</u> in a similar situation, so I was thinking about how to do this without endangering any of the actors. I walked them in about as far as I could for this shot, and then had other people on the far side who could pull them out. I put swimmers on the end, men who could take care of themselves. I know I had one lifeguard with me, and he actually played a part in the picture. In fact, I think most of the people in these shots were swimmers. I couldn't put the main actors through that, and I couldn't take any kind of a chance on it, so we had to devise a scene in the studio later and work it out with the special effects man.

Actually these scenes in the river are almost real. They duplicated each tree on the bank. The water tank had to be circular so that the water would revolve. You couldn't do it in a rectangular tank. They got a current going there that was very forceful. I think the tank was about five or six feet deep. We demonstrated that if anybody broke loose or got away, they'd just go about fifteen or twenty feet until they reached a point where the water was only about a foot deep. I suppose I went in and demonstrated it myself to show them that it was safe. Different fellows tried it and said that it was all right, so then everyone was willing to do it. The advantage of being able to shoot this type of shot in a controlled situation made all the difference in the world. It was certainly much different than the first time I tried to shoot on the river in Northern California.

DOWD: Did you have any Newcombe shots in this picture?

VIDOR: Yes. The French gunboats were all done with Newcombe shots. Whenever we had something that was too costly to build for one scene, we called in Newcombe. You could tell him how you saw it, or how you wanted it, maybe even make a sketch for him. I suppose I used two or three of these types of shots for every picture that I made. The Big Parade has a lot of them.

DOWD: How was the village massacre scene done?

VIDOR: If you put the whole thing on fire, as it was in the picture, you could only get two or three angles before the whole thing burned down. To control it, you'd put gas lines out from butane tanks and put the lines in the windows and on the roof so that they could be lighted at different times by special effects men stationed in the right places. When you blew a whistle or shot off a gun, they all lit up the flames and as it burned at full blast, you'd shoot your scene. When you gave another signal, you could have the gas lines shut off so that the flames stopped. We had men stationed with hoses who could put out the fire quickly if anything really caught on fire. Actually it was pretty safe.

DOWD: How does it feel to be in charge of all this? It seems like each picture becomes more and more complex, especially with equipment and special effects.

VIDOR: Well, I'm of the nature that I like it and I'm technically minded enough so that I enjoy it and handle it. In fact, I enjoyed it tremendously. It's like being the captain of a ship or a general in the army. You'd divide the work and responsibility up between different fellows. You would have an art director, a unit manager, and a couple of assistants. I had very good assistant directors and I had a second unit director named Norman Foster. He was an experienced director, too, and had been an actor. If something was too tedious for me to stop and do, like the Indian fight, I'd just go over the shots with him and I would let him shoot it. I could then go ahead and work with the principals.

When you're having lunch with eight fellows like my assistants, you can say what you want done, and remain confident that they will go out and do it. We had very good men working on this picture. I would try not to do anything that somebody else on my staff could do. When you have a good cameraman you're able to talk things over with, you can move along at a pretty good speed.

At the same time, I was taking photographs of the entire operation for Life magazine. However, they didn't get published. The war in Europe started that week. I took shots of everything: tents, shooting, locations, all things that were connected with the picture. I thought they would be a good record of what was going on, and I wanted to have them because I thought it would be the last of the big production expeditions.

DOWD: The massacre scene was very well done, yet you don't seem like the type of person who is terribly interested in violence.

VIDOR: No, I'm not. I think some of the good shots I had Norman Foster do, but that's the kind of story it was. We weren't as politically minded then as we are today, and we weren't as frightened to do something. That's the way picture making is supposed to be. We bought the book on this one. You don't argue with the book and say there mustn't be too much violence. Violence wasn't overdone the way it is today, it wasn't smeared all over the place as it is on television. I don't like violence today. I won't even go to see a violent picture, much less put it on the screen myself.

X

DOWD: The next picture for you was <u>H.M. Pulham,</u> <u>Esquire</u>. How did you feel about working with Hedy Lamarr?

VIDOR: I think the film was hurt to some extent because of the languid, European quality of her beauty. She was a star at the time, and she was quite a name for a picture to have. Robert Young was a very fine young actor then, certainly as good as Donat, but unfortunately he was not exciting material at the time. He was making a lot of pictures, but they felt they needed the excitement of Hedy Lamarr.

I think these kinds of compromises hurt the quality of films. I think it hurt the story. In looking back over my career, the main thing that stands out and continues to upset me over the years is that these compromises always stand out above the film, especially when I see the film later on. If you know the book, you know where the compromises are.

Nevertheless, the quality of the film as a separate entity would have been better with a girl like Shirley MacLaine in that part, a girl who had drive, ambition and so forth. I wrote a short story that has never been published, on that same theme. That's why I might have bought this book, because the idea of going back to an old, cold love and trying to revive it has always been a fascinating theme to me. It happened in my own life in a very sad way.

DOWD: I think one of the strongest scenes in the film was when Hedy Lamarr and Robert Young get together and try to start it up again.

VIDOR: That theme was the main interest I had in making that film. There were a lot of things in it that attracted me. In the opening scene there is a sequence that I especially like.

DOWD: There is a series of close-ups that establish the routine. You never see Robert Young's face. You just see his shoes and his hands.

VIDOR: I was glad I had done that that far back, to work that closely to isolate everything I wanted. It's supposed to be the ticking of a clock, and we did it with a metronome to keep it right. I liked that technique to establish his routine.

DOWD: You decided to keep the flashback structure of the novel in the film.

VIDOR: Yes. Again, this is another thing that fascinated me. The flashback idea was very interesting. Of course that had originated in greater or lesser form way back in the days of Griffith's silent films. I was still fascinated by it because you have a framework over the whole structure and can go back and progress from the end if you want to. It's sort of a Cavalcade idea.

DOWD: In keeping with the flashback structure, didn't you use two innovations? You had the voices over the scene where they read the letter, and you also had the telephone voices.

VIDOR: Again, we were breaking with tradition. When the sound men took over, it became the cliché to put all telephone voices through some sort of filtering device. This made it sound distorted and weird. It occurred to me, why should the audience strain to listen? The person with the receiver up there on the screen doesn't strain to hear the voice. There isn't any kind of mechanical distortion. I thought we should just direct it to sound the way it sounded to the person. The letter was an innovation that let the full recorded voice read the letter with no tricks, no distortion, and no filtering.

DOWD: I think it works beautifully.

VIDOR: Yes, it does. You get the full emotion of her voice. It is just as if she were sitting in the room. When you read any letter, it's the person speaking as if they were right there in the room with you. If you just put it in as an insert, and let the audience read it, it doesn't have the emotional directness and clarity. My feeling was to use sound with imagination as we had done with visuals. In Our Daily Bread, as I mentioned earlier, we shot some scenes silent and put the sound in afterwards, which gives you absolute freedom in doing the sound.

DOWD: Your early sound films weren't hampered by this?

VIDOR: No, because I shot Hallelujah with silent cameras.

DOWD: Still, a lot of people took to doing sound on location. Why was that?

VIDOR: They were bewildered. It was the era of the sound technician. They would say, "You have to have a table-cloth on the table," or, "They can't talk facing down." The technical minds were trying to tell us what to do. Well, when you get a technical mind around when you're making something with an artistic mood, you're licked, you're through. They took over for a year or so.

Cameramen had their day, too. They would say, "We can't shoot in this light." Nothing was more hampering to me. Today if I would like another angle, I would just override the cameraman. I used to be constantly faced with the fact that if I did another set-up, it would take another hour. When I look back, I see they had beautiful lighting, but it didn't have to be that beautiful.

DOWD: I have often wondered how it was possible for any emotional feeling to come out of a soundstage so encumbered with people, machines, and equipment.

VIDOR: My thoughts about that were very definite. In working on the script, alone in the morning or at night, I would visualize what I was going to do. I figured I wouldn't have the chance the next day with a hundred people standing around. They would all be asking questions and moving around and talking. To organize and think clearly under those conditions was very hard. As a result, I tried to have everything organized beforehand.

DOWD: Was that one of the big advantages to shooting on location?

VIDOR: Yes, it certainly was. Victor Fleming called them "happy days." He would look at all of the crew members, who were playing cards, talking, or reading the newspapers, drinking coffee and those types of things. On location, the tension is not the same as when you are in a studio.

DOWD: The war scene in this film had a certain similarity to The Big Parade. In a way, there was no real animosity between nations as when Young meets the German officer and offers him a cigarette.

VIDOR: I don't remember if that was in the book or not. It is close to The Big Parade, though, and reminds me a lot of the shellhole scene in that film. It's basically the same type of scene, only this time they're not in a shellhole.

DOWD: Then there's the scene where Harry and Marvin are together and she sort of fades into the darkness. I have never seen that done before. I thought it was beautiful how she was in a much darker light than he was.

VIDOR: Well, that was a photographic idea. I think it has a mood effect of getting her off into a secret, dark place. It uses lighting to enhance the value and mood of the scene.

DOWD: What did you use for snow in the snow scene?

VIDOR: Whatever kind of snow they were making at MGM at the time. I think it was from a machine. Sometimes we would go downtown in an icehouse and shoot snow scenes. Some brewery or ice company had a big room that was refrigerated. We put up sets in there and they had a way to blow ground-up ice into the room. However, I think this film was shot entirely on the lot at MGM.

DOWD: Another scene I thought was very well done was the scene where Robert Young marries Ruth Hussey.

VIDOR: There was a technique of double talk we used in that scene which we derived from the way Red Golden, my assistant director, and I talked. He was a double talk expert. He picked it up from the cameraman.

DOWD: This was from the Northwest Passage cameraman?

VIDOR: Yes, it was from the second assistant cameraman on that film. He could carry it to extremes, and it would amuse the hell out of me to listen to him talk to people. This was a very humorous idea, and it was popular with us on the set. I don't know how I ever got away with this at Metro Goldwyn Mayer.

DOWD: I was wondering about that. MGM was the big wedding factory for the pictures at that time. This is a little bit out of the normal treatment of weddings.

VIDOR: I think I got away with that because I was my own producer on that film. I just put it in, and it was too late when they found out about it.

DOWD: This film looks very modern.

VIDOR: Yes. I think it is because I treated everything very satirically. I was surprised and pleased to see that I did that so early. We probably made another version just as a safety precaution, in case we had to go back and restage it. We never did have to, though.

DOWD: The faces of the guests are funny. They all look as if they're having such a bad time. It's like a bunch of death masks. Did you notice Marquand's obsession with class distinctions?

VIDOR: He was very much aware of class distinctions. He later wrote an article for Life magazine about the upper middle and lower middle classes in this country. He was an analyst and an historian of this type of distinction. But still,

he had trouble in breaking down the class distinctions in Hollywood. One day we were sitting down to lunch at the studio
when someone came over and asked, "What is this H.M.S.
Pulham about, an over-age destroyer?" Marquand leaned over
the table and said, "Yes, by God, it is!" He has a little touch
of that English humor, although it is a bit reserved. He is
likeable in a way because he was always making jokes about
this class distinction that the English are very conscious of.
Most of his humor was based on that. He had lived in Japan at
one time. That was where he got all the material for Mr.
Moto.

DOWD: How did you feel about the ending when Harry
and his wife get back together?

VIDOR: I am not sure if that is a happy ending or not. I
think it was an honest ending, though. In looking at the film
again, the wife seemed to come across as being too cold for
my taste. I thought she should have been somewhat willing, but
she should have said, "I'd like to go, but it's impossible for me
to change so quickly." Then I would have believed her a little
more and the ending would have been better. Her transition
was a little abrupt from her former state to her latter. This
should have been in contrast to a very warm, affectionate girl,
the character of Marvin Myles played by Hedy Lamarr.

DOWD: There is a moment when Marvin and Harry get
back together, when she picks up the telephone and starts to
make a call, and she becomes very harsh and matter-of-fact.
You can tell she doesn't want any of that.

VIDOR: I thought that was a good motivation for them
not getting back together. I drew from an incident in my own
life for this. When Harry Behn and I were writing the script
for The Big Parade, I went back to Hot Springs, Arkansas to
see a girl that I had known many years before in Texas. She
was the daughter of a judge. There was such a dramatic
change in her whole character when I saw her in Arkansas, I
couldn't get out of there fast enough. She had gotten rough
and crude, very common. She had just become an entirely
different person. I sent a telegram to some of my friends
saying, "Please send me a telegram signed by Louis B. Mayer
saying I have to return to Hollywood at once." I had to get

out, and she tried to follow me. This was a tragedy to me because I had dreamed of this girl for a long time, and I had promised myself that I would take the first opportunity to go back and see if I could revive our old romance. When I finally did, it all hit me right in the face. I used all of this for the film. The great tragic thing is that you can't make it work. You don't have to tell the story in bold strokes. It could be that they just couldn't communicate any more. That would be enough to get the point across to the audience.

DOWD: I thought it was great when she puts on that old record, the warped one.

VIDOR: Yes. I had done that before in <u>Love Never Dies</u>. This had to be treated more delicately because of the way Marquand wrote. He had a different style of telling this type of story.

DOWD: Weren't you and he going to do a project on Lindbergh?

VIDOR: Yes. I liked working with him so much that I tried to get him to work with me on following projects. However, he wasn't too anxious to be a script writer. I tried to lure him away from his job as one of the Book of the Month Club editors. One day he called me up and said he had found something interesting. I went to New York and he gave me the galley proofs of a book by Charles Lindbergh and I was greatly moved by it. It was a wonderful book, and he introduced me to Lindbergh at one point.

DOWD: What did you think of Lindbergh?

VIDOR: I liked him very much. He was one of the weirdest fellows in the world, though. He'd come up and say, "Would you lend me a quarter?" He wouldn't have any money to tip the cab driver. We once walked down Fifth Avenue together. We went to lunch at a Chinese place. Nobody recognized him and I kept thinking of the film I had seen of his triumphant ride down Fifth Avenue for the ticker tape parade.

He was also very meticulous. The whole time we talked about the book, he took notes on what we said. He was trying to learn everything about the distribution of pictures so that he would know what was going on when we made his picture. One Sunday he called me and said, "May I see you?" He wanted to go over the notes he had taken the day before because he didn't understand something. That's why he was so successful with his flight. He weighed sandwiches individually to calculate how much fuel he would need. He even did things like throw out pieces of paper from his loose-leaf notebook to lighten the plane.

DOWD: How far did this project go?

VIDOR: Not much further. Lindbergh called me one day and told me that he had made a deal with someone else for the story. That put an end to it right there.

DOWD: After this film you began to work on An American Romance. Don't you have a story to tell that deals with "Fort Roach"?

VIDOR: Yes. I was working at MGM at the time. Norman Foster was working with me on the script, although I don't think he eventually got any credit. One day he said, "Let's go down to Fort Roach and see if we can go into the Air Corps for the Cinema Department." He said that we could probably go in as captains or colonels. We went down to the Roach Studios, which they had jokingly named Fort Roach and talked to them about joining up.

          They had taken it over for the use of the Air Force. It was the national headquarters for the Air Force film industry. Eventually both (George) Stevens and John Ford joined, although Ford went into the Navy branch. I believe Wyler also went in. At the time I thought it was the right thing to do.

          I'm not sure how far along I was with the script for An American Romance, but I'm sure we had done quite a bit of work on it by then. I felt I should make a film that many people would see. In other words, I was going to make a wide scope film of American know-how and productivity. I wanted to show what America was really about.

As you can tell, the film took the final priority over joining up at Fort Roach. I decided that people other than myself could make films for the Air Force. They didn't need me. The film itself would be my first effort to reach an ideal of the American democracy. At least that's the way the production began.

DOWD: Had you been carrying this idea around for many years?

VIDOR: Yes. It was part of that trio of wheat, steel and war. It was about the growth of the idea of steel production. I had once read a book called The Three Black Pennies about a family in the steel business. I had always wanted to make a film about steel.

DOWD: In your book you said that you were trying to make metals and men analogous, to show how men were refined.

VIDOR: Yes, that's right. The story was based around the town of Hibbing, Minnesota, one of the biggest open pit mines in the world. That type of work down there in the depths of the mine was really what you would call the bottom rung of work for the new immigrant who had just come to America. They all started at the bottom.

Louis Adamic had written stories about the immigrants who came to America and worked in these mines. He had come from Yugoslavia himself. From some of his case histories I got the idea for the basic story line. Some of the men he wrote about had got off the boat without enough money for a railroad ticket and had to work and walk their way from New York. These were all completely factual case histories.

At this time I was also still learning about colors. I was painting again and I was still trying to find out more about colors and the different effects they had. As the film goes on, the colors gradually get lighter and lighter. The colors of aluminum and magnesium become similar to the sky colors. The story moves to Gary, Indiana, then to Chicago, and the steel colors become red like the color of molten steel. I tried to avoid the Technicolor pretty blue sky. If we had a scene where we wanted to avoid the blue skies, we would paint our own backings and do it on the stage at the studio.

DOWD: What was it like working with color when it first came out? Was it difficult?

VIDOR: No, but the cameras were difficult. The cameras weighed up to 800 pounds in some cases, and it took a crew of five or six men to lift them up. You can see these cameras if you look at the stills from the production of Northwest Passage. I think those pictures show at least six men trying to move the camera back and forth for one of the dolly shots.

Anyway, the film had an analogy to the refinement of steel. The refinement of steel goes from iron ore to steel through the Bessemer process. As the process continues, the steel becomes harder and more refined. In some cases stainless steel is produced. The film itself is the story of a man who is, or becomes, the refinement of the immigrant. The colors are supposed to follow the same progressive uplifting refinement until the story comes to California -- the bluer skies, the oranges, and the general way of living. That's the pattern of the color in the film.

The original film included almost every state between New York and California. When the man is making the walk, I had signs of towns in practically every state that he went through, or was supposed to go through during the story. We had signs for places like Gary, Indiana; Chicago; towns in Minnesota; the Rushmore Monument; all kinds of places.

DOWD: Were they taken out?

VIDOR: Yes, all those were removed. The important points were from New York to California, so I went through and decided which ones were the most important and left those in.

DOWD: You say in your book that you got permission to do the film without having a word on paper. From whom did you get the go-ahead to start the film? Ben Goetz?

VIDOR: No, he didn't have the power to approve it. I told the idea to Mayer, and then Mayer had to tell the idea to Schenck. I told the story to Schenck after Mayer had talked to him, and it was Schenck who gave me the green light. I'm not really sure how much of the idea I had written out. They preferred to have stories told to them instead of reading anything.

DOWD: How did Schenck react? He gave a famous reaction to the story proposal for Hallelujah.

VIDOR: I can't remember his exact reaction. It's difficult to remember because they never really showed much enthusiasm for anything. They were well trained with the poker faces. They would just listen blankly as you talked, and it made things very discouraging if your idea did not seem to be winning them over. You'd think that they had missed your point completely. You never knew whether you were having any sort of success in selling the idea. They would never say anything like "That's good," or "That's great!"

DOWD: Is it true that your pre-production took almost three years?

VIDOR: No, the whole production took three years from start to finish. The first year was spent in writing and pre-production, the second year was taken up with the actual shooting, and the third year was spent in editing, music, and some post-production work.

We also spent some of that third year in taking the film around to various places to preview it and test the audience reaction. I forget what the running time of the first version was, but I know that it was quite long. I think it cost around $3 million, which is not terribly much by today's standards. We went on an Army post benefit tour that third year, which was popular then. It included camps and other types of benefit showings, and we even took it to Cincinnati, and the area around there. It was mostly done in states like Ohio, Indiana, and Kentucky. After each leg of previews and shows, we'd swing back to Cincinnati. I think the whole tour was arranged through the USO.

The reactions we got were that we had concentrated too much on the documentary side of the story. However, they all liked the human part of the story. It still is a bit heavy on the documentary side, even when you view it today. When I was in New York after the tour I got a call from Eddie Mannix saying that the orders had come through to cut out forty minutes from the film. In those days I was doing all my travelling by train. I wanted to stay in New York for four or five days, and by the time I would get back to the studio it would be at least another week. I asked him if the cutting could wait a week so that I could do it there. He said, "Oh yes, of course it can." I got my business in New York taken care of and went on to Chicago. When I was there one of the men from MGM said that they had just received a copy of the film and it was a lot shorter than that first version. I was absolutely shocked. I came straight out to California. When I got to the studio I went to the editor, Conrad Nervig. I asked him, "What happened?" He said, "The cuts have been so badly done that I just can't face you. I can't talk about it."

DOWD: Do you think this was a show of bad faith on the part of Eddie Mannix?

VIDOR: I don't know. I talked to Nervig some more and found out that the negative had already been cut and the prints had been shipped out. I simply went over to my office and packed up everything in boxes and got the hell out. It was too late to do anything about it. I had been the producer, director, and writer on the picture. I had worked on the thing for the last three years, and now that it had gotten to the final cutting stage, they edited according to the music track. They had cut the film under the supervision of Margaret Booth. She was the head editor at the studio and had her offices up front with the executives. She had cut the documentary portion of the film only slightly, but edited the story material extensively.   That was not the way it should have been done.

DOWD: Why did she cut it that way?

VIDOR: Because of the music track.

DOWD: You mean because the documentary scenes go well with the music?

VIDOR: Yes. Where there is a big orchestra accompaniment it is hard to take out short pieces as I had done with The Big Parade. So, you have to wipe out the big non-musical sequences in order to cut that much time out of a film. With music, you have to lift out the entire sequence. You cannot make inside trims where music has already been laid down.

DOWD: And you think that Eddie Mannix was behind this?

VIDOR: It was pretty hard to think that Mannix had ordered that. But, somebody had given the go ahead, and Mannix was the head of the studio at the time.

DOWD: At that point you had been working with Metro for almost twenty years. What was the studio reaction when you left?

VIDOR: I don't remember any definite reaction. Maybe they felt the picture wasn't worth all the work, effort and expenditure. I don't know. MGM had this policy that if you worked for them for twenty years with continuous employment, you would go on the studio pension plan. I somehow avoided overlapping contracts during this time. I would go out somewhere and make a film, and then come back. I didn't want to feel that I was married for life to MGM. It turned out that I wasn't eligible for the pension plan.

DOWD: Let's go back a ways. Would you talk about Ben Goetz and the casting of the film?

VIDOR: He was the man in charge in London. I was impressed with him, and he gave me the type of executive help I needed. He didn't interfere with the artistic part of the picture, but he could represent me at the top headquarters when I needed someone. He represented me during the casting. The perfect casting for me was Spencer Tracy in the part of the immigrant Steve Dangos, Ingrid Bergman for the role of his wife, and Joseph Cotten as his friend.

Just before we started shooting, Goetz assured me that we had the three stars that I wanted for the picture. I think Tracy was working on A Guy Named Joe at that time. It was a film about the Air Force. I went over to the set and saw Tracy and said, "Spencer, this story is written for you. I wrote this for you, and it's ideal." I told him all about the story and he said, "If you wait until this picture is finished, I'd love to do it."

In the end MGM persuaded me to use Brian Donlevy instead. It was always studio policy that they would find someone else for you. Then they had this girl named Ann Richards who they were hoping would take the place of Greer Garson. They asked me to make tests of her and she made excellent tests. I considered it quite a compromise. Cotten was in another film, and so was Bergman. She was working on Gaslight.

I was so enthused about the possibilities of my picture that I thought at the time that it would not be dependent on stars to carry the story. I didn't realize until later that personalities can make or break a picture. They all had symbols that they stood for, and you had to have the right people playing the roles. I really learned a lesson on that film.

DOWD: Did you get John Qualen anyway?

VIDOR: Yes, I did. You see, in the case of The Crowd I had used unknown people, but they were ideal according to my viewpoint. They were all unknown. I had been successful with Jimmy Murray. In Hallelujah and all of the other films I had been successful with unknown people playing the parts. I think Brian Donlevy gave a wonderful performance in the part, but he symbolized something else entirely.

You can't take someone playing a gentle, sweet part like Lillian Gish and throw her into the part of a prostitute and make it convincing. It just doesn't work, no matter how good the actors or actresses are. It takes more than just acting. It takes a certain quality that comes from the screen. But as I said, I learned a lot on this picture.

I think one of the greatest stories in America concerns the immigrants, what happened to them, and how they built this country. I was glad I made it for the war effort, but most of the reactions I got were through men in the service. There was hardly a man in the service who didn't see the film. It was used on all sorts of ships, in camps, and even in Europe.

DOWD: Did they feel it was inspiring and true?

VIDOR: Yes, I'm sure they did. I think they felt good about American strength, American know-how, and the American way of doing things. Evidently, once it was seen by the Army and Air Force people, they just pushed it and pushed it wherever they could. I suppose in theatres in the United States you could call it a moderate success. They probably didn't get behind it from a sales standpoint. It probably should have been a picture for art theatre circuits in this country.

DOWD: Hal Rosson was the cameraman, and you had worked with him briefly on The Wizard of Oz. I think An American Romance had some of the finest rear projections, just magnificent colors. He must have been a fine cameraman to work with.

VIDOR: Yes. You know, so few cameramen really have an appreciation for the great painters, the modern painters, and so forth. Hal really did. On our days off in Chicago we went to the art museum and discussed paintings. He recognized good paintings. This is very essential for a cameraman, especially a cameraman doing color films. He had a vast amount of experience to call on, and he was a sensitive artist himself.

DOWD: The opening with the rainbow is really lovely.

VIDOR: I think that was all done in the miniature department at the studio.

DOWD: You talked once about the painting of the schoolhouse up on the hill. There is a scene in the picture where Donlevy is going to meet Ann Richards and he is down at the bottom of the hill and there's a schoolhouse with an American flag. Is this based on a painting by Burchfield?

VIDOR: Yes, I was collecting American paintings at that time. I had an entrance hall in my home where I had a collection of Benton, Grant Wood, and Charles Hopper paintings. I tried to buy a Burchfield and a Hopper, but I never succeeded in getting the ones I wanted. I was influenced entirely by Burchfield for this shot. I don't know whether that exact setting with the house is taken from a Burchfield painting, but it was certainly inspired by him. The character of the house is entirely based on Burchfield's work.

DOWD: What about the locations? Was part of it shot in California?

VIDOR: Yes, I think it was shot in Wilmington. I used to have this policy that there was no use keeping the whole crew on distant locations with all the overhead, hotel bills, meals, and overtime costs for something that you could get around here. I sent a second unit out to get several shots that were too much trouble for the entire crew.

John Qualen went out with the second unit. At the time Donlevy was working on another picture and I used Qualen as a double for him. This was material that was supposed to take place in snow. I think it involved him jumping off a train and sliding into a ditch. I might have gone back later and shot it again with Donlevy. This took place when the character grabbed the last train out of the Mesabi open pit mine. I had the idea that he went right along with the ore to Chicago. He had been interested in what happened to the ore after it had been mined, and I had him ride one of these ore cars all the way to Duluth, where the cars were emptied. I had him slide right out of the chute with the ore. There was also a scene in the bunker of the boat where it all comes sliding down, him along with it.

DOWD: You mentioned once that there was a scene with a lot of danger in it that you shot in Gary.

VIDOR: This was when the men were passing the buckets of molten steel over their heads. The entire crew was right underneath these buckets. That was the number one fear we had. Eventually eighty tons of that passed over our heads. From time to time the molten material would slosh out of the buckets and come falling down. At first we would try to move over to one side and get out of the way, while still looking up. But as time went on, we just kept on shooting and didn't pay any attention to it.

In one area there was a section of the steel mill that was about thirty or forty feet wide. On one side of this area was the outside of the mill, where it was usually below freezing. Inside the mill, just on the other edge of this area it was at least 150 degrees. We had to take off our trench coats and mufflers to work in there. The men who actually worked in the mill were usually down to just a shirt. I remember that it was a strange scene with the freezing temperatures just a few feet away from this area where men were working in temperatures around 150 degrees. You don't often see such extremes that close together.

DOWD: Did you have any special protection for the camera?

VIDOR: Yes, we had blankets that went over the top of the camera to try to shield it from the intense heat. We were shooting right in front of the furnace a good deal of the time. Later on we had the camera up on a slight platform. This was because every once in a while some of the slag spilled over from the furnace and slid along the floor. As soon as it hit a bucket or a tank it sent up all kinds of sulphurous smoke, so much that you could not even see where you were standing. You didn't dare walk away when that happened. You just had to stand there and breathe that smoke. With the camera on the platform, you didn't have to worry about it getting hit by the slag.

DOWD: How did the people in the factories react to the film crew?

VIDOR: They were so busy working they didn't have a chance to pay any attention. They would glance up from time to time, and then go on with their work.

DOWD: When we saw the film there was a scene in a bar at Christmas when Donlevy is alone, talking to the bartender. You mentioned Marcel Pagnol then.

VIDOR: I was charmed and delighted with this type of French dialogue. I liked where they kicked an idea around in their conversation. I had never been aware of this but in a film of Pagnol's called <u>Harvest</u> there was a discussion about bread, and when I saw it I was suddenly reminded of this scene. I thought this was a fine thing to do with dialogue. This was a scene that I wrote with Donlevy. There are several pictures of Pagnol's that do the same thing. It is a very human scene that has a lot of philosophical depth to it. Unfortunately I think it has been cut from the release print.

DOWD: Was the speech that George gives one that you had actually heard?

VIDOR: Yes, it had been given at Beverly Hills High School. I heard it there and made notes about it. It was at my wife's stepson's graduation. It intrigued me when I heard it, and I later used the same idea for this picture.

DOWD: Is the sequence where Steve takes his car apart based on something you knew about?

VIDOR: Yes. I remembered that Walter Chrysler bought a car once and then took it apart. He took every piece and laid it out so that he could look at the thing. That appealed to me somehow.

DOWD: The Indianapolis sequence is indicated by just a title that reads "Indianapolis" now. Did you ever shoot a scene at the racetrack itself?

VIDOR: In the present version you just see the title and then you cut to the two men in the hospital. I remember that we shot a scene against a background that was supposed to be at the racetrack. We had these big wind machines going to give it a little realism. As we were rolling the camera, the wind machine started up and blew a little harder than it was supposed to and blew the toupees off against the painted background. Somebody remarked that the picture should be retitled <u>Victory Through Hair Power.</u>

DOWD: Was that just a painted background?

VIDOR: Well, actually I had some film shot at the race-track during the Indianapolis 500 that we used as background material in some places. I think there was also some kind of promotional thing involved there. We may have used a few of the new cars for that year in those background shots. We also shot inside a car factory. However, when we got in there we found that the military had taken over the facility to build aircraft engines. We had to take all these big radial aircraft engines off the assembly line after normal working hours and then bring in the cars. We had to take the fenders off the bodies, take out the seats from some of the others, and generally make it look like the cars were still being assembled. Some of the cars we got had been painted a dull Army drab color, so we had to paint them as well. We paid all the assembly line workers to come over and work while we shot the scenes. I did the scene somewhat impressionistically to pull it all together. I had to give it conciseness and brevity. In order to give each of the parts a different identity on the assembly line we colored and painted them different colors.

DOWD: How did you arrange to shoot in the assembly plant?

VIDOR: Keller was the head of Chrysler at that time, and he and Mayer were good friends. They were making all kinds of war vehicles there. I think they even made tanks at one point. Keller gave us full access to the entire plant, which turned out to be very useful. When I first met Keller, I walked into his office and found him sitting at his desk with his feet up on the table next to it. He was reading a book on Hitler. After that meeting he took me all through the plant. I found that he was completely familiar with all of the machines and processes that were used in that facility. He had a great respect for machines and precision.

DOWD: The documentary scenes in the film are very good.

VIDOR: The last sequence to that portion was supposed to be a look at how they put together one of the huge aircraft engines and airplanes for the industry. This super plane they were making was supposed to help the war effort tremendously. Originally we were going to shoot some scenes of the entire plant, but the plant was supposed to be made by the studio's miniature department to save costs. When the footage from these miniatures came back, we spliced them together and did some previews. It just didn't look real compared to the footage we had shot in the other plants, so I got permission to shoot at the Douglas Aircraft factory.

DOWD: Was that the Douglas plant in Long Beach?

VIDOR: Yes. They were makng the B-17 Flying Fortress out there. Those were the workhorses of the Second World War.

DOWD: Those scenes are very striking, especially when you see all the women workers on the assembly lines.

VIDOR: Yes. A lot of women worked during World War II. They quit doing housework and took jobs in the factories. They were mostly riveters, I think.

DOWD: Did you have them dress especially for these scenes?

VIDOR: No, not at all. That's all authentic. It was a beautiful factory, and we didn't have to change it at all. The assembly line process was really refined then. They had parts rolling off the line every five minutes and it looked great on film. There was a man who had helped initiate the assembly line for that kind of work. He had worked at North American Aviation in San Diego. When the war started he was called in to refine this type of assembly line and he did a fantastic job. His methods were used by a lot of other companies, including Douglas Aircraft. The demands of the war were very heavy then. They had to use those techniques to keep up with the orders.

DOWD: Pat O'Malley was the male lead in two of your films. Those films were Happiness and Proud Flesh. Wasn't he an extra in this film?

VIDOR: Yes. He only had a bit part in this film. It's very much like the typical story of Hollywood people. They are up today and down tomorrow. I watch for these people in my films. He was one of them. If you knew an actor, it was good to help him out all you could, especially if he was down.

DOWD: When we were watching the film, you said all of your feelings about machinery were in the film. I know you like machines. You're certainly not afraid of them.

VIDOR: The two places I've always enjoyed the most are hardware stores and stationery stores. During the war I bought all of the machine tools sold by Sears and Roebuck. I had a basement for them. When I came back from making this film I had all kinds of steel beams and parts that I took for samples. I have a lot of them to this day. I practiced working on them with my tools and I taught myself how to operate all of those machines. It was a fascination I had. It goes all the way back to my childhood when I was interested in motion picture cameras. I was interested in the function of the machine and how it worked. I was trying to communicate the idea of construction and movement, and how things are put together. It fascinated me and I hoped it would be interesting to other people.

DOWD: It is one of the few films to deal with this, and it also makes it very interesting. Most films that try to make industry interesting fail. The way you put the car assembly scenes together was very beautiful.

VIDOR: We spent a lot of time and money on that. It's basically not a documentary as far as the story line goes, but the documentary scenes of the plants and factories seem to be a little different from other films that deal with the same thing. I wanted to communicate some things that no one had done before. I remember that I was shaving with an electric razor once and it suddenly stopped. The action of the razor going off startled me, and I tried to communicate the same type of surprise by turning off the huge dynamos and motors in the plant suddenly. During the strike I had them turn off the motors. The entire plant suddenly comes to a halt. It comes across very effectively, both visually and dramatically.

XI

DOWD: Before you made <u>Duel in the Sun</u> you were offered another picture by Selznick. What was that?

VIDOR: He offered me <u>Tom Sawyer</u>. I wanted to take two weeks of vacation first, but he wanted me to start right away. I needed a rest and was thinking of taking a trip to New England. It was fall, and I had always heard that New England was beautiful in the fall. Anyway, Selznick wouldn't give me the time. He got someone else to do the film. As it turned out, they didn't start the picture for over a year.

DOWD: You mentioned that he had liked <u>An American Romance</u> very much.

VIDOR: He thought it was a great idea for a story, and a great theme. It could have been one of the top films if he had only had a chance to cast it the way he was famous for. He would have put a wonderful cast in that film, and that's really what it needed. That would have made it much better.

DOWD: You had left Metro and then received the offer for <u>Duel in the Sun</u>. How did this come about?

VIDOR: I think I was in Mexico at the time. I had an agent named George Vol, who at one time was affiliated with Myron Selznick. I got a telephone call one day from him while I was in Mexico and he said that David wanted to talk to me. I talked to him when I came back and he gave me a paperback book by Niven Busch. I know it was published in paperback, but I have never seen a hardcover copy of that book. Selznick said he wanted to make an intimate Western, a small picture, but one that would be very well done. He also wanted to have Jennifer Jones star in it. He was going to be busy with some other picture, and he said that I could produce and direct it. He would not interfere at all.

Oliver Garrett and I went to work on the script. I wasn't entirely enthusiastic about the first script, but it was getting the usual first draft treatment, and it got better as we went along. We had to get the story from the book translated into visual form.

After that point David began to get more interested in the project. He started to talk about an opening like the one in Gone With the Wind. He even got a print of the film and had all of us look at it again. He talked a lot about building it up. Without a doubt he was one of the greatest producers around. He could really give a picture the strength of a good cast. He was the one man who really deserved the title of producer more than anyone else I knew. As time went on, he got more interested in the story, and eventually he let Garrett go and took over the job of writing himself.

DOWD: What was it like with him doing the writing?

VIDOR: When we were not in production it was fine. But after we started to shoot the picture, he was never aware of what we were filming. I'm not sure if he just didn't know what we were doing, or whether he couldn't face it. He would often go to a party, have lots to drink, and then come home and start to work. He employed secretaries around the clock to help him. He did most of his letter writing at night.

As soon as we started to shoot he began working on rewrites. It didn't matter so much in pre-production because the order in which you got the pages from him did not matter. But it got to a point where he was doing rewrites of his own work, and the material he would rewrite was the scene we were doing the next day. When that happened, we would have to go ahead and shoot the first version of the scene because his new drafts would not come through until three or four o'clock of the day we were shooting that scene.

We really had high ideals about filmmaking then, especially David. We wanted this film to be a really grand picture. Since he had taken on the writing responsibility, it

was his task to both write and approve whatever script material we used. One day I got a call from the studio's general
manager, Danny O'Shea. He said to me, "Look, King, you are
going over schedule." I said, "Don't talk to me, talk to David. I
could keep on schedule if he would stop giving me all of his
rewrites." After I had finished shooting the film he still
wanted to shoot some more scenes. He even wanted to retake
certain scenes. I'm sure none of this ever was shot again, but
he certainly wanted to.

He'd usually come by with his new scenes, or his
rewrites and want to do some more shooting. When he came by
in the afternoon I would say, "David, we started this scene at
nine o'clock this morning. We're almost finished!" He would
then insist that I read what he had written. He would plead
with me to retake it. Usually it only amounted to a slight
difference from the way we had originally shot it. On one
occasion we called the actors back at four o'clock in the
afternoon when they were already taking their makeup off, and
we started to shoot a slight variation of one of the scenes we
had shot before. Needless to say, that didn't go over too well
with them. However, David was basically the producer and
writer, so at that time there was not much we could do about
it.

In one scene, David came back to me with
another draft of a sequence, with the only change being that
Joseph Cotten had his arm in his lap instead of on the arm of
a sofa. We really did shoot some scenes over with things like
that being the only change. David would always think that he
was going to make big changes in scenes, but when it came
right down to doing them again, he never seemed to have the
time to write much.

He did a few scenes after I had finished direct-
ing the majority of the picture. He liked to use several directors on his big pictures, especially if it involved a lot of action
or some kind of special scene. We went to the Directors Guild
on a few occasions to determine what film I had shot and what
film another director had shot for him after I left. The
changes he had made were so slight that we all had a hard
time figuring out which was which, but finally it was evident
that I had shot about eighty-five percent or ninety percent of
the film.

He thought that having several directors' names on the picture would make it seem very impressive. The Screen Directors Guild didn't want that to happen at all. It is a common practice to have a second unit director at times, for instance if you are going to have scenes that require lots of extras, but the credit is always as the second unit director. This way, the main director can spend his time working with the main characters, so you don't have to pay the actors' salaries while the director works with the extras. Selznick liked to put all of the second unit directors' names in the credits. Let's be honest, he wanted to belittle the importance of any one director. I quit after the shooting was finished. I think I even quit within a day after we stopped.

DOWD: Was your idea to open the film where Joseph Cotten and Jennifer Jones arrive at Spanish Bit?

VIDOR: Yes. We ran Gone With the Wind and looked at the area around the big house, Tara. We planned it so that all of the big backgrounds would be in the opening scene. That was what set the atmosphere as they approach the house, where Joseph Cotten goes to meet Jennifer Jones and she gets out of the stagecoach. We would explain what had happened and the fact that she was reluctant to talk about it when she first meets Barrymore and Lillian Gish. My plan was to explain the story up to Jennifer's arrival with dialogue while we were looking at this tremendous ranch and all of the land that went with it. Later on David wanted to blow up the picture to a bigger size. He wanted to open with a big splash, open with the Mexican dance hall, which I felt was very unreal. It may look fine now, but at the time I didn't want to do it.

DOWD: When we were watching the film, you said that Selznick always wanted to explain everything in his films.

VIDOR: Yes. I had the problem of becoming too literal, doing too much explaining. I remember seeing a play with Ethel Barrymore in which she used dialogue to explain part of the story. It is an old technique of the theatre. If you are showing one bit of action, such as Cotten meeting the girl at the stagecoach and then riding up through a ranch, to show a lot of space, a lot of cattle, and the immense size of the ranch, it is only natural to have some dialogue over that to help set the scene. That way you have the double interest of having the story set up and the scenery being shown at the same time. On the other hand, if you tell it all in the beginning, if you lay it all out on the line, you're going to be redundant the rest of the picture. That was my feeling about the opening.

Maybe that spectacular dance hall thing in the beginning has an appeal that is more pronounced today than it was back then. However, I think I may have used a little too much dialogue in that sequence. It became obvious to Selznick that when he did the big prologue, he would have to cut some of the lines of dialogue. He had a good point there. He may have been right to explain things so that nobody is left puzzled about the story, but sometimes dialogue can paint a thing more graphically than by showing it all on screen. At that time we were still experimenting with those techniques, and to a large extent we were still experimenting with and studying sound.

DOWD: I could imagine that it must have been terribly difficult to have Selznick as the producer during the time he was so obsessed with Jennifer Jones.

VIDOR: He definitely had an obsession. He would breathe hard when he watched her scenes on the screen, and even as they were being shot. At times he could be a great asset to a picture, and at other times he could be terribly annoying.

He was famous for the long letters he used to write. One time they gave him a birthday party and for a joke they gave him a cake that was decorated with all kinds of letters and memoranda in just the same style as his. I think writing these letters was basically a catharsis for him as he was trying to grope around to find the real core of the story or the ideal that he was pursuing. He was doing it with the idea that he would sooner or later run across what he was looking for. And in the end he would be satisfied that during the whole process he had exhausted every possibility in his pursuit of the film.

He was constantly going into infinite detail with every department on the lot. He conferred with people about costumes, photography, editing, anything that had to do with the film. We'd have a meeting after we finished shooting for the day and he would talk about photography with the cameraman, art direction with the art directors, anything that pertained to the production aspect of filmmaking. I think Josef Von Sternberg came in on a couple of those meetings. The slightest detail would send Selznick off on a wild chase, even if it was just the way a scarf was arranged on Jennifer. He never let up on this effort. Sometimes we would order a hundred horses for a shooting day and about five hundred would show up. We would panic and say, "My God, what happened?" They would tell us that Mr. Selznick wanted to be sure that we had plenty.

DOWD: But he never objected to the expense, did he?

VIDOR: No, he had no feeling for money. He did the same for Portrait of Jennie, and that was supposed to be a small picture. He blew it up into a major production with beautiful storm effects and other photographic tricks. He really shouldn't have gone to all that expense. He certainly did not need to. The fellow who wrote the story wrote it with an idyllic sort of mood in mind, but Selznick blew it up more and more until it damn near ruined him. That was one of the pictures that didn't make him any money. He spent far more on making it than the picture was capable of earning back. It was lucky for him that Duel in the Sun made a lot of money. He eventually had to sell Gone With the Wind to MGM to get the money to make his other pictures. He simply had no realistic idea of money. His father, Lewis J. Selznick, had taught him and his brother absolutely no lessons about money. I think his father was actually a gambler as a matter of fact. His basic philosophy was: The more you spend, the better it is.

DOWD: Was Jennifer Jones a difficult actress to work with?

VIDOR: She was one of those actresses who would really show whatever they were feeling in their facial expressions. I don't know whether they're really called actresses or not, but they certainly are a very photogenic group. She was definitely one of them, and I enjoy working with them. Their inner feelings show up very well. If you can make them feel something inside, it will photograph on the screen.

We had to start each day by telling her the story from the beginning. I didn't mind that because I felt that she had a special quality. It is very hard to express what she had in words, but a lot of silent film actors and actresses had it. In other pictures when she tried to really act, she wouldn't arrive at it from the inside. She made a lot of grimaces, and the effort on her part became very obvious. I discovered that if we worked up to it gradually, she would sustain that special quality all day. When she could achieve that, she wouldn't let anything interfere. She stayed in her dressing room a lot. She isolated herself and somehow preserved it all day long.

DOWD: Wasn't Selznick trying to turn her into a big star?

VIDOR: Yes, of course. He was madly in love with her. Everything he did was for her benefit. He spent more time working on her scenes than anything else. He also realized that I knew how to handle her. He felt that I had an understanding of her talents and possibilities. We worked together on another film, Ruby Gentry, later on. During the production of that picture, we made a deal that he would not be allowed on the set. We simply couldn't afford his emotional reactions to things that involved his wife's work. I think one of the main reasons that we were able to work out a deal was that he was not the producer on that picture, and didn't have as much control as he did on Duel in the Sun.

DOWD: There were some fantastic close-ups of Jennifer Jones. It must have been a lot of work to do all of those so carefully.

VIDOR: Of course the cameramen knew what they were supposed to do. If they missed in any way making her look as good as she should, they would be made to go back and do it over. They knew what their number one objective was, and that was to make her look great. Nobody rushed them at all when it came to photographing her. The two men who worked on her shots were Ray June and Hal Rosson.

DOWD: Wasn't Ray Rennahan a cameraman on this picture?

VIDOR: No, he was the Technicolor man. I think Lee Garmes also worked on the Technicolor staff.

DOWD: How did it come about that Hal Rosson was fired?

VIDOR: We had a strike in the middle of the picture. It came about twelve weeks after we had started production. We were interrupted for about a month or so.

DOWD: What kind of strike was this?

VIDOR: IATSE, I think. Hal Rosson was very difficult. Sometimes the cameramen can be more difficult than the worst actor. As I remember, he was quite difficult. Although he was a good friend, and I liked him very much, he could be very irritable. I don't know whether he was doing another picture by the time we got back to work on the film. It may have been that Selznick just thought that it would be a good idea to bring Lee Garmes in. After the IATSE strike was over, we had the option of using the same people who had worked on the first part of the production, or using new people. At that time we started up again with Lee.

DOWD: Lee Garmes is certainly one of the best cameramen around.

VIDOR: Yes, and he is a very pleasant man to work with. Hal's nickname at MGM when he was working with us was Putt-Putt. He was always fussing around. Probably the most annoying thing about cameramen is that sometimes they can be irritable, and sometimes they just stop talking to you when they get angry. Hal certainly didn't start off being that way, but it just evolved over a period of time. I believe there was a little pressure from Selznick that contributed to it eventually. After all, he wanted his wife to look perfect. Lee came on and was always agreeable, pleasant, and a joy to work with.

DOWD: He shot the scene in the bar with Charles Bickford. He also shot the scene where Lionel Barrymore meets Harry Carey on a hill. I believe he said that he was influenced by Rembrandt in lighting that scene.

VIDOR: Yes. One thing about that scene with Lionel Barrymore was that we designed it for strictly controlled lighting. We had the choice of going out to a real hill, but what would we have gotten? Either a foggy sky or a smoggy horizon, or a pretty blue sky, which we really didn't want. It was done right on the stage because a fellow named Mack Johnson, who has since become an art director, was the designer on this film. He designed the look of the picture with all of his drawings and paintings. He did most of his original artwork for the film in color.

DOWD: He was the production designer, right?

VIDOR: Yes. I think later on William Cameron Menzies, one of the all-time great production designers, came on and helped him a bit. They did a set that was used for the dance hall scene. It took place in the patio of the house. As a matter of fact, another man named James Basevi worked on this, too. I saw his name on another picture of mine. I think it was The Big Parade. He actually did quite a few pictures for me.

There was a constant demand from Selznick for nothing but the best, and if it took several people to do, that was simply what had to be done. That's one thing that deserves nothing but praise. David Selznick had a wonderful organization that could really get a good job done. They would handle the casting, organizing, pre-production, and everything else that is so important. All the director would have to worry about would be directing. You could work on the script if you wanted to, and if that took a little rewriting, they didn't mind as long as you were improving the production. As far as the film's production value goes, this one had a lot more of his attention than Ruby Gentry, since he did not produce that. He certainly tried, though. He wrote lots of letters to try to get a small hand in the making of Ruby Gentry. Also, the difference in the budgets of Duel in the Sun and Ruby Gentry was quite large.

DOWD: How was the scene done where the clan gathers together, with all those hundreds of horses in the shot?

VIDOR: We were out on location in Tucson. Otto Brower, a second unit director who had had a lot of experience with Westerns and horses, worked with us there. He was a good man for handling lots of action shots. He would sit in on the readings and sometimes I would get together with him in a hotel room after the shooting was over for the day and we would start to plan out the next action sequence. Sometimes we did it in between shots on the set. I would draw out the shots as I saw them in my mind, and he would take this paper and go out and shoot it at the same time we were shooting the main scenes with the actors. It was simply great to have two units going at once.

        I remember a close shot we had of Gregory Peck racing after Jennifer on horseback. There was no acting in this shot, but it was a great action shot. It takes a good fellow to know how to get a shot like this, and Otto certainly got it right. He was in a camera car racing alongside Peck.

        Getting back to the whole second unit director problem, there was just no reason for me to take time out and shoot a simple scene like that when I had people like Lillian Gish and Lionel Barrymore waiting to do their scenes. Just to have them sitting around would have cost the company a lot of money. I was grateful to have Otto working with me.

DOWD: Isn't there a famous story about D.W. Griffith coming out to visit you on the set? Where did that happen?

VIDOR: That was in Culver City at the studio. I imagine Lillian Gish was in touch with him over the years, and she asked me if it would be all right for him to come out and watch us on the set one day. Barrymore, who had been a Griffith star, was also excited about it. I was pleased because at one time I had worked for him as an extra. I had never met him before, and I certainly didn't know him personally.

        When he came out to visit us he was no longer directing. I think he had been teaching at one of the colleges. He brought his wife, but I've forgotten who she was. I supose we selected a day when two of his old stars, Lillian and

Lionel, were both working. He came and he watched us shoot the scene. I was very flattered and pleased and certainly excited to have my mentor there watching. Lionel started to forget his lines. Lillian seemed to work fine, and remembered hers very well. Lionel just got more and more in trouble as he tried to work. The Old Master gave him the fear that he couldn't remember all that he had learned. We kept doing it for over an hour, and finally I went up to Lionel and said, "I guess it's because D.W. is here." I asked Griffith if he would mind going behind the set for a few minutes. He remarked that he had been there long enough, and he left.

DOWD: What kind of shape was he in then?

VIDOR: He was fine. He was the same imposing figure he always was, tall and very good-looking.

DOWD: What was it like to direct Lillian Gish again after you had directed her twenty-six years before?

VIDOR: It was a difference of her playing a teenage seamstress in the first film, and a grandmother in the second film. I suppose we had kept in touch. Ever since La Bohème we had remained good friends. She is a marvelous old pro, always on the job. She knew what she was doing, and she gave it everything she had. I can think of nothing but joyful things when I recall our work together.

DOWD: There was also Walter Huston. Wasn't he wonderful to work with?

VIDOR: I think he stood absolutely alone in his excellence as a character actor. There was a man who knew how to act. I don't think there is anyone who can surpass his work, and I don't think anyone could ever take his place. I knew when he died that it was going to be very difficult to replace him. Who would we get to do the roles that he had done? He was just an amazing fellow. We needed him for about three or four days. His agent asked us for a minimum of ten weeks per picture, which in today's acting market seems cheap. They wanted $40,000 for ten weeks of his work. It seemed like an awful lot back then, but Selznick just said, "Let's go ahead and do it." He knew that if we were going to spend some money and get some good actors, we might as well do it right. Selznick was a good person for me, especially since I am inclined to economize, and sometimes that happens in the wrong places. It was wise to put Huston in, and it was certainly worth $40,000. We had ten weeks with him, and we brought him into more and more of the story. Selznick brought him back once for a scene that wasn't going to be shot until the end of the schedule. It was a dance scene, which means that we had to pay him for extra weeks at the rate of $4,000 per week. We had decided to use him all we could since we had him for ten weeks, and David went all out.

DOWD: How did Von Sternberg get into the production?

VIDOR: I don't know what he is credited for, but David had a lot of admiration for him as a director. He wanted to do something for him, and he also thought that Von Sternberg could do something for Jennifer. I think he was under this impression because of the work he had done with Marlene Dietrich. He could certainly handle women well. Dietrich had been helped immensely because of the careful lighting and the little touches he had given her. It was fine with me, and I liked him as a person.

          Now that I think of it, I think he was listed as a color advisor. He probably suggested that we use a spotlight somewhere, or he may have suggested some sort of scarf or hair arrangement. He was giving advice on those things while I was off planning something else. He may have been doing this while I was working on the script. He did a lot of work in the preliminary tests that were done before the actual shooting started. Joe directed the lighting, makeup and photography tests so that we would be ready to go when the script and pre-production were all finished. After the production started, he would do anything I wanted him to do. He was around as an assistant, but he was definitely more artistically valuable. He was certainly not commercially oriented, and he never confined his work to simple tasks. He contributed quite a bit to the artistic nature of the film.

          Down in Arizona we shot a scene where Jennifer was supposed to be sweaty with all of the heat, and Joe decided that he would throw a bucket of water over her. He enjoyed doing that. One time I had an appointment with a doctor around five o'clock. I had rehearsed a scene that was slow going, really hard to get all planned out with the lighting and camerawork. I had to leave, so I just let him shoot it himself. Over a week or so later Selznick said to me, "My God, he shot until eight o'clock that night!" I had given him one scene to do of the sheriff entering the room. I thought it would take about one or two takes to complete. Selznick told me that he had shot 4500 feet of Technicolor negative on the scene. He had kept everyone there late, incurring all sorts of overtime expenses. I guess he was just eager to do some real directing again.

DOWD: You've said before that you were opposed to the extreme violence in the character of Gregory Peck and that you didn't like the railroad scene. Why?

VIDOR: I think that blowing up the train was just not the right thing to do. I thought it was going too far. I didn't shoot it, it was shot after the picture was finished. I saw the picture with that scene included and I begged David to take it out. He said, "I want to make Peck the worst son-of-a-bitch that ever was in a film!" I tried to argue with him by saying that the bad aspect of his character was there in every scene he played. It was part of his character, and it was just inherent to the man. I pleaded, but it didn't do any good. He may have been right, but I don't know. I just thought it was in bad taste.

DOWD: You also said that you had to fight some censorship. How was Selznick involved in this?

VIDOR: He was not involved with the censorship. The office would read the script so that they would know when a scene would be shot, and they would show up on that day and we would have to go through a little dance routine with them to get them to let us shoot it. There was one scene in particular I don't think they let us keep in the picture. Although we did shoot it, I don't remember seeing it in the final film. It was a seductive dance around a tree, but it was really too much to be released with the picture. I guess they objected to the amount of nudity, but I don't think there was that much. They also objected to the possibility of how the man and the woman came together in that scene. I think it was Geoffrey Shurlock of the Johnston Office who was there watching me that day. They always wanted to have someone there so that they didn't have to fight that battle later on. They figured that if they could get you to stop shooting it, they would not have to fight you later. I don't think they ever actually stopped me from shooting a scene, though.

I remember we were shooting as the war with the Japanese ended. We were shooting the scene with the colts. I had a disagreement about part of it with Selznick, and he became very upset and caused quite an uproar. I told him that I would face any criticism he had if he would call me over to his office, but as for blowing up on the set, I wouldn't stand for it. I'd had a lot of experience with Goldwyn and I told Selznick that I just wouldn't take it. There had been a scheduling problem because there were only a few cameras around, and we had to time the shooting of that day's work so that both the second unit director and I could do what had been planned. Selznick showed up on the set when I was starting the scenes we were supposed to finish that afternoon. I had been waiting for the cameras, and I was a little uneasy. He came in and we got into an argument, and I told him that I would take two of these blow-ups, but when the third one came, I would simply walk off the set. I told him I was going to leave, and he started to kick things and began to scream at me. He was trying to bawl me out for the cameras not arriving on the set on time. While he started this routine, I took off the megaphone I had hanging from my belt and handed it to him. I said, "You sound like you think you could do it better. If you want to direct this picture, here's your chance." With that, I walked over, got into my car, and left. He was left with all of the cattle and all of the extras waiting for some kind of instruction. He had the second unit director there, and it was an important scene. I didn't like to do that, but I really couldn't stay under those conditions.

DOWD: Was this in Arizona?

VIDOR: No, this was up in Thousand Oaks near a place they called Lasky Mesa. The next morning Charles Glet, who was the business manager, called me up and then David talked to me and said, "Please, will you come back?" I told him that I couldn't possibly go back.

DOWD: Did he apologize for the things he said?

VIDOR: He apologized for a few things. He said, "Think it over and come back and finish." As it turned out, there was only about a day of locations and a day of studio work left on the schedule. I just couldn't, though. It was emotionally too difficult. Today, I probably would have gone back. I am more in control of my emotions now.

DOWD: Was that the first time you ever quit a picture?

VIDOR: Yes. I threatened Goldwyn the same way, but I never walked off. Actors used to do that all the time. They would say, "If so-and-so does that again, I'm leaving!" I would say, "Well, don't threaten me! I'll beat you to the door!" I think I said that to Spencer Tracy once. I don't think he walked off after that.

DOWD: You really had two bad experiences in a row. First there was the problem with An American Romance where MGM cut it without you, and then came these problems with Selznick. Weren't you feeling pretty discouraged about film-making after all of this?

VIDOR: Yes, I was. I wasn't tired of filmmaking, but I was tired of all the people who just seemed to get in the way all the time. I remember shooting up in the mountains in Arizona. All day long these big black cars would be carrying those famous memos from Selznick, who was up in the Santa Rita Hotel. That was just ridiculous. It certainly didn't help things when Selznick got mad on the set and started to kick things. That was entirely impossible for me to deal with. That type of thing would just undermine the director's authority, and he did it repeatedly. I couldn't stand around and give empty threats back to him. I wanted him to know that I meant what I said, and by walking off I finally showed him that I meant it.

DOWD: He later asked you to work on <u>Ruby Gentry</u>, so you must have resolved things.

VIDOR: Yes. Soon after the picture came out I was up at his house again. When he died, he was trying to get some story for me to direct. He sent me books by Herman Hesse which are now being made into films by other people. He sent me a lot of other stories, too. I don't know why he didn't try to get me on the Scott Fitzgerald story, <u>Tender is the Night</u>. He talked to me once about doing a story that involved an Air Force general and the Chinese wife.

DOWD: Was that <u>Flying Tigers</u>?

VIDOR: No, it was going to have Rex Harrison in it. We went up and talked to Rex about it. When that didn't come through, I went on to do a show for television, and I never got to do the film. We were good friends after that, though. He was at my house quite often.

DOWD: I think Gregory Peck was better in this film than any other film I have seen him in.

VIDOR: I had an idea of what to do with him, which I took from <u>Porgy and Bess</u>. In other words, he had the hat tilted forward, the cigar in his mouth, even the walk, which I knew how to do. It was the walk of a tough Negro man, a guy who thought he was a hotshot. I had a similar character in <u>Hallelujah</u>. I described this character to him and how he should play the scenes. He was supposed to be somewhat of a slicker, like a black man with a very sinister character. Ed Garner told me later that Greg had said that he had a very clear vision of what he was doing with that character. I was able to tell him what I wanted more than anybody he'd worked for, even in the years afterwards. He remembered this, and it impressed him. I would agree with you in saying that he was better in this than in anything else I've seen him do.

DOWD: He did most of his own stunts, didn't he?

VIDOR: Yes. One day he did all of his stunts on the horse. He had a scene where the horse drew up to the camera and he slid off the back of the animal and landed on his seat.

The animal's legs weakened, and it sat down right on top of him. I panicked because I thought the horse would have broken a couple of his bones, but it didn't hurt Gregory at all. He got up and right away started the next take. I was amazed. There was another accident where they ran into something while he was riding the horse. He was thrown over the horse's head, and the horse cut himself on something. The horse was cut badly, but Gregory wasn't hurt at all.

DOWD: Was Ray Rennahan, the technical representative for Technicolor, on the set all of the time?

VIDOR: He actually functioned as a cameraman, and he was there all the time. Back in those days you had to have a representative from Technicolor on the set. They would always send over Natalie Kalmus. She was the wife of Doctor Herbert T. Kalmus, the head of Technicolor at the time. She would come over and spend about a half hour on the picture, but her name always had to go in the credits as an advisor. Ray came along as a more serious advisor. He was actually trained as a cameraman, but he was working for Technicolor at that time. He didn't always direct the lighting, but he did most of the second unit lighting. Because of union laws we used our own lighting man to light the stars, and Ray just made sure that nothing went wrong.

DOWD: Did you actually have a contract with Technicolor in which their representatives had to be present?

VIDOR: Oh, yes. That was a definite part of shooting any Technicolor movie.

DOWD: Would Ray do the lighting if one of the stars were doing a stunt or action shot?

VIDOR: It's hard to say exactly how that worked out. He would definitely be there advising. It may have been a case where he and the regular lighting man worked out their own system as to who was responsible for lighting those types of shots.

To mention Gregory again, I wanted to tell you about another time he tried something. One night a photographer from <u>Life</u> was taking pictures of him. They had him ride a horse into the dining room of the hotel where we stayed. They put rubber shoes on the horse so that he wouldn't damage the wooden floor. I was having dinner with Selznick, and in came Gregory on the horse. The floor was slippery, and David nearly fainted when he saw his star riding in on that horse. He thought for sure that the horse would slip and fall, thus permanently hurting Gregory. I never saw him more surprised in all my life. It really looked great. They rode in and then the horse stood up on its back feet. It sure made a great photograph.

DOWD: Selznick didn't know anything about it?

VIDOR: No. He looked over and happened to see the star of his picture on the back of this horse. He jumped up and ran over and said, "Stop this! Don't do that anymore. I forbid that!" Greg was getting a big kick out of it.

DOWD: I understand that <u>Life</u> did quite a photo essay on the film.

VIDOR: They certainly did. They liked to get as many photos of Jennifer as they could. There were lots of things they were interested in. There was one scene where she was supposed to crawl through the brush on the side of one of the mountains. The terrain was so rough that she got cut up a bit from all the crawling. So, we had a rubber suit made so that she could do all of that without getting hurt any more. The <u>Life</u> people really liked that for their story. They also showed how she was instructed in shooting a gun. Selznick wanted an expert to teach her how to shoot so that it would be right for the film. I knew how to shoot a rifle, but he wanted a real expert to come in and give her lessons. And in addition to that she had dance instructors, riding instructors, and she was taught how to do everything she had to do in the film. The reporters covered all of that. They thought it made great copy.

DOWD: Seeing the three Selznick pictures, <u>Bird of Paradise</u>, <u>Duel in the Sun</u>, and <u>Gone With the Wind</u>, I realized it must be very difficult ending the stories where the heroine has to die or get murdered. Was that the thing Selznick really liked to do?

VIDOR: Yes, he was interested in that. That is the way he saw the ending to a lot of stories. He thought he could milk that kind of thing for a lot of action and drama. He wanted to squeeze the last drop of emotion from every film. That's the way he thought they should be done. To illustrate the way he thought, he once sent me all of the drafts for Gone With the Wind. I directed that for just one weekend. It took me a whole weekend to read them and it was really quite a mess. I went back Monday and found that Gable had asked for Victor Fleming. They took Fleming off of The Wizard of Oz and I took over the last days of shooting on that film. I was just glad to get out of Gone With the Wind because they had turned it into such a mess with all those drafts of the script. But in that mess you could see that Selznick wanted to do the same type of ending he was famous for. It was really his baby. He was so very determined to do it his way.

DOWD: Did you like Duel in the Sun when you first saw it?

VIDOR: No, I didn't do the editing for that picture. During the long strike that occurred in the middle of production I was able to work on a little bit of the editing. I started out with a vision of a very intense story, very similar to Zinnemann's High Noon. That was what I was striving for. I wanted just plain good acting, with no blown-up or overacted scenes. I wanted a good artistic Western film, with good color and a good cast. I thought it had a great chance for the Academy Awards. But Selznick wanted this overly dramatic thing that just grew bigger and bigger, as was his style. There were some scenes I didn't go for. I didn't like the beginning, and I didn't like the shot where he blew up the train. He was definitely inclined to overdo things. I basically liked the film, but I thought that he went too far in a few places. It was a little embarrassing to me in a few places like that. When you are close to a film and you see it another way, these things affect you more. As the years go by, you just sit there and you can observe it as an ordinary human being finally. You can't do that if you have visualized it another way. That was the situation here. Back then some people called it "Drool in the Sun" or "Lust in the Dust." Today, since so many films have nudity, it seems pretty tame.

XII

DOWD: The Fountainhead was the first film you made at Warner Bros. after you left MGM. What was the difference between working for MGM and working for Warner Bros.?

VIDOR: It is rather hard to define quickly. Warner Bros. was sort of a one-man studio and it was run by Jack Warner. On this picture I had Henry Blanke as the producer. They had already cast Gary Cooper to do the part. They signed me as the director. The interesting thing, and this occurred to me yesterday as we were watching the film, was that it was so much in line with what I was thinking at that time. I reread Jung's Psychology of the Self just the other day. It is mainly the self against the mob, against prevailing public opinion. I opened it up and saw that I had marked all the pages with notes. I was surprised to discover that influence on the film.

The point is that one has a tendency to feel that you're not perfectly cast, or not exactly suited to do a certain picture. But both War and Peace and The Fountainhead were films that came to me through an agent, and I did not set out to do them as personal projects. It was a coincidence that I was set to do this new film, because I had just gone through Jungian analysis a few years before, and I was then very conscious of this recognition of the self, the dignity of the self, and the power and divinity one has. I had been approaching this in my own way, and not exactly through Jungian techniques. What was so startling was the thought that I would do these films after the thinking I had been doing. I was very much in accord with this story, and I would ask myself later, "How could they be so perceptive about my own beliefs and thinking, that they would assign me these pictures?"

This same feeling came over me when I watched the film again the other day. It was almost as if the feeling I had and the search I had been going through had been an absolute secret, and then suddenly they came up and asked me to do these pictures which were exactly in line with my thoughts.

My first feature film had been inspired by Buddha and The Light of Asia. I ran home after seeing the play and wrote the story. The Fountainhead and War and Peace are very much alike in this respect, and in War and Peace the character is even fat and round, like Buddha. It's a man's search, and apparently the films I had done were able to communicate that this type of story would be good for me to do, since it would be an ongoing continuity with my previous work. This tremendous feeling is what I had when I started to work for Warner Bros.

DOWD: Did Ayn Rand have any kind of requests for you at the beginning of production?

VIDOR: I don't think she did. They had bought the novel and she was not active in the making of the picture at all. I activated her participation in the picture. That's another old story. I've probably talked about it before, but I believe somebody's inspiration to write a book or a story is very valuable. They feel it very deeply. To then discard them as an adaptor or writer has always been very hard for me to do. It seems stupid. In other words, I always feel like bringing them in on the project, to let them participate and write a script. Even if they don't know how to write a screenplay, they can do it with a little bit of help and guidance. But as a rule, they're not going to mess up characters they've originally established. They won't mess up the most important thing, which is the motivation and the depth of feeling for the whole story.

The studio had excluded Ayn Rand and had put in a husband and wife writing team to do the script when I came onto the project. They wrote a script that spoiled what the book intended to be, and what the characters had to be. They just chucked it all out. I certainly can't explain why. I had studied the book and when I read the first script I said, "This is just throwing the whole story away. Why did you buy the book?" So we talked around with other writers and finally brought in Ayn Rand herself. She volunteered to do it for free, providing we didn't change any of her dialogue.

DOWD: This sounds just like the character in the film.

VIDOR: Yes, that's right. I rather welcomed that because actors, when they become uncertain and insecure, always blame it on the writer. I had a wonderful excuse if an actor would say, "I can't read that line," or "That line isn't right," or so forth. I'd say, "We'll get her over here and talk about it, then."

"How long will that take?"

"Oh, just about an hour. Let's call her up."

After that they would get back to work and they'd do it. I think we only had to bring her over once, and that was to change something just a little bit.

For the most part, the film is the same as the book. There is no contamination or dilution of the book. I disagreed with the ending, however. I didn't like them blowing up the buildings. Today, I agree with that ending, and I like the dramatic power of it. I have a little more perspective on the film now and it doesn't seem so startling. I do get a little uneasy over some of the bombings and violence that goes on today, though. Warner advocated that type of thing in the picture. Since no one was hurt in the buildings, I guess it was justified after all.

I had done a picture with Gary before, Wedding Night. In that picture he had had a little trouble memorizing all of his lines. We had to cut back and forth in every scene to get around that difficulty. He could only learn one line at a time. In The Fountainhead he had a speech of about six pages in length for the courtroom scene. It was a long, very important speech. When we approached that, he looked at it and said, "God, I don't know whether I'll ever be able to say that." I said, "Well, I'll cut it up and shorten the takes a little bit." I think he ended up doing about a page at a time. It doesn't help on the set to have this kind of problem with an actor. We ended up making a record, a disc recording, and he took it home and played it over and over again to learn the lines.

DOWD: Did you shoot a master of that entire scene?

VIDOR: I don't think we did one of the entire scene. I probably did a master of the beginning, the middle, and some small parts here and there. When we'd get into a good set-up with the jury and Cooper, it was only natural that we would run the camera until he finally forgot his lines. We'd stop then and figure out another shot we could cut to, maybe a shot of the judge or something. We had to have cuts anyway, in case it turned out too long. Sometimes the audience would get fidgety when you had a scene that ran too long.

Looking at the picture again, I was quite pleased with it in general. Ayn Rand had a definite idea about the integrity and permanence of this artist's work. That's what the book is all about, and that is where the title comes from. I think it is a most interesting theme. If I made a film today, I would think of making a film with the same theme, about the integrity of the self against the mob -- against advertising influence, mob psychology, mob thinking. That's where the neuroticism comes in. It happens when people try to conform to the way other people do things.

DOWD: Did you get along with Ayn Rand?

VIDOR: Yes, very well. I liked her because she was a woman with a particular idea. Back then it used to offend some people because they had been taught some vague definition of unselfishness. It's stupid to go through life justifying everything by being helpful to other people and thereby messing up your own life. People don't quite know what it means, but they think that the thing one should always do is sacrifice oneself. This picture damned sacrifice and rightfully so. You can only help people by helping yourself. The characters really grew from Ayn Rand. Her individuality, her slant, her peculiar mixture that would bring forth this story, was very special.

Another thing that strikes me is the photography. It looks modern, especially the lighting. The composition was also fairly modern, except when we wanted to give a false

Victorian influence on the publisher's part. We tied the phoni-
ness to her. The publisher was still influenced by the past, by
the mob, and therefore had a Victorian state of mind, and we
used some of the architecture in those scenes to emphasize
this. I made a very good study of Frank Lloyd Wright and his
career, as well as his work. I was already preparing to go to
Arizona to meet him when Jack Warner heard about it and
cancelled it.

DOWD: Why?

VIDOR: He was afraid that if we went there and something turned up in the picture against him, that Wright would
have a case for a suit. He was afraid of a possible problem
with him. There were probably half a dozen of his buildings
here, and I photographed those and I began to get a definite
feeling of what he was doing in architecture. I got so interested that other buildings done by a less talented man looked
horrible to me.

The art director on this film was very good. His
name was Edward Carrere, and we were able to fashion the
architecture to look much like a building that is now in Century City, and some others in New York that Wright did. We
were actually becoming involved with glass walls, much like
the modern buildings of today have. It was a great joy to be
able to project trends and influences in architecture. I have
always been interested in that subject. I've built seven houses
of my own over the years.

DOWD: I know that the house you had in Bel Air was
designed with a noted architect. I think it was the house on
Tower Road. You also had one on Summer Ridge Road.

VIDOR: That was with Wallace Neff. I had two houses
that he designed. He had a definite style of his own. I designed
the outside appearance of both of those houses, and he did the
rest. I think making films has a lot to do with architecture,
telling a story and constructing it well.

My interest has always been very strong in this
area. We had a fairly modern looking building in The Crowd in
1928 and Cedric Gibbons had developed a modern style of

interior for the penthouse rooms. In working with him on that film I developed a good sense for architecture and began to appreciate it. Again, on the architectural side, this picture held a big interest for me.

Of course Gary Cooper wasn't the image that he had presented on the screen, and you didn't connect him with the idea of arrogance. When you read the book you probably think of a more arrogant performance, something Bogart could have done. Tracy was not right for it, but perhaps Gable could have been. They would all be more arrogant than Cooper, who was a soft-spoken man. But really, this turned into a plus. It wasn't the arrogance, it was simply his assuredness, the confidence, that he had in his own work. Confidence does not necessarily have to be arrogance. It took me quite a while to see this. It was probably a couple of years after I finished the film before I realized that his quiet strength was better for the screen than if he had played it more arrogantly.

DOWD: I think he is just perfect in the role.

VIDOR: Yes, that is the way it looks to me now. That type of character could simply say a "Yes," or a "No," and it would hold a lot of meaning because of the strength and character behind it. He really was convinced that he knew what he was doing. He had a grasp on the importance of self.

Today, I know that the self is the only evidence of what we call God. That is the only place to find God, in one's own self. If you can't find God in the expression of man, then where do you find it? Now I know. We've only been thrown off by repentance, long suffering and the ideas of the church -- eternal sin and all that has been putting man down. Where do you find God -- in a church, a priest, a Pope? Truly it is a man's consciousness and his own self that represents God, and that speaks for God in its own way. None of the other outside authorities can ever do that. It really is a fine basic theme.

That phrase, "Give the public what they want," has always stopped me cold. I have never been guilty of giving the public what they wanted because I always thought they never knew what they wanted. You do something that you like very much and you can get other people to like it -- that's the way it works.

DOWD: This picture reminded me very much of <u>The Crowd</u> in the way it was lit, the sets, and in the expressionistic look about it.

VIDOR: Yes, it is very similar. I was very fortunate that it came out so well. I think I chose the cameraman from seeing some other picture. He was a Warner Bros. cameraman named Bob Burks. Carrere and he did a wonderful job. It was a great combination and we all agreed in the approach needed to get this effect. I thought the miniatures and backings we used outside for the windows looking out over New York had a very real feeling about them.

DOWD: They were very well done, and I believe you did this with a long, open stage, especially for the newspaper office in back of his desk. That reminded me of <u>The Crowd</u> also.

VIDOR: It's exactly the same thing that I did in <u>The Crowd</u> with all those desks on the stage with no set, no building, nothing but a stage and a little set in the foreground. There was a little set that housed the office, and there was a glass wall that surrounded it that you could see through, and then we had all the backdrops. This was done with a minimum amount of money because the main thing determining the realism of the set was the lighting. Everything else was minimal. I think we just pulled the desks out of the prop room, so they didn't cost us anything.

For the final scene where we went up over the building we had a helicopter rise up over New York. I don't know how low they got, but we had process plates with the stuff from the helicopter. They had a lot of trouble with the vibration from the helicopter at that time. So, we went back and had it reversed. We turned the film around and let it come down, instead of rising up. It looked a lot better that way, and I think that was the way we finally used it.

For the scene where she was in the elevator, we had to shoot from way up on top of the stage. I don't like heights but they built a nice system of railings and I got up there and shot it. We were up there because the screen had to be forty-five degrees below us. We had to shoot down so they had the screen angle correctly placed. It was tough to do.

DOWD: I don't think it suffered from not being in color.

VIDOR: It was probably much better in black-and-white than it would have been in color.

DOWD: The shadows are beautiful. In color films, the shadows never seem to look quite right.

VIDOR: Yes. It prettifies the picture when you don't want it. This is the same thing that Peter Bogdanovich told me about The Last Picture Show. He wanted it in black-and-white specifically. I don't remember if we ever had the option, but I'm certainly glad it was done in black-and-white. If it had been in color, it would not have had that stark, definite effect.

DOWD: All the reproductions of Wright's work were done like that. The books that you would see at that time were all black-and-white. It was very much in keeping with the style. I've noticed that effect in different ways. I've seen photographs of Japan that always come across much better than pictures of the same thing in color.

VIDOR: Yes, that's true. It is a peculiar thing. I couldn't have given a lecture on what Wright was trying to do, I couldn't define it. At that time people were damning Wright and what he did. However, he had the right idea. I spent days and days looking at his books, studying them, and I began to realize that the effect I wanted was exactly as I saw it in those books and drawings. There is a certain style that blends in harmoniously with the entire story, and his style matched it. It began to work on me subconsciously.

        This was an interesting thing. I wasn't entirely intellectual about it. I picked up a certain feeling, and since it seemed right, I went with it. That was really what the character of Cooper was trying to do in the picture. It was similar to what I was going through with my own pictures. The slightest change by Thalberg or the studio would just wreck the whole thing if it was done in an insincere or careless manner. I wasn't spouting off about this, and I certainly wasn't writing about it, but I sure felt it. My early pictures were exactly the way I saw them, without anyone else coming in and changing them. That was the way I liked it.

DOWD: Here you were making The Fountainhead after having two bad experiences with An American Romance and Duel in the Sun. It must have struck a very responsive chord in you, especially after you had been interfered with so much.

VIDOR: Exactly. After I saw it the other day, The Fountainhead looked very good to me. I was thinking that perhaps I shouldn't try to do another picture. This one has a lot of my ideas and beliefs in it, and it expresses them very well. If I don't make another picture, I'll be perfectly happy to stand on my record because I've got some good material here. That picture is so much of what I believe, I could die happily, knowing that I had made it.

DOWD: How did you cast Patricia Neal? I don't believe she had done much work before this.

VIDOR: No, she hadn't. She was under contract to Warner Bros. and she had done one picture, which I believe David Butler directed. It was a light marriage picture.

Ayn Rand wanted me to try and get Garbo, and made me promise that I would try. I gave the script to her, but I found out that she wasn't doing films. She used to take a walk up near my house, so I just called her up and asked her if she would read the script. She did, and I told her I'd like very much to have her. My heart wasn't in it, although I thought she was the greatest. She told me why she didn't think she should do it. I didn't fight her very hard, but I satisfied Ayn Rand that I had tried, and that's why she did not end up doing the film.

Patricia Neal is tall, and has a certain strength. The studio said, "We have a girl under contract right here on the lot." I went out to talk to her, and I found her riding a bicycle. I called to her and gave her a copy of the script. She liked it, and I liked her. She had a lot of strength and vitality. We ended up becoming good friends.

DOWD: Is there a story about how you were going up to Fresno once? Was that to shoot the quarry scene?

VIDOR: Yes, that's where we started.

DOWD: And you and Cooper were in the car?

VIDOR: I think it was Patricia. I don't think Gary was along with us. I remember I picked a gardenia and gave it to her. Then Gary came later on, on his own. The three of us had dinner together when we got there. They fell immediately in love. It was a big, terrific romance. I used to have drinks with them, and I could see it happening.

DOWD: That must have been very nice.

VIDOR: It really helped in the picture because they were really in love with each other. I was with them a lot, and it certainly influenced their performance. When they looked at each other in the picture it really meant something. It was very convincing.

DOWD: Did you ever get to meet Frank Lloyd Wright?

VIDOR: No. I remember later when I was in Phoenix I had made all of the arrangements to go and see him when a tremendous windstorm came up. People said that I better not go, that my car would have the paint blasted off from the sand. The storm was really that bad. So, I couldn't drive out then. I would have liked to have known him. I think we would have gotten along very well.

DOWD: You've told me that Marquand gave you a set of paints. I notice that a lot of the pictures you've painted around your office and home have the same kind of forced perspective that appears in your films. It is also evident in The Fountainhead.

VIDOR: Yes, in The Crowd it was the stairway, the hospital corridor, and the building. I don't know what it is. I don't know too much technically about painting, but I do know about perspective. The last two paintings I did are both perspectives. One is a railroad track across the desert, and the other one is a corridor that I saw in Munich once. They both have a lot of forced perspective in them. It ties up with my psychological life somehow.

DOWD: Yours and Wright's, both.

VIDOR: I suppose so. I identify with him, with his long, horizontal lines and balconies.

DOWD: Was the columnist based on Alexander Woolcott?

VIDOR: Yes. Woolcott exercised a certain control with his column, and he had a certain dominant attitude about everything. I don't know how it came about, but they are out of the same mold.

DOWD: The Fountainhead was certainly a very popular film, wasn't it?

VIDOR: Yes, I think so. I think it is still being run. You see, Cooper was better known for his Western films, and neither one of the films I did with him were Westerns. He was a writer in one of them, and an architect in the other. People identified him very much with the character he played in High Noon. But he was very pleased with this film. He named it as one of his favorite films several times. I think it was very successful. As a result, Warner Bros. wanted me to stay there. I made two more films. I didn't feel as good about them as I did about this one. I thought they were compromises, and they had some difficulties I wasn't able to overcome.

DOWD: Max Steiner did the score. Did you choose him?

VIDOR: Yes. He was at RKO and he had done Bird of Paradise, and I really liked everything he did. He was my favorite at the time.

DOWD: It really is a beautiful score.

VIDOR: Yes. I must have gotten him approved to work on the film rather quickly, because that quality in his work takes time, and he did a lot of work on that score.

DOWD: Between the release dates of Duel in the Sun and The Fountainhead there is a time span of nearly two years. Were you doing anything else between these two pictures?

VIDOR: I was working on an idea of getting some directors together, somewhat along the lines of United Artists. I wanted to get Tay Garnett and Howard Hawks. We tried to get four directors. We had it rolling, when Hawks objected. He said he could make more pictures outside the organization we were setting up than he could within it. The idea was to cooperate on each other's pictures. I spent a lot of time getting it together. Unfortunately it never quite came together. I was still working on the idea of having my own set-up. It really appealed to me. There were several other people who wanted to join, but somehow or another it always fell through. I wanted to have an organization that allowed the other directors to step in if one became sick or unable to work. Each fellow would make his own pictures, but they would each participate in some way in the profits of all the pictures.

It finally ended up with Garnett and I going together. Then I realized the story he wanted to do was so different than what I was thinking that I couldn't contribute anything. The same thing happened with him. He couldn't contribute much to what I wanted to do. I think it would have worked better for four directors instead of just us two. But it did give us the chance to get together and discuss our ideas. I think Victor Fleming was in on it at one time, along with Hawks, Garnett, and myself. That would have been a nice group.

———————

DOWD: Beyond the Forest was your next picture at Warner Bros. How did you obtain the property? Did you buy the novel, or did the studio assign it to you?

VIDOR: As a result of The Fountainhead they liked my work, and I liked them. I thought they gave me everything that I asked for during the production of The Fountainhead. I wanted to continue, but I only had a contract for that one picture. I think I moved away for a while. Then they came up with the story and the star for this picture. They were always more oriented towards the star. They bought the story for Bette Davis and then asked me to read it. I accepted the assignment, and this time I signed for two pictures instead of just one. I tried to change producers, but apparently they wanted me to continue with the same ones I had worked with on the last film.

Actually I had looked around at the stories the studio owned at the time, and wanted to make a different picture. I had seen the script for The African Queen, which they owned, and asked them to let me make it. They wanted me to do the Bette Davis picture. There were things about Beyond the Forest that I liked very much, but I wasn't as enthused about it as I have been on other films. However, I went along with it anyway.

The studio wanted Joseph Cotten, but they couldn't get a yes or no from him about the project. We were to leave for location and Warner Bros. sent a message to Myron Selznick, Joe's agent in New York, that read, "Tell Mr. Selznick to send a message back immediately about Cotten, or prepare to send a check for the $100,000 he owes Mr. Warner." Of course, Selznick called back. He had been stalling for two or three days, and would not give us an answer about Joe. Joe didn't want to play the part. I guess he thought it was too weak or something.

Then I sent a telegram to Joe because we were old friends. We used to go to football games together. Anyway, I sent a telegram to Joe and politely asked him to do the film. Joe called me later and said, "What do you mean that this script is the greatest story ever written?" I told him that I hadn't written any such thing. Later on I found out that the telegraph office at the studio was near Jack Warner's office, and that Warner himself saw most of the telegrams that were sent out. If he didn't like any of them, he would rewrite them. That's what he did to mine!

DOWD: So Warner was personally involved with the projects at his studio?

VIDOR: In that manner. He probably ran all the rushes. Sometimes I would go to him. In one case there was a point in Beyond the Forest where in both the book and the script, she doesn't want to have the baby. Joseph Cotten says, "You've got to have the baby, and we've got to stay married until you have the baby." She decides then to go to another town and have an abortion. She puts on some rough clothes so she won't be recognized, and Joseph Cotten sees her getting onto the bus.

I had a scene in the abortionist's office. I didn't put a sign up, but by the way the women sitting in the office looked, and the way the nurse spoke when she came to the door, you could tell that it was not a legitimate office. The nurse said, "The doctor will see you in a few minutes," and she was an absolute phony. The studio cut that sequence out. They went directly to the scene with the attorney where Joseph Cotten, having found her at the office, says, "Come on home."

It took the foundation right out of that scene. She continued to work on having the abortion on the way home, and had him look for a robe in the back of the car, and when he went back she jumped over the side of the hill and had the abortion that way. But it was determined by the Johnston Office, or the fears of the people at Warner, that the abortionist's office never be shown.

I'm amazed all those gangster pictures were made there. It just seemed so ridiculous that a studio that had made all those pictures about crime and violence would not let us put in that scene. Children wouldn't know what it was, but it just amazed me when I saw their lack of courage.

DOWD: Did you try to fight that?

VIDOR: No, I didn't. It was done after the picture was finished. I would usually go away and take a little trip after I had wrapped up production on a film. This decision was made between my final cutting of the picture and the release. I didn't even know about it until I saw it in the theatre.

DOWD: So you had no final cut, then?

VIDOR: No. It is one of the most difficult things to get.

DOWD: Do you remember any critics remarking about
this?

VIDOR: Oh, I remember some discussion on it. Somebody
asked me, "Why did you have it like that?" She did say that
she was going to get divorced and apparently going to a lawyer
could make quite a little scene, but it has none of the power
that originally was there with the other sequence. The whole
point was her trying to get rid of the child, and she finally
dies as a result of her efforts. The divorce had a little something to do with it, but the main thing was she wanted to get
rid of the child.

DOWD: Surely Warner had seen the script, hadn't he?

VIDOR: Yes, but he got scared later on, I guess. Always
during the production of a picture, I would do something unex-
pected. I would have the emotion of a particular scene go
beyond what was obvious in the script. I would just carry it
beyond, once I felt like doing it all the way. In another
instance, this offended Blanke. It would shock them a little bit
and then he'd go to Warner and he and Warner would decide on
cutting it out. I'm thinking of one love scene in Lightning
Strikes Twice particularly. They would gang up on you, just as
they did on the writer, who was Lenore Coffee.

            I think it was a nice part for Cotten, though,
who didn't get the girl in Duel in the Sun. He's more or less
that type that gets the short end of the deal, and as far as I
was concerned, he should play it. I was amazed at Bette Davis
and what she could do to enhance her acting performance by
using her eyes. She evidently did a lot of thinking about her
character.

            I mentioned while the picture was running the
other night that there used to be a painting I liked of a girl
walking down a street in New York. She's wearing yellow and
there's a very forceful style to her walk. I can't think of the
painter right now, but it was certainly contemporary. I took

some shots that were exactly like the style I had seen in this painting. I remember one scene when I saw it in the film, and that was where she was walking in just the exact way I had seen the girl in the painting walk. I had forgotten about that until I saw it in the film.

Bette Davis was full of ups and downs as an actress. She had a temperament that changed quickly from hot to cold all through the picture. She was pleasant to work with, though. She was cooperative and helpful. There was one point where she became very high-strung, and she was almost impossible to work with for two days, but once she got over this, it wasn't so bad.

DOWD: I bet they were memorable days.

VIDOR: One of them took place where she was throwing a bottle of medicine that had been prescribed for her character, and I thought her action looked a little weak. I insisted that we do it again, and she evidently took offense at what I was saying, although she eventually did it the way I wanted.

She did take direction rather well. Of course, I was not one to sit back and let the actors work everything out for themselves. I just didn't direct that way. We had a rough spot with that scene, but that didn't last long. I didn't like to act for my actors, I just told them the way I thought they should do it.

On the last day of production she said that she wouldn't work unless I was taken off the picture. Both the producer and Jack Warner said that I would not be taken off. They were perfectly happy and satisfied with my work. When they told her that, she said she wouldn't go to work unless they cancelled her contract. She had been with them for eighteen years. I suppose she had a twenty-year contract to begin with. They jumped at the chance to cancel her contract because they thought they were paying her more than she was worth. After they signed the release, we went back to work.

On the last day I had lunch in the executive dining room and Harry Warner told me the the story. I didn't know what had happened until she was already released from her contract. They didn't want to tell me because they thought I'd take it out on her or that it would affect our work together. As it turned out, she came up to me at dinner on that last night of work and told me how much she had enjoyed working with me, and that if I ever had any stories she could do, to please let her know. I guess she had forgotten the incident by then. She was preparing herself for freelancing and if I came up with a good story, she would like to play in it.

DOWD: How serious was that one incident during production?

VIDOR: She was very upset. Then when that last incident happened on the final day of production, no one had come around and said, "This is your last scene and your last day." The very next day after production finished, they came in and started moving all of the furniture out of her bungalow and back to the prop room. She told me later that no one had told her good-bye when she left. I think she would have behaved differently if she had known that it was her last day of production work before the picture was finished. That's typical of a big studio. When you're on the way out, you don't really expect it, and it comes as quite a shock.

DOWD: What did you think of her acting?

VIDOR: I thought it was very good. In fact, there was another scene where we had a problem. I had rehearsed a scene where she was dancing, and I think she was also embracing David Brian. He was rather large and I had the camera in such a way that you could just see about half of Bette Davis's face. You could just see her eyes as she turned. During the take they turned differently and I said, "Why don't you do it again so that we can see more of your face." She got upset and made an absolutely tremendous speech, one of the best performances I've seen.

At the end of her speech I said, "That's fine with me if you don't want to do it again. I'd just as soon not see your face." That worked quite well. There was a quiet hush over the stage the rest of that day, but I got the scene shot the way I wanted to eventually. It was almost like child psychology.

DOWD: You never really had big arguments with people that you worked with, did you?

VIDOR: No, I didn't. My voice isn't very loud. I used a megaphone sometimes when I had to, but I talked quietly most of the time. I preferred to address actors in a quiet, intimate voice rather than yelling through a megaphone beside the camera. If any dispute ever came up, I didn't like going into it right there in front of everybody else, so I would take them a few steps away and we would talk about it.

I always tried to treat them in a friendly manner. If they blew off, I always figured that I could blow off more than they could. If any of the actors said anything about walking off the stage, I always said that I could run pretty fast and beat them out the stage door. It would sort of take the wind out of their sails, and they'd realize that they couldn't go any further.

DOWD: Do you think a director is a democratic person?

VIDOR: No. They're looking for a father figure a lot of the time, and they find it easy to get mad at the father. Usually it's a love affair because he takes the place of the audience, the applause. It's the director's compliments and his praise that makes up for the lack of any response. The crew is not going to do all the applause at the end of every take because the director may not agree with them. If some big scene is done, sometimes they'll applaud at an obviously marvelous performance. I would go through each take by saying, "Gee, that was great. Could you do that again?"

I never tried to throw my weight around. It was too much of a family affair, as it were. Occasionally there were times when I had to step in, especially if one actor was getting a little out of hand. But I never liked to do it. I didn't like to encourage any animosity. I never let myself be dependent. I always thought that I could quit just as fast as they could. I can get along with someone even if another director is assigned to a picture I'm working on. That has been my attitude from the beginning. If I don't make pictures anymore, there are still a lot of other things to do.

DOWD: You didn't cast Bette Davis in that role, did you?

VIDOR: No. She was under contract to Warner Bros., and they bought the story for her.

DOWD: Who did the choreographing for the dance sequence?

VIDOR: It must have been Busby Berkeley. By that time his fame had peaked, but they brought him back now and then to do things.

DOWD: Didn't you also say that Billy Wilder really liked this picture?

VIDOR: Yes. Wilder copied the scene in The Crowd for his picture The Apartment and he asked me how many desks I had had. I used to hear quite a bit that he liked Beyond the Forest, but he also talked a lot about the ending and the symbolism for the last scene. He told me that he'd seen it three or four times.

DOWD: The ending is really beautiful.

VIDOR: I always tried to come up with something different. I wanted an episode for this film that would symbolize the whole story in a way, to pull all the essence of the story together and summarize in a few shots what the picture was all about. I'm sure this ending was not in the book. I certainly doubt that it was ever in the script.

DOWD: It's beautifully edited. It is like one of your silent films, except it has dialogue.

VIDOR: I think Rudi Fehr was the editor on this film. He was quite a good editor, and I think he went on to become a producer. I don't know whether he is still with Warner Bros., but he was a good, sensitive editor. We didn't plan any dialogue for that end sequence. I remembered when I saw the picture the last time that the scene in the house is the last place where there is dialogue. I knew when we were working on it that I could play the music up a little bit, as well as the sound effects. I knew from then on that I wasn't going to have any more dialogue because the rest of the sound and picture would give the right crescendo effect to end the film.

DOWD: The character of Rosa Moline seems to be an unusual heroine for you. Most of the women in your films are very generous and courageous.

VIDOR: Yes, this is true. It was out of my line, true, but it is more in line with films today. Naturally, you're supposed to be maturing. Look at Disney. For all of his films with children there's nobody more violent than Disney. In the Haunted House at Disneyland they have all kinds of gruesome things going on. You have to be flexible. You have to do things a little out of the ordinary once in a while. I suppose I was getting away from the small town ideal that I had started out with. I suppose I was adapting myself and trying not to be frozen or restricted in my work. I believe that to restrict yourself in the work that you do will only limit yourself as a person. This represented a bit of growth and development on my part. I might have been stupid enough in my first few pictures to put out a creed that I wouldn't make pictures with violence or sex.

DOWD: You did that?

VIDOR: Yes. Adela Rogers St. John probably wrote it, and I signed it. It was an advertisement, you know. It said that I wouldn't have anything to do with violence, and that I wouldn't have any emphasis on sex. Right after it came out in the paper I got arrested for playing dirty poker in a sixty-cent poker game. The headlines were pretty awful. It didn't go with this idealistic statement.

DOWD: Where were the locations for this film?

VIDOR: We looked for a small lumber town with a mill. I guess we finally wound up near Tahoe, and from there we heard of a town named Loyalton, which is up in the lumber country about thirty or thirty-five miles north of Reno. It was along the Truckee River. This town was exactly the kind of town that the story called for. The name in the story was not Loyalton, but I changed it in the script so that it would match perfectly with all the signs.

At that point we still didn't have Bette Davis. She was just finishing up another picture. For her scenes where she is supposed to be walking down the street, we went out to Chatsworth and at the same time we rented a railroad train and used the street right across from the station. For the other shots, we just used the backlot at Warner Bros.

DOWD: You didn't have a long-term contract at Warner then, did you?

VIDOR: No. My contract was only for two pictures.

DOWD: What was the "Milly" story that you had been working on during the previous few years?

VIDOR: One time I had a flat tire in Colorado and there was a man who had a gas station there who was a sort of leading man character that interested me. It was like a drug-store in a larger town, only in this small town, the gas station was where everyone came to meet people and talk. I thought of making it in Loyalton at one point. Then I had an idea to put across a character that looked the furthest from being a saint as possible, dressed in blue jeans and a checked shirt. This down-to-earth type of story had a lot of spiritual questions in it. The closest thing to it might be something like La Dolce Vita.

"Milly" was a story where a girl, who had been picked up in the mountains and brought into town, touches the lives of the people. Up until that time there was always some mystical character I wanted to show and I was trying to do it with a very down-to-earth character in the other films. I wanted to have a character that people would ask, "Where did she come from?" There would never be quite a full explanation as to who she was and where she came from. She comes into town, works at the gas station, and gradually she becomes the answer to everyone's problems. This story grows out of my psyche, the feminine idea, the feminine archetype. It's called the soul figure in Jungian philosophy. I could always tell the story, but when people read the scripts I wrote, they never quite got the idea.

DOWD: Did the inspiration for Milly come from someone specifically that you had met?

VIDOR: It came from a dream that I would have about someone. When I was actually working on the production of the picture at Allied Artists I was interviewing girls and I had a terrible time trying to find the right girl. Occasionally I'd see someone who might be the one, and I would pursue it, but I never quite found it. This model came from a dream I had of going into the depth of my own soul. In other words, what I lacked as a male for completeness in a soul, Milly could supply. This was an image of integration that this male lead character lacked, and this girl came along and integrated him, and then helped the other people in the town, and finally got on a bus and continued on her way.

DOWD: Did he stay there or did he return?

VIDOR: He returned to what he had been doing. It was a deeply felt thing, otherwise I would have given it up instead of sticking with it for ten years. I had good writers, and I spent a lot of money and time, and I almost got it going.

DOWD: Did you ever come close to finding the person to cast in the girl's role?

VIDOR: Yes. We almost had it. I was ready to take the closest one to the part for the production. I had a terrible time trying to find the person, though.

XIII

DOWD: Let's move on to Ruby Gentry. Why did you choose to do another picture with Jennifer Jones and David Selznick? Did you think it would be any different than working with them on Duel in the Sun?

VIDOR: Our disagreement on Duel in the Sun was forgotten. Neither David nor I had any animosity about it. He was the producer for that picture and on this picture he wasn't. That meant a lot right there. We just made an arrangement with him for Jennifer. I think the arrangement was that he would not come on the set, and he kept his word. I had the job of co-producing the film and directing, so I would not have any time to read any of Selznick's letters. He was in New York and had Jennifer with him when we were negotiating. One day he said that he wouldn't make any agreement to let us use her unless I agreed to answer all of his letters during the production of the film. The other producer, Joe Bernhard, said that I had to answer the letters if we were going to get Jennifer.

          So, I went home and sat down and answered all of the letters David had sent already. By the time I finished with them, David had answered all the questions himself. Then there was nothing to write about. For example, sometimes he would suggest having some dress designer like Jean Louis, and then three letters later he would say that I shouldn't use someone like Jean Louis. The same would go for actors, photographers, and all kinds of positions and details. Finally there was a point where there was nothing more for me to write about. I actually was prepared to send him one short letter, but I didn't mail it.

There's a book out now called <u>Memo From David O. Selznick</u> that has a lot of his letters gathered together. I have a copy of it, I think. They didn't even come close to using all the ones that he wrote. They would have needed twenty volumes.

DOWD: What was the story about Jennifer and the costume?

VIDOR: Here she was playing a swamp girl in blue jeans, although she eventually brings herself up in the world later on. David was going through the usual pain that he went through for every picture he did where he considered every dress designer in New York at one time or another. He thought that we must have the best to do her clothes for this picture. That is one of the traditions of Old Hollywood. She had some costumes made in New York and arrived with them when we started production. We made some tests with them and they didn't look very good, so we just used the dressmaker that we had working on the other clothes for the picture. Most of the dresses that she had brought from New York were never used in the film.

DOWD: This was the second film you made with Joseph Bernhard. He also produced <u>Japanese War Bride</u>. <u>Ruby Gentry</u> was distributed by 20th Century-Fox, although it was made as an independent production.

VIDOR: Right. Spyros Skouras was the head of the studio at that time, and his son put up twenty-five percent of the money for the film. That was hard money to get. The hardest part of the deal was to get the initial capital. Once you had the initial money and a few stars interested in it, the rest of the money was easy to raise. After Skouras's son put up that first sum, the connection with Fox was made. I think Bernhard was actually working for Fox at the time, though I'm not sure.

DOWD: Was it Selznick or Bernhard who came to you with the idea for the story?

VIDOR: I was brought in a week late on <u>Japanese War Bride,</u> and I had not prepared for the story at all. There was a young producer on that film named Anson Bond who also helped tremendously. Anyway, after that picture was finished, Bernhard and I continued to work together, and we looked for more stories to do. I liked Ruby Gentry because I thought it was good, brief, well-told, and generally good motion picture material. I was somewhat in the mood for a Tennessee Williams type of story. Together Bernhard and I had a partnership and went out and bought it.

DOWD: And then you interested Selznick in it afterwards?

VIDOR: Yes. I think the trick to that kind of deal is that you have to have a name star ready to go. But usually those deals include the approval by the bank or by the distributing organization. Although we made tests of lesser known people, Jennifer was really the one for the part. We thought she would be a good addition to the film and had box-office appeal, so we went to Selznick. I thought that we could do it, and he thought that I was a good director for Jennifer.

DOWD: What method did you use to direct her this time?

VIDOR: I thought that she had a very expressive face. As I said before, I think her thoughts flow across her face with great rapidity and a definite quality. I had known this for a long time. The key was to use this quality as much as possible. This is really evident in her other picture, The Song of Bernadette. I think this method proved successful in Duel in the Sun, and it was well worth the effort.

As in Duel in the Sun, I used the same type of storytelling technique to get her into the mood of the shot. She must know what she's thinking about and what she's feeling. She takes all this in and lets it build up inside her and then it comes out in her performance. In some of the other pictures she made you could see the uncertainty and insecurity showing on her face because she had not been adequately prepared. It shows in the form of a quivering in her lips and a strange tense expression on her face. That simply means that she hadn't been caressed with the story sufficiently. That, I suppose, is the reason that after we made this picture,

David was always trying to get stories I would like that would suit Jennifer as well so that we could work together again. Jennifer was happy with my work and I was happy with hers.

DOWD: In the opening of the film there is a familiar white house, actually located right down the road here in Paso Robles, even though the story was supposed to be shot in North Carolina. It was shot right here on your ranch, wasn't it?

VIDOR: Quite a bit of it was shot here. They didn't have the money to take everyone down to North Carolina. Once we started to add up all the costs of doing it down there, it got to be way too much. Then we started to figure out how we could do it around here. We have moss in this neighborhood, you know, and that helped sell the idea of doing it here. I think I only shot about two or three days right here on the ranch, and then we went over to Morro Bay with the fishing boat, and we did the scenes at the beach in Pismo Beach. That is the only beach that looks like a Southern beach in all of California. Now that I think of it, we did some of the deer hunting scenes on my ranch also.

DOWD: Last night as we were watching the film you mentioned that Karl Malden was one of your favorite actors. Why?

VIDOR: He is not like an actor. He's like a real person. He seems so real, so believable. He has a crooked nose and he's never tried to straighten it out. He is a fine actor and all the things he does and feels as an actor look real on the screen. He makes me believe they are happening. He is a loyal friend, and he is easy to get along with. I am always happy when I watch him in a picture. When I see him in this picture I'm even happier because of what he was able to contribute to the film.

DOWD: You used a narrator for this film.

VIDOR: Yes, the narrator was the doctor. Then I had another narration with Malden. That was the idea, I think, in the story. The doctor from the North originally had more perspective on the story. I think we kept that from the original story, but it might have gotten a little lost in the later versions. He was the one who could look at the whole thing with some distance. You see, it starts off with the shot of Jennifer after the whole story has taken place. The first scene is actually after the story is over. At that time the use of narration over a scene like that was very popular. It seemed good for this story, too. Then I thought it was a free idea, free use of film. I liked to feel free to do anything I wanted if there was a reason for it. To me it was all right to leave out the narration there, and just stick with one narrator.

DOWD: Did you choose Charlton Heston?

VIDOR: Yes. He had just done one of DeMille's pictures, but his salary at that time was not high. I think it was somewhere around $50,000.

DOWD: How do you feel about the pace of this film?

VIDOR: One thing I learned from silent pictures was that even when you were shooting a scene that you thought was fast, when you got it up on the big screen it would sometimes take forever. The thing you have to learn is how fast you can move people and still not sacrifice anything. There is something that happens to pictures and sounds when you put them on a big screen that makes them slow down. I was very much aware of this feeling, so I may have been pushing things just a little bit.

DOWD: The ending is very abrupt and definite. It is a picture without much hope.

VIDOR: No. For that reason I suppose it is more in the contemporary mood. It is an anti-hero type of film. While it was going along, I'd forgotten the ending and I was wondering how to end such a story -- how do you end characters that react toward each other the way these do, and how does the story wind up? We ended it the only way I could think of. The ending came along and I said at the time that that was the natural way to end it. She was supposed to be committing all of these sins, but nevertheless there was no reason to bump her off. It seemed to have a good ending in my opinion. It seemed to have the ending that the previous scenes pointed to.

254

DOWD: There seems to be a certain affinity between the character Jennifer plays here and the one she played in Duel in the Sun, and even the woman in Beyond the Forest. There is a certain common self-destructiveness in these characters. It is rather unlike the other women in your films. Was that something that you were doing deliberately?

VIDOR: I don't know. I'm not too conscious of what was going on there except that when you look back you see that these are true girls. The film we ran before, The Texas Rangers, has a girl who is the stereotypical good, sweet, pretty, loving, romantically inclined young girl. But that really is a stereotype. I think I was trying to get away from the nice image and more into a realistic type of woman and the character that a lot of women would like to play. I presume I was trying to get more vitality into the women.

          I was on the edge of my seat watching The Texas Rangers thinking, I hope this doesn't get too maudlin and sweet. Jean Parker sort of brought it off in a way, though. It's nothing that a woman like Jennifer, or Bette Davis would be eager to play.

DOWD: Did Ruby Gentry somehow conform to the image that Selznick thought she would be on the screen?

VIDOR: I believe so. He saw her as a femme fatale and a terrific sex image. However, she has a childlike quality about her, very insecure and childish at heart. The funny thing during Duel in the Sun was that the microphone actually picked up Selznick's hard breathing when he was standing off to the side of the camera as he watched her. He liked this part for her, and he thought she should be built up for all of the sex and mystery that she could have. The Song of Bernadette had none of that and I remember she was good in it. But that was just the way Selznick guided her career. There are a lot of producers that don't earn the name of producer, but you certainly can't say that about him. He was a very smart fellow about a lot of things, and casting was one of them.

DOWD: You had money troubles on this film, didn't you?

VIDOR: When you went out on a restricted budget to make a film, you couldn't afford any delays. Jennifer broke her hand in the scene where she is supposed to be fighting with Charlton. The normal budget in those days was around $800,000 or more, and ours was budgeted at $525,000. We had to make the same picture -- the same costumes, the same sound, the same camerawork -- for $300,000 less. If you lost a day or two, especially toward the end, you'd start to run out of money quickly.

There were a few scenes we weren't able to do. One had to do with a funeral and the other was something about waves dashing against the rocks. There simply was no more money left. I think I was able to do a few quick shots that could be used in the editing later on, but it is very hard to shoot that way. With actors to pay and a budget like that, you know that as soon as the money runs out you aren't going to have them around anymore. That was why I had to think of a few shots we could use without any of the actors. I remember shooting the scene where the wreath is thrown into the hearse, and we cut from that to the shot we had done before of all the people. We couldn't afford to pay them overtime. Sometimes it is just as good that way. I went down and shot the scene with the waves dashing against the rocks myself. I used an old Eyemo camera that I have had since 1928.

DOWD: Who was Al Brown?

VIDOR: I had a fellow working for me at the ranch. He was my foreman. He was famous for always telling everybody what to do. I used to have to get him out of the way whenever the county agricultural inspector came around because he'd tell him what to do. He was just an old cowboy, and I never thought he knew anything about movies. He had never seen a film being shot, so I didn't think he would bother anyone by telling them what to do. But by God, he did!

We were there setting up a camera in one place and he said, "I think it would be better to put it over there. It would be a nicer shot." I'm sure he never saw a movie in his life, and had probably no interest in films whatsoever. Later on I caught him telling the sound man that he wasn't doing something right. It got to be pretty funny after a while.

DOWD: How did you get started on your next film, <u>Man Without a Star</u>?

VIDOR: My agent called me up one day and asked me to come down to Universal to talk with him. I went down there and we met with Borden Chase, who was the writer, and they told me that they had negotiated to sign Kirk Douglas for four weeks. This was about three weeks before the picture was supposed to start shooting. They asked me if I could shoot the film in four weeks. I told them that if anybody could, I was the one. It turned out that they had managed to get Douglas to squeeze in this film between two others. The script they had started to work with was unacceptable to them, so we had script conferences each day. We had to begin and end the picture on certain predetermined dates. I think the original schedule called for a production time of twenty-four days for principal photography. If I remember correctly, we were able to do it in twenty-two days. We shot the entire picture at the studio, except for a few shots that we did at Lasky Mesa, which was only about an hour away from the studio. It was out in what is now Thousand Oaks. That was the same area where we shot <u>Duel in the Sun.</u>

DOWD: In an interview I had with Borden Chase he says that you told him that you were going to make this film for a nickel's worth of cakes all in the studio backlot. What was it like to work with him?

VIDOR: He was a nice fellow and a rather good Western writer, but he had a habit of acting tough. I don't think he was very tough at all. However, he was able to write tough stories, and they were very good.

     Aaron Rosenberg was the producer. He used to be a star lineman on the USC football team. He would play an entire game, and then come off the field looking all beat up. He was one of my idols as a football player. After he got out of school, he went to Universal and became a producer. It was an interesting experience working with him in my own field.

When all of us would sit around together -- Douglas, Chase, Rosenberg, and myself -- they would only use four-letter words. I guess they were trying to put the toughness and roughness of the script into themselves somehow. One Sunday we were working on the script, and the maid at my house came in and said that she was going to quit because we were all so loud and foul-mouthed. I moved them to another part of the house and we continued. But even before I could move them they began to swear again. I suppose they just wanted to get into the mood of the film.

DOWD: The script moves quickly and the dialogue is very good.

VIDOR: Yes, I think so. In order to have a film go well for a director, every scene must be perfectly in tune with what the director thinks it should be. Every scene should be the way you dreamed about it. This film was supposed to have a stampede at the end, but we couldn't get all the cattle. Most ranchers will not let you stampede their animals because it runs off too much of their weight. I understood this, being a rancher myself. I had to leave to go and start War and Peace, so I let a second unit director do this scene. Unfortunately, it did not come out exactly the way I wanted it. I felt disappointed and let down when I finally saw it, but it seems to look all right now. As long as a viewer never knows what the director was dreaming about when he planned the movie, it comes out looking all right. That's the way it is with all films.

DOWD: What was it like directing Kirk Douglas? When we watched the film you commented about the scene where he does the monologue about a star. I think you said that you didn't like the way he smiled.

VIDOR: An actor will decide on how he is going to play a character, and it struck me that he was smiling just a little too much. It was a little bit of a grin, as he is apt to do. It was as if he were taking everything very lightly. I didn't really detect that through the shooting, or else I would have asked him to do it differently.

I think at this time he was forming his own production company, and he was planning on being his own director. In looking back on it, I'm glad we didn't get into a big argument about the way he was doing his part. It might not have been made if he thought he could do it with his own company. Even as we were shooting, he was moving into the director's area of work, and he started to play around with the planning I had done for some of the scenes. He began to tell me where to put the camera and I eventually had to nail him down a couple of times.

DOWD: Isn't it difficult for a director to work with a star like that?

VIDOR: Certainly. You can take it for a short while, but then you start to see that it is hurting the picture. You just can't go around in an unhappy mood, or feeling that you're constantly frustrated. You start to come home, wake up early in the morning and say to yourself, "I'm going to put an end to this crap today!" That was what I did. I let him have it. I won't use the words that I used then, but it got the message across.

It wasn't a negative experience, either. That night when I got home, I found a magnum of champagne waiting for me. He realized what he had done, and he was apologizing for it. The scene that we were shooting when this happened goes by very smoothly now, and I couldn't tell that we had a big argument during that time.

All in all, it turned out pretty well. There are some shots in the film that I find very smooth. Sometimes when you shoot a scene, you use a special technique to make the visuals work. Looking back at the film today, I can hardly tell what types of tricks we used to make different shots. It really looks that smooth. That's the mark of a good film.

The only thing that stands out to me today is the scenes I didn't shoot. Those stand out very clearly to me. There's one shot where the train is shown. It's like something out of The Great Train Robbery. It is just a stationary shot with a train going from one side of the screen to the other. Maybe in my teens I would have done such a shot, but you learn to either pan with it, or you get a shot where it's closing in on the camera. In other words, the camera should be in the same mood that the scene is in. Here's a big train rushing by and the camera is absolutely static, unable to move. I'll bet a thousand dollars I had nothing to do with that shot. It must be either a stock shot or something that someone else shot after I left.

DOWD: There are some very nice scenes with Douglas, especially in the bar where the kid comes in dressed up in his new outfit and he says, "What's that? I'll kill it with a stick!" Were scenes like those improvised?

VIDOR: I think so. Douglas's problem was that he should have been more human. Douglas has to fight the same thing Yul Brynner has to fight. They both have these images as strong, macho men. Sometimes they have to change this. They want to be strong all the time, but now and then they have to be weak.

DOWD: I think those moments come across well in this film. You can see that aspect of his character.

VIDOR: Yes, I agree. That was what we were trying for.

DOWD: Chase has a very nice comment in the interview. He talks about the scene where Douglas is dancing with the banjo. He said that that was pure King Vidor:

> Again, I had written the words and all that sort of thing, but I did not dream of having him dance with the banjo. That was a special touch. He came up with these wonderful touches, and you can tell that this film was influenced by a wonderful director.

I think that's a nice comment.

VIDOR: Yes. The fact that he wraps his arms around the girl and then keeps his banjo looks nice to me even now. I don't know where that idea came from. But again, it was part of my whole attitude. I wanted to avoid the usual, the ordinary. I try to train myself to think in terms of the unusual. If I am not doing that, I am doing something any other director can come along and do.

DOWD: You must have had a good cameraman on this. The lighting was very nice, and as you said, the bar scene was done very well.

VIDOR: The fellow was a very good cameraman. His name was Russell Metty. These were the days of the big Technicolor equipment. It really helped to have a photographer who knew what he was doing. This all ties in with the directing style again. When you have a cameraman like this, you can concentrate on doing the special touches that make the film different. For example, during that banjo scene, I could just tell the cameraman what I wanted, and I could leave the rest to him. Then I concentrated completely on directing the scene. It gives that extra edge to your work.

It really gets back to your basic approach to making films and directing them. For example, in shooting the scene with Douglas I could have just read the script and told the actors what the script said. But I always felt that I could put something different into what the script called for. The obvious thing is to have him put the banjo down and start dancing without it.

Kirk worried about doing this scene during the entire production. He worked himself up to the point where he came to me and said that it couldn't be done the way I wanted to do it. I just told him that he shouldn't be worried about it. He'd practice and practice, but he still was very uneasy about it. So, when it came time to do the scene, we used all kinds of special techniques to help get the effect we wanted.

There was a part where he fires the gun. We photographed that scene over and over again so that it was really done in short bits. We photographed him pulling the gun out time and time again, almost as if he were practicing on-camera, but it came out looking fine when we edited. We shot other portions with different techniques. In one scene he had to flip the gun over his shoulder and catch it.

With those short shots you could do it in reverse, if it happened to be easier that way, or you could do it over and over again, or you could do it in such short segments that it never really was very hard for any particular segment.

Luckily, I knew enough about camera technique, and had a first-rate cameraman, so that I could get Kirk through that difficult scene without it becoming a nightmare to shoot. I'm sure I did a lot of stuff in reverse for that scene. But it looks good. All things considered, I think it is a pretty good film for a schedule of twenty-two days.

DOWD: It really is a wonderful picture. I suppose it could have come off like a big cliché, with a bunch of cliché characters like the whore with a heart of gold or something like that. Douglas is not an actor I like very much, but in this film he comes across very well, and he is successful in his role.

VIDOR: That is a nice compliment, because it shows what part a director can play in keeping the people in a picture believable. When you get into a Western there is probably a great tendency to get into the usual clichés. My job from the beginning was to make the people convincing, and not just to have them follow some stereotype.

I have to admit, though, that everyone helped a great deal on this film. For me, this was just a straight salary job. I think the picture meant a great deal more to Douglas than it did to me. It turned out to be a financially successful picture, too. I remember when I went to Italy to work on War and Peace, Man Without a Star was playing in Rome. When I drove along the street, I could see young children practicing twirling their guns like Douglas did in the film. They practiced the quick draw and all the other cowboy moves.

DOWD: Borden Chase did a lot of research for this script. Even though he was born in Brooklyn, he was obviously a fan of the Old West and he knew a lot about it. The first bunkhouse scene where they are all having lunch is a good scene.

VIDOR: It looks real, doesn't it?

DOWD: Yes. That must have been your doing also. They are sitting and chatting over lunch and you can hear these two guys killing one another.

VIDOR: Yes, it's a little different. Although you can hear these two guys, you never get to go outside and see them.

DOWD: How did you feel about directing Westerns? You did about six or seven of them at least.

VIDOR: I liked doing them very much. They open up all kinds of possibilities photographically.

XIV

DOWD: How did you get interested in doing <u>War and</u>
<u>Peace?</u>

VIDOR: I got a phone call from Dino de Laurentiis in
New York asking me if I would like to do the picture and I
said, "I would rather do that than anything else I know of." At
the time Mike Todd was also working on a film from the story,
and he was going to produce it in Yugoslavia. I believe he had
Fred Zinnemann ready to direct it. I think Selznick entered the
race at one time, but Dino beat all of them. He went ahead
and sent me a script. It was 506 pages long. I read it and he
started to talk about the cast, and I got hold of Ray Stark's
agent and told him to be ready to discuss the deal. They were
talking about who would play in it, and they talked about Jean
Simmons and her husband, Stewart Granger. He was mentioned
for the part of André. One time we went up to their house on
Mulholland Drive and talked to them about the picture.

          I didn't like the script very much. I told Dino
not to let anyone else look at the script then. It would be too
difficult to explain in detail what was wrong with it, but it
was very disconnected and disjointed. The origin of the script
was when Mike Todd got the idea to do the story and went to
de Laurentiis and Carlo Ponti to get some financial backing.
After they talked to Todd, they decided that it would be a
good story for them to do, since they figured it was in the
public domain.

          After a while Ponti dropped out, but de
Laurentiis figured that the way to beat everyone else to the
punch was to have a script put together as quickly as possible.
He employed about five or six Italian writers to work on it. He
assigned each of them a segment of the book and just pieced

all the segments together when they were finished. It only took them about two or three weeks. Then he got six translators to work on translating the script into English. He gave them only a weekend to do it in. It was a terrible translation.

With that script he flew into New York and on Monday morning went into the Paramount office and talked to the man in charge of foreign production. He laid this big script down on the desk and said that he was ready to go with the production of War and Peace. About a year and a half later, near the end of the production of the film, I talked to the man in charge of production for the studio and asked him, "Did you ever read the script?" He said no. He said the thickness of the script impressed him. That was all that it took.

Well, I agreed to do the film, but I told them that I would be in Rome in no less than six weeks. That was how long it would take to get my affairs in California settled. We were selling our home then. I set a goal for myself of reading fifty pages of the book per day, with careful studying of the sections and lots of note-taking. What I wanted was lots of time to study the book. I decided to take a ship over there to give me more time. I brought along a production man and an art director to help along the way. The production man was Arthur Fellows and the art director from Paramount was Franz Bachelin. By the time we got to Naples I had a complete outline of how I saw the script.

De Laurentiis was in California at this time. I had talked to him and he finally admitted that the Italian writers he had used were not good. We talked about getting another writer and we settled on an Englishman by the name of R.C. Sheriff, who had written some very successful plays. He was supposed to have been working on another outline for the story while I was doing mine. When I arrived in Rome I was told that Sheriff would not be there. He had decided that he did not want to leave his farm in England. That was the end of that.

DOWD: What was de Laurentiis like to work with?

VIDOR: He is very aggressive. He'll jump on a plane and fly anywhere at any time to do something. You really have to slow him down a bit. He reminded me of the better American producers in that he aimed big, and his sights were always high. He wanted to make a very fine film. American producers will promise you anything and agree to whatever you want whether they can come through with it or not. But he had very high artistic aims, and I admire him for that. He was a hard man to pin down, but he had lots of energy and ambition.

DOWD: Do you remember the first time you read War and Peace?

VIDOR: I read about 200 pages at the time Selznick talked to me about it. I read enough to know that it was a great book. I spent a great deal of time trying to straighten out the characters and their relationships. I finally worked with a book that had all of the characters' relationships written out in a little pamphlet that came with it.

DOWD: What attracted you to it?

VIDOR: I think it is one of the greatest novels of all time. The strange thing about it is that the character Pierre was the same character that I had been trying to put on the screen through many of my own films. My first full length film, The Turn in the Road, had a character who spent the entire story searching for truth. That was the same theme Pierre had in this story. He was motivated by certain tragedies, and particularly the tragedy of Napoleon overrunning Russia. Pierre was a man who was really searching for a truth. That is always my favorite theme and I was working on a new film, also called Turn in the Road that was modelled somewhat after the first film, and it also had the same type of theme. I had also been working on the "Milly" story for years, and it was very similar in its search for truth. It was very easy for me to identify with Pierre and Tolstoy. Many times during those months I thought about how well we would have gotten along.

DOWD: Did you feel a tremendous amount of pressure in writing the script?

VIDOR: Yes. It was still in the running with Mike Todd's and Selznick's productions. But when we started to shoot with Audrey Hepburn, they bowed out of the race. The fact of the matter was that de Laurentiis had an Italian director all primed to go and shoot some of the winter scenes when I came in. I had to start shooting with almost a quarter of the script unfinished. But at least we knew where we were going because we still had my outline to work from.

What happened was this: When I found out that Sheriff was not going to work on the film, we had to get writers immediately. We called the Paramount office in London and they sent down two writers, Bridget Boland and Robert Westerby. They hadn't worked together before, but the two of them were sent down. I had a very clear idea of the things in the book that we couldn't put into the film. It seemed to me to be a very clear outline. I gave them this outline and they proceeded to do a rough script. Four weeks later we finished the first draft.

At the same time de Laurentiis called and told me that he'd heard from Audrey Hepburn's agent and he said that I had to go right to St. Moritz and talk to her. He had heard that the film she was going to do had been cancelled. It was arranged later that they would drive down into Italy a short way and I would meet them in a small village, where I could tell her what I had planned.

The village we met in was very small. It had only one hotel. I met them near the border and we got a room overlooking the town square. The people in the town had heard that she was going to be there, and they gathered in the square. Mel Ferrer, her husband at that time, sat on one twin bed, and Audrey sat on the other. De Laurentiis was there, and as soon as we were settled, he told me, "Go ahead." He couldn't understand English too well, but he pointed to me and managed to say something like, "King, tell them." I had an outline and I had rehearsed on the automobile ride, telling the story to Dino's secretary in the back seat. In the hotel room I realized that I had only one chance. There had to be no hesitation and it had to be a great performance.

DOWD: Were they antagonistic?

VIDOR:　　　No. They wanted to be convinced that it was going to be a great film. By then we wanted Mel Ferrer for the part of André. I thought he was perfect for it. Luckily, they were married at that time and we hoped that would have some positive effect. But anyway, I walked up and down at the foot of the two twin beds and told them the story. I don't think de Laurentiis stayed in the room. I think he left and came back quite a bit later. I was using notes I had stashed in my pocket so that I could refer to them if I got lost. I really gave a performance in telling the story. It must have taken two hours because I told them as much of the story as possible. When I finally finished, they applauded. One of them remarked, "You can really tell a story when you want to!"

We had to catch a plane very quickly, and that meant a very fast drive into Milan. We all went downstairs and got into the cars. Audrey and Mel and their agent were in the rear car, and I was in the front car with Dino. We started off at eighty miles an hour, and every so often the cars would stop so that de Laurentiis could switch cars to do some further bargaining. This went on at speeds much too fast for the roads we were on, but by the time we got to Milan, the deal was set.

Suddenly we found ourselves with a start date, and a tremendous amount of production work to do before we could start to shoot. We had to get costumes and locations and all the art work had to be done. Fortunately, we had a great crew working for us, and that work went fairly smooth. If we had stayed with the art director from Paramount I'd started out with, I think we would have been in big trouble. Fortunately, we had a great art director from Italy who did a splendid job. His name was Mario Chiari.

After this step, de Laurentiis wanted to get another big-name writer to work on the script some more. He made a deal with Irwin Shaw. I wasn't too enthused about the deal, but I did make an agreement that we must work together, because we didn't have time for Shaw to go back to Paris, where he lived, and work on the script himself. He said he would come to Rome, which he did not do. He did exactly what I didn't want him to do. He went to Paris, and sent the material down to us as he finished it. He said he would stick to the outline that had been done already, but he didn't even do that.

With all the experience I had in trying to save time on the script and get it right, instead of relying on rewriting to save it, I was dominated by de Laurentiis and Shaw, and the script came to be much to my disliking. We got Shaw down from Paris a few times and I told him my objections. I don't know whether he agreed or not, but as the time grew closer to the shooting date, we didn't have a script that I wanted to shoot. I had to go ahead with making all the location decisions, designing sets, and working on the script that the two English writers had done. We made all the decisions on the basis of that script. That way there would be less confusion as to what we were following as a guideline for the production.

We finally got an Italian novelist named Mario Soldati. He had lived in America and his English was very good. He and I worked very hard and fast and I found him very flexible and agreeable. We started to write the final script. But we were only about halfway through the script when the day came that Audrey was supposed to start work on the film. We delayed it for two more weeks. We were still a quarter of the script shy of being finished, but I had plenty of material to shoot then, so we started. I started filming and Soldati finished up the script.

To cast Pierre, I had gone to London to do some interviews. On the way I stopped in Paris and talked to Peter Ustinov. I wasn't sure how he would fit in with Audrey, so I went on to London to see Paul Scofield in a play. He wasn't absolutely right, although he was a great actor. We came back and by then we had a cable from de Laurentiis in Hollywood saying that he liked Henry Fonda. I think we voted for Scofield, but he was committed to some other engagement. I wasn't staunchly in favor of Ustinov, a fact which I've regretted many times since, because I think he would have been ideal, and would have given the film much more stature. Anyway, de Laurentiis cabled to say that he had made the deal with Fonda, so that was that.

Usually in shooting a picture you let the second unit director shoot all the battle scenes. I reversed this process. Soldati, who was also a very good director, did some of the scenes with the cast, and I did some of the battle scenes myself. I was not quite satisfied with some of the exaggeration he did. He seemed to be too Italian, filled with exaggeration.

This was the problem: De Laurentiis's English was not very good at all, and I had to have an interpreter assist me whenever there was a disagreement about something. We would have great arguments between myself, Soldati and de Laurentiis. Usually the two Italians would start screaming at each other about what they thought should be done, and I would be left completely out of it. They would speak so quickly that the interpreter could never keep up with them. They would yell at the top of their lungs, and it made the room feel like it was about to explode. I would have to start screaming in English to get them to stop. When I would get a little bit angry and lose my temper, Dino would say, "That's the King I like. I thought you were sick."

Anyway, we eliminated some of the scenes Soldati did, but he was a big help during the production. His work helped me to spend most of my time directing Audrey. He didn't work with Audrey or Fonda, but he helped me quite a bit.

DOWD: Were you disappointed with Fonda?

VIDOR: I don't know whether he read the book or not, but I don't think he is the type of actor that would devote his life to a search for the truth. I don't think this philosophical search interests him at all. One time I was talking to him about a scene, and I was quoting Tolstoy from the book. When I got through with this he said, "I've been listening to you for an hour, and I still don't know what the hell you're talking about." I think more depth could have been helpful in his acting. It would have helped if he were really groping for the truth.

DOWD: How did you cope with something like that?

VIDOR: You just have to get the scene another way. Someone asked me once if I could make a book out of all the things we had to go through to make the film. My thoughts were that I could write a book about any one particular day that we had to go through. It was constantly one obstacle after another.

DOWD: Did you write on this?

VIDOR: No, unfortunately I never did. I did write some stuff afterwards about that period, and I have a complete diary in my memory about it. I have written pretty extensively to come out with a new edition of <u>A Tree is a Tree</u>, and this could fill a large portion of it. I remember everything about it because it was so difficult just to get the simplest scene.

DOWD: Tell me about how you shot the Battle of Bordino.

VIDOR: That was one of the big tragedies in my life. This was really something I wish I had a chance to do again. I laid out the battle scene and I had a wonderful idea to have a small valley filled with 5,000 or 6,000 troops, 800 cavalry and 500 foot soldiers. I just wanted to fill a valley with all of these men. I found a perfect location for it, and I went ahead and put up stakes where the cameras would go.

About two days before we were going to shoot this scene, de Laurentiis came and said that we had to shoot it on the cavalry post itself because it had to be shot at a certain time and date no further than one hour from Rome. I had taken all that time to lay the scene out at my location, and I began to cry, but he still insisted that we do it at the post. He had bribed the general by saying that we would use his mistress in some of the studio scenes or something. It ended up that we had to shoot it on this military reservation. Five thousand troops were simply swallowed up by it. It would have been so much better in the original location. It lacked all of the feeling that I had planned for it.

DOWD: Could you have refused?

VIDOR: He probably would have had someone else shoot it if I refused. If I did it over again, today, I would know how to handle it. Whether I would refuse to do it or not, I would pretend to refuse. I would just quit, and that is the only thing producers understand. I would hold out until the last minute.

DOWD: How many cameras did you have?

VIDOR: Only three.

DOWD: How long did it take for the opening shot?

VIDOR: It took about three or four hours for that shot. We had about 6,000 men the first day, 3,000 the second, and 1,500 men on the third day.

DOWD: You had shot battle scenes before, hadn't you?

VIDOR: Yes.

DOWD: What kind of effect were you looking for?

VIDOR: My feelings were that instead of being carried away with the details of the scene, I would concentrate on the motion. Most people think you have to pay all kinds of attention to uniforms and all that, but really all the audience recognizes is motion. You have to have the men moving in the right direction. That way you can tell immediately which group is the French Army and which group is the Russian Army. I insisted that all of Napoleon's directions and movements were from left to right. The Russians all moved from right to left.

DOWD: This was at the height of Anita Ekberg's popularity. How did she become involved in the film?

VIDOR: We had already cast someone else in the part, and in fact we had already made up all of her costumes. At the last minute she decided she couldn't do it. We were confronted with this decision of who we would get to do the part. The part called for the actress to speak English very rapidly. Anita was still learning English at this time. She was shipped in quickly from Hollywood or somewhere. The clothes were all readjusted to fit her figure and we started with her in the part. She still had the problem with not being able to speak English as quickly as the part called for. I had to push her and push her to get it as fast as possible. After the picture was finished, we got another actress to dub her lines in. The dubbing job was so good that even she didn't realize that we had dubbed in her lines until someone told her.

DOWD: Is there a story about Clare Boothe Luce that involves this film?

VIDOR: Yes. One afternoon I was shooting and we had about 600 extras. De Laurentiis came onto the set and said he had gotten a call from Clare Booth Luce who wanted me to be in her office by five o'clock that afternoon. So, we had to quit and let everybody go home. We went over to the American Embassy and she asked him, "Mr. de Laurentiis, how many workers do you have that come from the Communist agency?" He said, "A few, but not many." She said, "Twenty percent of your workers come from the agency." She had all of these figures, and he got angry and he tried to get some of the other people we brought with us to defend him, but they didn't know anything about it. She had talked to some labor leader who had found out all of these figures. Her main objective was that any project with American dollars behind it would not be associated with the Communists.

DOWD: How did this affect you?

VIDOR: Actually it was really between her and de Laurentiis. They just exploded at each other. I checked the production about two weeks later, and I found that the actual number of people who were affiliated with the Communist party was fewer than ten percent.

DOWD: How long were you in Italy?

VIDOR: I was there about a year and a half. Of that, about six months were spent in actual shooting.

DOWD: How did the editing go?

VIDOR: It went well. I liked the table equipment they had there. The first running time of the picture was around six or eight hours. The first release print was three hours and forty minutes. It is such a production that there should be one show of it per night. There was no reason to cut it down just so you could show it three or four times per night so that the theatres could make more money.

DOWD: What scenes did they take out?

VIDOR: I have a list somewhere. The approach they took was to cut away whatever they could without making any noticeable jumps in the soundtrack, which was already complete. They didn't even have the courtesy to call me up and tell me that they were going to do some cutting on it. They didn't want to spend any more money in making a new score for the picture so that the editing could be done more judiciously. It was another painful thing to have to go through, especially after having the same thing happen to my other films as well.

––––––––––

DOWD: After doing War and Peace why did you choose to do a big film in Europe again?

VIDOR: As soon as I came back from War and Peace, I had a call from MGM. They wanted me to direct Ben Hur. I considered it for a day or two, and then strangely enough, I turned it down. I turned it down because I wanted to stay in California. Then, along came the offer to do Solomon and Sheba. They weren't going to start that film for at least a year. I had turned down Ben Hur for the second time in my life. First I had turned down the silent version, and now I had turned down the big screen version. However, I accepted Solomon and Sheba because they were going to work on the script here. I thought this would be a perfect chance to get the script in shape before we began, but they kept deferring my participation in the script.

     I didn't have a good script before we went to Europe. I wrote a letter to United Artists protesting how bad the script was. They said, "Well, you have lots of time." I took Arthur Hornblow Jr. along so that I wouldn't be doing anything behind his back. As a result, he resigned from the picture. Edward Small participated in the script some, but very little. Very quickly after that I had to go to Spain to approve the locations and sets so that we could start building. We were supposed to make the picture in Italy, but at that time <u>Ben Hur</u> was occupying all of the stages in Rome and we had to move to Spain. I sent a cable to Small saying that unless I got a writer as I had been promised, I would have to leave the picture. Suddenly a writer appeared. I think his name was George Bruce. After Hornblow left, Tyrone Power's agent became the producer.

DOWD: How did this agent become the producer?

VIDOR: He was in the business department of the studio.

DOWD: Had you made the decision to cast Tyrone Power?

VIDOR: Yes. I don't know how we got George Sanders, though.

DOWD: Were you interested in this subject at all?

VIDOR: Yes. What I remember about it was the issue of God against the pagans, and I felt that I could give some feeling against pagan worship.

DOWD: Do you remember whom you wanted for the role instead of George Sanders?

VIDOR: No, I don't.

DOWD: Did you know Tyrone Power very well?

VIDOR: I knew him, and I liked him on the screen. He respected my ideas and he tried to give the film what I felt about it. If you have a rapport between the director, the star, and the writer, it can go quite well.

DOWD: You said once that you intended Power to be more gentle, but still divided, in the role of Solomon.

VIDOR: Yes. This again is the story of basically flesh and spirit. This is a basic theme for me, too. Power was a fellow who could interpret that physical pull of Sheba. He had been through it too, and was willing to do it. In the scenes we shot you could see that he was torn, but it is a subtle thing. Unless somebody can express this, you can't make them do it. They have to do it for themselves. Brynner certainly has the quality of strength. He plays that way all the time.

DOWD: You started with Power in the role. How much did you shoot with him?

VIDOR: I shot about half the picture. Had we done the love scenes before the battle scenes, we could have used doubles and finished the picture. After we found out that he had died, United Artists signed up Yul Brynner. He couldn't double it to the scenes we had already shot, and there were too many close shots that we hadn't done. So, we had to start over.

DOWD: What about Gina Lollobrigida? Was she a difficult actress to work with?

VIDOR: With Power she was all sweetness and honey, but when Brynner started to come on and throw his weight around, she tried to keep up with him and she started to swing her weight around. The main trouble we had with her was that she would always get her clothes set, take photographs in them for our costumers to work from, and then she would decide that she wanted to change them. Sometimes she would not even come to the set if she was having trouble with her costumes. She would arrive later and later all the time. I finally got fed up and Ben came over at that point.

DOWD: You mean Ben Goetz?

VIDOR: Yes. He came over to take on some of the authority and help me with some definite backing.

DOWD: Was he with United Artists?

VIDOR: No. He had retired, and Small hired him. They sued her for the entire day's losses since she had agreed at the beginning that she would not hold up production. I think we sued her for $1,000. She had her husband fly home and settle for half that amount.

DOWD: Did she show up late anymore?

VIDOR: No. You can let actors go just so far before you have to put your foot down. She was at the height of her popularity then. To settle the suit she had to give up her interest in the picture. She had quite an interest, too.

DOWD: Did you have any choice in who would replace Tyrone Power?

VIDOR: No. United Artists made the deal. They had to find someone who was available immediately. Yul Brynner was in a tough spot, too. He had to wear some of Power's costumes, which we altered to fit him.

DOWD: What was it like shooting in Spain? Was it cheaper?

VIDOR: For example, there is a courtyard scene where Gina drives in. To shoot that in Hollywood would have cost $60,000. In Spain it was only $20,000. We had extras there for a dollar a day. They would have cost thirty-five dollars a day in Hollywood. For a scene with 1,000 extras, it meant a difference between $1,000 a day, as opposed to $35,000 per day.

DOWD: Who was your cameraman?

VIDOR: His name was Fred Young. He was excellent. He did Lawrence of Arabia, which was one of the best photographed films ever.

DOWD: Did you have the problem of last-minute location changes, as you did on War and Peace?

VIDOR: No. However, I had to do a lot of stuff ad-libbed. For example, I saw a chariot go over an embankment. I shot that and included it in the picture. The problem went back to not having a finished script before the production started. I finished up this picture saying that I would never do another picture unless the script was completely worked out. On this film I was writing scenes between shooting other scenes.

DOWD: What was it like when you heard that Power had died?

VIDOR: We were working on a Saturday. We finished one scene and then we quit after we heard the news. They took him to a hospital but I think he died on the way. He was still in his costume, I believe. People said he had been doing strenuous work, but actually we had been using doubles. It wasn't that at all. He had done a couple of shots, but that was all.

XV

SHEPARD: I've been curious about something. <u>War and Peace</u> was your second-to-last film, and also one of your best films. Were you prepared to hang it up after just one more picture and retire from the making of features? Had you expected to stop?

VIDOR: No. I never have thought of the word "retirement." I've never had it in my vocabulary. Making films was to me a great joy. It isn't as if I had some dull, monotonous job. It's not like I was in love with golf or fishing. I used to play golf, but I don't like fishing. So, there was nothing better that I wanted to do than to continue making films.

Occasionally I would quit right at the height of my career because people would try to mess around with a film that was a personal statement of mine, and that would discourage me. I had to fight with all kinds of people after a picture was finished. It's very much like what happened on <u>The Fountainhead.</u> I would say to myself, That's the last personal film I'm going to do. But then a few months would go by, and I'd forget it, and try to do another one. At the end of <u>Solomon and Sheba</u>, when Tyrone Power died on the film the producer went to pieces. But I was able to reassure United Artists, and in not too many weeks we brought it off, and got the picture finished.

When I came back to New York and met with the office there, they said that they wanted me to continue working for them, and that they didn't want me going anywhere else. I thought that was a pretty good invitation, and I also wanted to continue with them.

I'd been working on the "Milly" story. Years after the release of my first film, The Turn in the Road, Sid Grauman remembered the success of that film, and the impact it had had, and he bought it. Then he got hold of me and said that he wanted me to update the picture, make a modern version of it. I thought that times had changed, so I said that I would do it. I started work on it. But then I was interrupted by something, and in the meantime he died. I went on with the story, and that eventually became the "Milly" story. I had been working on it for five years before either War and Peace or Solomon and Sheba. In fact, I was also working on another project, which was Hawthorne's The Marble Faun.

Having this offer, as it were, from United Artists, I went back to California to complete work on the "Milly" story. I rented a few offices over at United Artists, and I had a writer, whom I think I had worked with before, and we just buckled down and accomplished what we set out to do. It was one of these stories for which I had a personal feeling. Sort of what you might call "out of my guts." That's the way The Crowd was made, and that's the way Hallelujah was made.

There were other projects, such as The Big Parade, that I felt very deeply about. They didn't always read too well, or show up on paper in script form well -- if I'd had to put The Crowd into script form as a screenplay and submit it around to a lot of people, it wouldn't have been made. Even with a picture like Show People, it was the same thing. There was a certain mood to it. MGM and Thalberg had been so pleased with the success of The Big Parade. When they first saw it, they were elated and surprised because a lot of it wasn't in the script at all -- it grew from the script while we were shooting. When The Crowd was written, they were afraid to turn it down because I might come out with a surprise.

This all related to the "Milly" story. Max Youngstein, who was in charge of United Artists, would look at the scripts we were writing for the "Milly" story, but he wouldn't understand what I was doing. The others would say, "When we listen to you, we get the feeling, we get the idea. But when you give us the screenplay ..." They just didn't understand what I was doing, putting my own individuality into the script. It was like a painter telling someone what he's going to paint. After a while I started to think that the screenplay was not fine enough, not articulate enough, and I started to go back and do some revisions. For a time I believed that the only way to get the story down on paper was to write a book.

I spent a lot of money and a lot of time trying to put this picture over and get it made. Three times -- once with Darryl Zanuck at Fox, once with Allied Artists, and once with another company, I tried to get it made. Darryl turned it down because he thought it was going to be a high-budget picture. But with Allied Artists we went so far as to choose all the locations up around Truckee and Stockton, and I even went around and put stakes in the ground to mark the camera angles. I hope the stakes are still there. At Allied Artists, (Steve) Broidy and I started interviewing people and having readings. We had a deal set for $600,000. There were a lot of backers who said that it couldn't be made for that much, and they finally dropped out. Inasmuch as I'd made War and Peace and Solomon and Sheba, and they had both turned out all right, especially after saving Solomon and Sheba from being a complete disaster, I finally thought that I could do the films I wanted. But after a year with the writer, I don't know what happened. I just gave it up. I quit.

It's the same story with the new project I then started. I guess someone came along with an idea of doing a story about Cervantes as a young man. I think it was Ilya Salkind. He came over and they paid me and a writer to do a script, and I thought we had a marvelous script. It's based on a book called A Man Called Cervantes. We worked very hard on it. It progressed to the point where I went on to Paris to get ready to do the film.

At this time Salkind had invested in a film with Orson Welles, and suddenly they ran out of money. So, we took the project to Madrid, and eventually someone else bought the project. This man told me, "I think we should have the part" -- not Cervantes, but a secondary part -- "changed to a girl instead of a boy." I said, "My God! We've been working on this part for a long time!" He said, "We can get Jane Fonda to play the part if it's a girl." I guess she was twelve or fourteen years old at the time. I said to myself, Here we go again, screwing it up! You see, I believed that if I worked on the script, at least with a writer, and dictated the sequences and the action, it would add a personal touch to it. I think that is what's wrong with pictures today. They don't have that personal touch. That's what makes a Hitchcock picture what it is, that's what makes a Capra picture what it is. It's the men getting their own individuality into the films they make. That's what I wanted to do then, and not to let some financier dictate what I should do. We need more personal touches in films today.

Well, when this project was shipped over to Madrid, this new fellow turned out to have very little money. Then he wanted me to talk to someone else in Madrid. I guess I just sort of lost enthusiasm for it. I said to myself, I'm not going to run around and try to promote it just to get it made. Eventually they put some other director on it. I think his name was Sherman. Nobody ever heard of the picture, Cervantes, but I would have gone to see it if I had ever seen it advertised. The picture was made, though. I think it had Eddie Robinson and Gina Lollobrigida.

I was glad to get out of it. They were diluting every idea, changing everything, and I was at a place in my life where I didn't have to prostitute these ideas and make these compromises. In The Fountainhead Gary Cooper blows up the whole building because they change the facade and some of the other sections of the structure. That's what I felt like at that point. I'd had enough experience with that before. Even today, if I watch Hallelujah and see the Irving Berlin song in it, even though I'm a Berlin enthusiast, I feel like getting down on the floor and hiding my face because it didn't belong in the picture.

So anyway, I had to give up the "Milly" story, and I never made any progress on The Marble Faun. It was too nebulous, maybe too steep. But it had lots of spiritual meaning, and that is what has always driven me, because right along with my filmmaking, I was interested in the facts of life and the science of being, which is called Ontology. I'm really an Ontologist, and I can pursue that interest without making films. I think that films are for the public, and perhaps it is not right to put your own progressive ideas before the public.

Perhaps they don't want that. But then again, I will turn around and argue that if you do a thing clearly and well, they'll buy it.

About that time I went to Paris and bought a Beaulieu 16mm camera, and I thought I would make a film on my own without asking anyone whether they liked it or not. I came back from Paris and I sat down and thought, What would I do if I could just shoot what I wanted? I started to write a narration, which I called Truth and Illusion: An Introduction to Metaphysics. I shot it, narrated it, wrote it, and it became a twenty-five minute film. I showed it to a bunch of people. Some didn't understand it, while others did. I showed it at Caltech out in Pomona when Eric Sherman was teaching there. He said it was the best film I had ever made. I showed it to other people, but I never did anything with it. I thought the public wasn't ready for it, but after he told me that he thought it was one of my best films, I thought about it again. I'm now in the process of changing the titles. I had an assumed name for the directing and writing credits.

SHEPARD: Why did you have the assumed name?

VIDOR: Because I didn't want to have WRITTEN BY KING VIDOR, PHOTOGRAPHED BY KING VIDOR, DIRECTED BY KING VIDOR splashed all over the titles. A number of people have recently said that they think I should have my name on it, so I'm doing that now. When that's done, I'll send it over to my daughter in France, and perhaps it can be released with the Wyeth film over there.

I started a film about the anatomy of a small town, Paso Robles, and I've shot a lot of material on that, but it's not yet complete. While I was in Paso Robles I met a doctor who was a movie-making buff. He had a lot of 16mm equipment. I asked him if he would like to work with me on the Paso Robles film. He said, "I'm not too crazy about making a film on Paso Robles, but I want to make a film about you." I agreed, and I dropped the Paso Robles film temporarily. We started to shoot some interview stuff with me, but I don't think it was too good. I'm not sure he was technically ready. But two or three days after we started shooting, I got a letter from Andrew Wyeth saying that The Big Parade had been a big influence on his painting. I said to this doctor friend, "Wouldn't it be great to incorporate that in the picture about me?" So I called Wyeth, and asked him if he would talk about it if we came back to Pennsylvania. He said he would be happy to. Instead of the doctor, I thought I'd better hire a cameraman, so the doctor brought his daughter along to operate the sound equipment.

We went to Detroit first and did a couple of days of shooting with a psychiatrist friend of mine who has since died. This doctor and I talked about metaphysics, and got some good material out of that shooting session. From there we packed up and went out to Pennsylvania, where we shot for three days, going to the places Andy Wyeth talked about, looking at the paintings that had been influenced by The Big Parade, and then we ran the film. I think I had taken along my own copy. Since then, Andy has purchased one for himself. After we got back, this doctor and I worked on the film for a while, but then he moved away. I took over the film then. I bought some better editing equipment and took it up to the ranch, and then started to really assemble and edit the film. I put it out in rough form, but I later took it back and didn't show it to anybody. We re-shot a lot of stuff with me and the ranch and so forth, and then I thought I should drop it for a while and write a book or something.

Early this year, 1980, I completed work on it, and began to show it to people. There have been a lot of wonderful reactions. The Los Angeles Herald-Examiner had front page articles about it in both the Sunday and Monday editions. I'm now in the process of sending a videotape of it to someone in England, and I'm going to send a 16mm print of it to France so that my daughter can see what French television wants from it. The local PBS station here, KCET, liked it and they sent it on to Washington. That brings us up to date and covers all of my activities in film.

SHEPARD: On personal films such as Truth and Illusion and the Wyeth film, do you have a specific scripting process, or do you feel like you can write them as you work in the editing room?

VIDOR: For Truth and Illusion, I wrote a narrative of about four or five pages. I would use that to provoke the shooting. Another thing about Truth and Illusion -- it was always said that you can't photograph thoughts. Producers always liked to say that, if the writer put in something that a person was thinking. That stuck with me, and I wanted to see if I could reproduce thoughts on film. Another thing about it was that I wanted to see what the limits were to an individual filmmaker without having to pay actors. In other words, it was a professional home movie, without building sets, without the costumes, without the technicians, all of that. It was the same process as student filmmaking. I spent very little outside of the film stock and lab work. The few actors in it were friends of mine. I just contrived everything I needed. I would think, How can I shoot this line from the script? and then experiment with trying to illustrate that thought, to make someone feel it. That was the way it got going.

SHEPARD: Did the original script end up as the narration?

VIDOR: Yes. It was predominantly narration with images. The Wyeth film was made in just the opposite way. It was entirely ad-libbed, just between us. I made a tape recording of the dialogue in the film and had it transcribed. Two or three weeks ago was the first time I had a script all written down for it. If I ever talked to someone about distributing it, they would ask if I had a script. Now I have one. I can also look at the transcript and see what editing should be done.

SHEPARD: So you don't regard it as finished yet?

VIDOR: Well, it's thirty-five minutes long, and PBS might want it to run twenty-eight minutes, so I'm ready to cut.   There's some possibility that I could get Truth and Illusion down to twenty-five minutes, and if I could, we might be able to put it together with the Wyeth film, which I've titled Metaphor, and call the whole thing An Hour With King Vidor.   That's a slim possibility, but I think the interest may be different in the two films. The only other pending project I have is to finish the Paso Robles film. Just how I'm going to do that, I don't know.

SHEPARD: Do you enjoy the process of making personal films less, as much as, or more than doing commercial films?

VIDOR: I think the perfection you can achieve in the commercial films interests me more. There are a lot of people to deal with, and a lot of minds that can get contrary, but on the other hand, I never had a lot of interference while shooting. I would have to say that the commercial films that expressed myself were most satisfying.

Now that brings up a point you asked about before. What do I think of my films with this perspective of many years? I have discovered that even though I wasn't always aware of it, much of my own individuality as a person rubbed off on those films. I see by the fan letters I get that they're seeing me in those films. They're seeing something about me, because they go beyond those letters from people who just see the films and are entertained by them. The people don't say they liked the picture and would like to see another one, they're telling me that the films say something about me, the individual filmmaker, and every time I read some of those letters, I have to say, There has to be a lot of me in the film. Otherwise, they wouldn't write such a letter.

SHEPARD: Weren't fan letters in the old days almost always sent to the stars? Or did you receive letters like that when the films were new, too?

VIDOR: No, I didn't at all. But I received many, many more later on. I remember the letters I got, even from school children in Japan, when I was writing the first part of my autobiography. That amazed me. Those were the first worldwide letters I received.

SHEPARD: Once the "Milly" story, The Marble Faun, and the Cervantes story fell through, did you get any more offers?

VIDOR: I had a few scattered offers, but not many. There were offers for films I simply would not do. I had a plethora of people wanting me to read scripts of nebulous projects. I found that I could spend my entire time reading scripts, and they could pick my brains for nothing. After quite a while of doing that, I said, The hell with this! I noted that the stars' agents demanded a definite offer before a star would even read the script or look at it. I thought I would do the same thing, unless it came from some reputable star or agent or producer. I got very few.

I had a feeling they were looking for youth or sensationalism, like Sam Peckinpah. When censorship was lifted, they just didn't envision me as a popular director, as they did in Europe. I was turned down by a couple of agents here. I tried to get a good agent to represent me, and they said that they had all they could handle. It just didn't seem right for me at that time. It went along that way for a while, and then eight years or so ago, they rediscovered me. During that time I was invited to go to festivals in Spain and France, and I went to all of them. That's still going on. Right now I have an invitation from Barcelona, one from Ireland, and so forth, but I probably won't go.

SHEPARD: At what point did you develop the script based on the life of James Murray?

VIDOR: That's a very active thing. Let's see -- it started roughly four years ago when a French producer named Pierre Coutrelle asked me what projects I would like to do. He wanted to make a film with me, and I told him about several. He was interested in the James Murray thing. But then he went off and started doing something else. Later on I met Francis Coppola someplace, and he asked what I had. He wanted to make a picture with me, and I gave him the James Murray project and he said, "Perfect!" That's what he wanted to do.

That was just before he started working on Apocalypse Now. By that time I had an agent, Phil Gersh. Coppola said he'd have his agent and mine get together. Then the two agents started quarreling. Gersh said he was insulted by the offer, and they started to call each other names. Kate (Kate Finley, King Vidor's companion at Paso Robles) had just arrived, and I talked to her about it, and she said, "Why don't we do it?" So, we wrote the screenplay up at the ranch. We sent it to Coppola, but he was in the throes of making his film down in the Pacific. What he did was publish the announcement without consulting me that we had made a deal to do the film. I could have sued him, but I didn't. They eventually paid me off for the treatment, but I sent it to a few other places in the meantime. Nothing ever came of it, though.

SHEPARD: But the script is still going around, and Coppola is still interested?

VIDOR: I don't know. I haven't pushed him since Apocalypse Now went into production.

SHEPARD: You also taught film at USC.

VIDOR: Yes, for two semesters. The first class that I taught was called Film Directing, and the second course was called Aesthetics of Film. I realized that if I was going to teach them, I really should be on the set when they shoot their student films. We did a lot of preliminary talking for several months. The films weren't very good. The guys got self-conscious about them, and started to cut them to pieces until there was nothing left. I think Freddie Zinnemann had the same idea on going through the filming with them on the set. The other class, Aesthetics of Film, I don't know what the results were. I just talked about it in class, and I don't know how much rubbed off.

There's a big question in my mind about all universities. It seems that the biggest element to success in self-expression is to really get it out and get it down yourself. So much of it is really a do-it-yourself effort. That's pretty obvious in film, I suppose. Where I grew up, there were no film schools, you just had to do it yourself and learn the hard way. I made a lot of two-reelers. I don't know whether the teachers in film school are really capable of conveying the knowledge. They usually are just graduated students of another film school. All they can do is theorize and tell the students what books to read. I've never gone in for that. I think Russia has a better idea. They take someone like myself, Hawks, or Capra, and match them up with a young director, and they go through a whole film together. They discuss everything. That way, you're really getting the benefit of all the experience and it's all going to up on the screen eventually.

SHEPARD: When you go to universities to speak, what kinds of things do you find the students wanting to learn from you?

VIDOR: The questions are usually very intelligent. I'm amazed at how perceptive the questions are, and I suppose that indicates they're not getting it where they are. Then suddenly along comes someone like myself with all of this experience, and they ask how I happened to do something or other in a film. A month or so ago I spoke at a place called Sonoma State University. I decided to speak on Philosophy and Filmmaking. This is something I discovered when I was enroute to a university one time. Just before I got there, I thought, Why must I separate philosophy and filmmaking? Don't keep them apart, put them together. Make philosophizing and film-making the same effort, the same medium of expression. Since then, I've borne that in mind.

This was the first time I gave a talk on that theme, how what a person feels philosophically gets into the film he is making. It is the personal viewpoint, the thoughts, and philosophy that make a film interesting. This goes for writing a book, painting a picture, acting, and everything else. Take Gary Cooper or Spencer Tracy -- it is their particular individuality that comes through. Their acting technique is not so vastly different, one from the other. They're trying to make you believe what they're doing. I notice Robert Redford is able to convey what he's thinking very easily. The same must be true of a director. You might ask, How does he get it onto the screen? It's a general viewpoint about everything that does it. What you let the actor do, what you don't let him do, the costumes, the locations, all of these things enter into it. This is a discovery, although it is not particularly new, but I've been more aware of it lately.

SHEPARD: In that sense, if you were to go back into the act of making feature films would you want to be responsible for all aspects of the film?

VIDOR: Yes, definitely. That's the auteur theory. The French have a word, cinéaste, which they use instead of "director."

SHEPARD: The French also apply that term to directors who simply take whatever project comes along the day they finish the last one.

VIDOR: It's not true of Truffaut. It's a question of whether or not the director was able to put his trademark on it after he took on the project.

SHEPARD: What is your assessment of some of your films, as compared to the way festival audiences react to them? For example, I know you always regarded The Champ as a commercial assignment, but it's become a great favorite.

VIDOR: Well, I was aware of that comparison even back then. I said I would do Street Scene as an artistic means of expression, and then I would do The Champ to keep up my box-office reputation. The joke was that for a while, Street Scene almost eclipsed The Champ as far as box-office results were concerned. I think today's audiences are right. Back then audiences were just ignorant of something that people didn't discover until later. We had good reviews at the time, but generally they've attracted more acclaim recently. I am very pleased and happy that people can discover and enjoy films like Show People and The Crowd.

The first year of the Academy Awards, The Crowd was up for an Award for Best Picture. Back then the voting was done by five people -- Mary Pickford, Douglas Fairbanks, Joe Schenck, Sid Grauman and Louis B. Mayer. Sid Grauman called me early in the morning and said, "I held out all night for The Crowd, but finally I had to give in." I found out later that Mayer wouldn't vote for it because it had not been a big box-office success. It was a critical success, yes, but not a box-office success. He voted for another picture, Two Arabian Knights, a picture that hasn't been heard of since. What I'm trying to illustrate is that as far as Mayer and the studio were concerned, it was not a successful picture. That was hard to overcome in Hollywood in that era.

As the years go by, nobody gives a damn about whether or not a film was a box-office success. Today, people just look at it as a motion picture, and they're all very happy about it. In the case of Marion Davies in Show People, I think there was so much resistance to Hearst's publicity, they couldn't accept her in a comedy role. People can look at it now and enjoy it. I've always said that if it's a bad wine, aging doesn't help it any, and vice versa. I think these were good pictures to begin with, and they only get better with age. I had some very good criticisms, but I appreciate it that they are better known today. In the letters I get they mention all these films -- <u>The Crowd</u>, <u>Hallelujah</u>, <u>Street Scene</u> -- and I'm wondering where the hell they're seeing them. But, the good thing is that they're seeing them, and they're not judging them on whether or not they were box-office successes.

One night we were showing <u>The Crowd</u> to Ryan O'Neal and his agent, Sue Mengers, with the thought of doing a remake of the picture. Ryan said, "We've got to do this story!" He came up and put his arm around me, and Sue Mengers piped up and asked, "When <u>The Crowd</u> was made, was it a big success?" I said, "No." For just that reason, they dropped out of the deal.

I must tell you one more story that comes to me about <u>The Crowd</u>. Two years ago I had an introduction to David Merrick. He asked me what ideas I had for films. I told him that one of my ideas was doing an update on <u>The Crowd</u> in today's mood. In a short while he dropped out of the picture, but a little later it was turned over to a man named Arthur Jacobs. Jacobs called me up and asked me to have lunch with him one day. We met at La Scala, and I told him my feelings about making a new version of <u>The Crowd</u> for today's market. He had run it recently, and I told him what I would like to do. He said, "When can we go to work?" I said, "This afternoon!" I got hold of a writer and we started working immediately. They were having a Writers Guild strike, so we worked here at home. Jacobs kept calling up once or twice a week to ask how it was going, and if he could read some of it. After three weeks I called up his office and told him that on Friday I would show him the material. That Wednesday, he passed away. That's how close I came to making it.

SHEPARD: You attend quite a few film festivals. What's your motivation in accepting so many invitations?

VIDOR: Oh, I don't go everywhere. I just turned down an invitation to London for June. I don't accept everything.

SHEPARD: You're very accessible to younger filmmakers, and you're willing to share. What do you get out of doing this?

VIDOR: I suppose I've heard Capra talk about this, too. I get a kick out of imparting some information to students. In other words, if I cannot give of myself to films, then the next thing I can do is to express myself to students and young people. There is a great delight in doing that. If the traveling conditions are not too terrible, I like to do it. If, on the other hand, I get a request from a place where the people are just going to come because they can see a movie for free, I won't go. However, in most places there may be at least one film-maker, one fellow who will come forth and ask you for help and advice, and that alone makes the trip satisfying. It's been my experience that most students are a little shy on produc-tion questions, but they're pretty alert on the aesthetic side of films.

SHEPARD: Who are some of the young filmmakers with whom you are most friendly, and what are the bases for these relationships?

VIDOR: I would say Martin Scorsese, James Bridges, people like that. I meet them, and they're probably impressed with the name, so they ask me to have lunch with them. That's how those relationships get started. There was one fellow, a month or so ago, who had a script and wanted me to be his mentor, he wanted to pick up what he could from me. As I say, Russia is much superior for this type of thing. On their recent trip, one of the Russian directors was proud to say that he was a student of Girasimov.

SHEPARD: That was Kulidjanov, the head of the Associa-tion of Soviet Filmmakers.

VIDOR: It makes much better sense. I'll tell you, I've been puzzled why this kind of thing hasn't been going on here. Frankly, I'm surprised that over the twenty years that have gone by since I directed my last film, people haven't taken advantage of my experience and willingness to teach. I've spent many years going to see lousy films and wondering, What is it that they're not realizing? It's obvious they need talent, but maybe they're not looking for it.

It just leaves you cold. You wonder what the hell the film was about, and why it was made. I wonder if they think, He's too old, if my name ever comes up for directing a picture. That might be true today, but it certainly wasn't twenty years ago when I stopped directing films. My opinion of the films that have come out over these years is such that I know I could do better. I admit I've been through psychoanalysis, but I've progressed so much mentally, and I have become so much more aware by being in touch with students all over the world. I just feel that I could do a better job.

SHEPARD: Tell me about the experiences you had recently as an actor, and whether or not through those experiences you saw any difference between the way a director functions today and the way you worked.

VIDOR: I did it as a lark, mainly. But at the same time, I wanted to see what goes on. It happens that this particular director was more of a writer, and I think he was leaving a lot of the camera work to the cameraman. It was all very simple, just one light -- which was a great benefit because it lets them shoot in real interiors where you don't have much light. At least they don't sweat you out. But, it seemed very much the same. I would have been more involved in photography, but on the other hand, there may have been a lot of my contemporaries, like Cukor, who were not involved in photography. They had good cameramen like Gregg Toland and George Barnes to take over for them. I even used to say to myself, You're thinking too much in terms of the camera, you've got to spend more time with the actors. I was very precise about the camera set-ups and lighting, mainly because I started my career working with the camera, and I felt I knew a lot about the camera and lenses. In this experience I just finished, the director was more of a writer and was leaving it up to the cameraman. The main thing I noticed was that they used far fewer lights on the set.

SHEPARD: Do people who come to make films about you perceive you any differently than the way you perceive yourself?

VIDOR: I don't know if I can answer that. There was a film made by Richard Schickel, and I like that one very much. It's my favorite of the ones that have been made about me. I saw a half-hour of it at the Teacher's Association, and it was very good. I like the films in that series The Men Who Made the Movies.

Kevin Brownlow also likes to record material about me. One time I was at his home in England. Every time I go over there, he grabs a tape recorder and follows me around. This one particular day we were sitting in his living room talking and he was recording me. I told him that I had to leave since I had an appointment in the country. His wife called a cab, and he followed me down the steps and into the cab all the way down to the train station. He got on the train with me and kept recording. It was about a forty-five minute trip, and when I got off at my stop, he followed me until I met the people who were waiting for me. I said, "So long, Kevin, I'll see you later." He finally said goodbye and went back on the train.

SHEPARD: A lot of critics see your work as representative of an American character. They say that the optimism and joy of life that comes out of all your best films is something unique to the artists of this country. I'm wondering whether you agree with that.

VIDOR: Yes, but at the same time you have guys like Peckinpah shooting everybody up and cutting their hands off.

SHEPARD: Yes. However, their careers didn't last as long as yours.

VIDOR: The answer to that is perhaps I'm a typically American guy, therefore the subjects I worked on were good American subjects. But then maybe it's just that whatever it is I have, people like to call it American.

SHEPARD: It is obvious that the enthusiasm of a young culture infuses your pictures. There's no time for melancholy. I'm wondering if you see any differences between American films and the films of other countries with respect to that.

VIDOR: I've noticed that quite a bit. I don't have any cynical viewpoint at all. Someone said not long ago that I never had any villains in my pictures. Looking back, they're probably right. I've had a few bastards like Gregory Peck's role in Duel In the Sun, but he wasn't really a villain.

I don't have a negative way of life. My philosophy and religion are such that with negativism, the buck stops here. I try to live that way, and I try to express myself in that way. I try to avoid the negative aspects. Also, I grew up in the era of the happy ending. I don't necessarily believe in that now, but I don't necessarily believe in the unhappy ending, either.

That leads to something else. What happened to me in 1959 was because they viewed me from another era. I was always trying to think of myself as going along with the progressive ideas of our culture, such as the lifting of censorship. That's why I was going to universities and colleges. I had to keep abreast of what was going on. I felt that I owed myself the benefits of moving along with the kids who were in their twenties. I was never frozen in a certain period, which is the case with some filmmakers. But I guess people don't always see you the same way you perceive yourself.

SHEPARD: Do you think the energy, optimism, and outlook of the people you meet at colleges is different today than with young people years ago?

VIDOR: There was a pioneering spirit back then about movie-making. Nowadays you have students making films, supposedly under supervision. Somehow or other, my attitude back then was that I was ready to work in any aspect of film-making. I used to go to Universal Studios and go to every department -- acting, props, camera -- because it didn't matter which one I worked in. I wanted to learn anything I could about all those departments. I knew I wanted to be a director, but I looked on the other jobs as learning experiences. You don't get a feeling of that now. Everyone wants to start off being a director.

I met a young fellow last evening who I like very much. His family is in the clothing manufacturing business. He tried that, decided he didn't like it, and then tried several other things. Now he's going to Lee Strasberg's school. I imagine he's thirty, but he tried a lot of things before he started acting and directing. This is the real spirit of pioneering as it was back then, with people trying all sorts of things before deciding on one certain thing.

I hear all sorts of talk about drugs. I don't see it because none of my friends are involved in it. Wallace Reid was the only figure you'd hear about who had a drug problem in the old days. Now it seems very commonplace. I think people then were more naïve, they didn't have the millions of things they have to worry about today. They had simple houses and simple automobiles. They lived in flat apartments or in bungalow courts. They didn't have all the opportunities and Rolls-Royces and affluence. I don't understand how stars today can get $2,000,000 per picture and not have great problems, either from people trying to take it away from them, or just dealing with it themselves. It was a much simpler life then.

SHEPARD: How has your career work affected your private life over all these years?

VIDOR: Well, you have to look at it from two angles. You have a life outside movie-making, and you have your movie-making career. I suppose that I had enough offers and enough of a name and reputation so that I could choose what I wanted to do through most of my life. The accomplishments were there, they were real. That was all very satisfying. When you think of it, it's like children or marriage. You are really married to the films, as much or more so than to anything in your private life. I suppose we have no choice. If you're going to make a film, and it involves shooting in the middle of the night or early morning, it takes that much dedication to do it. With the other part of your life, you take it, come what may. If a woman can stand it, if she likes it, if she enhances it, fine. If she doesn't, why, you don't have time to worry about it. You can only say, "I'm sorry, it's been a nice experience, but that's it." You do it because a dedication to filmmaking is complete. If it comes down to the point where you have to go to Spain and she doesn't want to go, you say, "That's too bad. I'm going to miss you." It affects your life quite a bit. However, I think the relationship I've had with my three daughters couldn't be better than it is. We're very close. But they went through tough times. Their mother took them to France, and I had to kidnap them.

SHEPARD: What periods of your life have been the happiest?

VIDOR: When you say, "happiest," I guess it's really when you accomplish something, when you come up with a successful venture and pull it off. I was proud of The Crowd. But in talking about happiness, one thing I've lacked was the ability to protect myself from being talked into doing something I didn't originally plan to do. In today's world I can say "no" much better. My big regret in making War and Peace was that I said okay when I shouldn't have. The way to handle a producer like de Laurentiis is to scream and say, "No!" It's not always easy to say that, and to know when to say that. Intuition is not always firm enough. That's why I could have made a better picture in the last ten or fifteen years. I can see myself more firmly now, and I could very easily say "no" just when it needs to be said.

SHEPARD: How important is it for you to know that these films you have made will probably go on being admired as long as there are any films around to be admired?

VIDOR: I read something this morning during breakfast. The article was talking about using certain words. One line impressed me, and it said that if the word "death" is used, substitute "immortality" instead. I like to think of the films as being immortal, if possible. And as much as you put your self into your films, that is immortal. The immortal self is the divine birthright that we are given. I think everyone has it, but most people don't have the opportunity to find it. It takes an artist to find it, and it takes a good artist. That's why I said I wanted to make more pictures. I'd learn more about myself. The Crowd is very definitely of myself. That was a great experience for me.

For an artist the thing to remember is, Know thyself. I think it's true of everybody in the art of living, whether you're doing an artistic thing or not, it's the art of being a person. We're all very distinctive individuals, and that's what it's all about. Have you ever noticed these art sales, like the ones they have in Greenwich Village and here in Beverly Hills? I remember walking at least four blocks along the street in Greenwich Village looking at the paintings and thinking, Why is not one of them any good? How can they paint so many of that that are no good? Accidentally, the law of averages should have at least made one of them good. The reason is they're not painting from themselves. They're painting from some other painting they saw. They're not painting what they are as individuals. It's hard to put that on canvas. It's easy in a book, but it's tough in a movie because you have a hundred people around. Today we're getting at the immortal self, and to my way of thinking, that's God. He's not in an altar, not in a sunset, not in a sermon, he's inside. It all comes from inside, and that is the place of art.

Film Title Index

299

300

General Index